Praise for *Humanity Under Siege*

"We live in a society where anxiety, depression, and isolation have become the norm. The rates of self-harm and suicide alarmingly continue to rise, and problems are getting darker. Many are stumped for answers.

That's why I'm thrilled that my friend, Dr. Natalie Atwell, wrote *Humanity Under Siege*.

Natalie skillfully explores the spiritual dimension of the mental and emotional battles we face and ultimately points readers toward hope, healing, and the freedom found only in Christ. It's time we get prepared, and this book is an awesome tool. Do yourself a favor and pick it up!"

—Josh Doyle, host of *No Longer Nomads* podcast
and managing partner of Uncharted Adventures

"A bold and timely examination of the intersection between mental health and spiritual warfare. Dr. Natalie Atwell brings her clinical expertise, biblical conviction, and genuine compassion to one of the most important questions of our generation: 'What power is behind the ever-present battle for the mind?'"

—Bo Kennedy,
author and host of *The BUMP* podcast

HUMANITY UNDER SIEGE

DEFENDER
CRANE, MO

Humanity Under Siege:
The Unseen Realm and the Spiritual War Against the Mind

Dr. Natalie Atwell

Defender Publishing
Crane, MO 65633

ISBN: 978-1-7325478-2-7

Printed in the United States of America.

A CIP catalog record of this book is available from the Library of Congress.

Cover designer: Jeffrey Mardis
Interior designer: Katherine Lloyd
Editor: Angie Peters

CONTENTS

Part Five
Overcoming Unseen Dark Influences
Clinically and Biblically

INTRODUCTION

If you're a pastor, pastoral counselor, mental health professional, or someone who has for many years simply sat with people who have shared their stories, you may feel at times as if nothing can surprise you anymore. Admittedly, after more than twenty years of being a professional counselor, I've often thought I've heard it all. Yet, there are still moments when I find myself researching, consulting with colleagues, and praying for wisdom as I help clients navigate their way through challenges I've never encountered before. Despite years of counseling a plethora of clients, each with unique circumstances, I've recently noticed an uptick in strange occurrences—not just in my practice but among fellow professionals as well. The trend is clear: Cases are getting more unusual, and the steep escalation of this strangeness has prompted me to pay closer attention to these peculiar cases and behaviors.

As I started digging deeper, I couldn't help but notice parallel societal changes also affecting my clients. When I zoomed out, the larger societal shift became clearer. I noted an increase in suicide rates, in the number of abortions, in the frequency of cult and occult engagement, in instances of overall social isolation, and in the number of mass/school shootings—all evidence of a growing darkness, a sense of disconnection, feelings of despair, and the presence of evil influences pressing in on humans.

As a believer in the Most High God—the One True God of the Bible—I also saw changes within the Church in Western cultures. Megachurches have risen and fallen. Many pastors have appeared more like narcissistic leaders than loving shepherds. Younger people have been deconstructing their faith or leaving churches in mass numbers. Trust within church leadership structures seemed to be deteriorating, largely due to scandals. I watched as people I know and love, those who used to be strong leaders in churches, struggled to find congregations to join. The difficulty wasn't because of any selfish desires, but possibly because of their inability to trust leaders, a lack of solid relationships with others in the community, and a shortage of opportunities for serving and finding purpose.

Around the time I noticed the rise in "strange" things and observed the broader societal and cultural changes within the Church, I also experienced a personal battle I would define as spiritual warfare. It began when I stepped into the work of combating the darkness of human trafficking in my local community. The timing didn't feel coincidental. As I began to think things through—not just as a counselor but as a believer in Jesus—the oddities seemed to outstretch the scope of my mental health training and experience. So, I began researching not only in psychology journals but through a *biblical* perspective.

Many therapists believe integrating spirituality into counseling is important. Christian therapists believe it's essential to incorporate a biblical worldview into their practice, yet many (including myself, at times) fail to assess—or realize—the influence of God's enemies in addition to the consequences of humanity's sinful nature. At this point, I wondered about and explored what's behind the human struggle: Who is for us and who is against us? The unseen or supernatural realm became my unavoidable focus; it's absolutely real and is gravely affecting folks' mental health, among other things.

My research of the unseen was intense. The lessons were life-changing, but the changes were essential; they involved shifting how I view human struggles, how I view many problems, and, finally, how I conduct therapy. Now I want to share what I've learned with others: those in the mental health field, those in the Church, and anyone who's seeking answers to their mental health concerns.

This topic is vital to all of us today because the darkness is encroaching among humanity faster than ever. Mental health professionals need to be educated and equipped to diagnose effectively and identify doors that are open to sinister influences. Pastors and ministers need to learn how to brace themselves for the battle and embrace those struggling in love and with trauma-informed care. Individuals need to know what the darkness is, how it affects their mental health, and what to do about it.

This book begins with the things I noticed and what led me to dig deeper; it includes the discoveries I made about a supernatural worldview; and it ends with a suggested treatment plan for mental health and the unseen influences.

Mental Health and the Unseen Realm is designed to:

- Encourage people to look at society, church, and their own lives in light of mental health issues as seen through a divine council worldview.
- Equip individuals with detailed theological explanations about the origin of all mental health problems.
- Provide answers to questions about how to discern whether problems are related to mental health or spirituality by reviewing definitions, causes, and symptoms.
- Offer a biblically and clinically sound treatment model of darkness/evil that manifests as mental health.

Disclaimer

This book is a work of creative nonfiction drawn from my professional experience. While every story reflects the essence of real events, all names and identifying details have been significantly changed to protect privacy and anonymity. Events, conversations, and settings have been recreated to the best of my memory, and certain characteristics or circumstances may have been altered. Any resemblance to actual people, living or deceased, or to specific events is unintentional and purely coincidental. The material in this book is offered for educational and informational purposes only and should not be considered a substitute for professional medical, psychological, or therapeutic advice. Readers should consult qualified professionals regarding any personal concerns or conditions.

PART ONE

The Growing Darkness in Mental Health: In Practice, Society, and Church

Chapter 1

STRANGE OCCURRENCES AND INCREASES IN UNCOMMON SYMPTOMS

If we don't tell strange stories, when something strange happens we won't believe it.

Shannon Hale

"Do you have a minute?" I've heard this question echo through the doorway of my office almost daily for years. Counselors have frequently stopped by to consult on a client's case—an occurrence I've come to value deeply. I love helping my team help others. They've shared a variety of challenging stories over the years, and I've helped many in their healing journeys. These days, however, my colleagues have been saying things that are more unusual, like, "Got a strange one for you," and "I need consultation on this one." Recently, a fellow counselor said, "My client said she was bitten by a guy who indicated he was a real vampire." Many times, hurting people come in to share stories with us that they've never shared with anyone else because they're afraid no one will believe them.

As a therapist and practice owner, I strive to help people feel safe and heard or believed to assuage their biggest fears. When a stranger helped me once—a person I truly believed was an angel—I wasn't sure whom I could safely tell. So, I find it very encouraging when my practice's therapists provide an environment in which their clients can feel comfortable enough to tell their difficult stories. Yet as the reports grow increasingly strange, it's more and more difficult to provide the "believed" aspect of their sessions.

One recent example leaps to the front of my mind. A staff member consulted me about a client whose parents had brought her in to receive counseling for anxiety. However, during the session, she disclosed dissociative symptoms (temporary disconnection between thoughts, consciousness, memory, and identity, usually resulting from severe trauma or stress). On the surface, nothing added up. She had experienced no known trauma, her parents were supportive and loving, she had a seemingly normal family dynamic, and she was thriving in most areas of life. Oddly, however, she couldn't recall almost an entire year of her early adolescence. She didn't forget just a few events; an entire year was simply "gone" from her memory. This is *not* normal and is a relatively new circumstance for me. I've never seen clients *without* trauma express dissociative symptoms, but recently it's happened more than once. When I observed it the first time, I was challenged to think about diagnosis and treatment from a different perspective. It required me to seek the Lord's heart, study God's Word, pray, and consult with other licensed professionals. Thinking through these situations with others kept me from feeling "crazy"; we can't hear these types of narratives and simply process them alone.

Recently, a pastor told me he wasn't sure how to help a woman who had become obsessed with death and things associated with darkness. He indicated she had anxiety due to these thought patterns. Obsessions with darkness or death in and of themselves aren't specifically assessed in therapy; we more typically look at issues such as family, trauma, and behaviors. While these are important factors to evaluate, the increasingly atypical symptoms made me consider whether we're asking questions that actually lead to the root of the problems.

At first, I noticed even more peculiarities about the symptoms experienced by my clients. Dissociation, sleep paralysis, gender dysphoria, personality disorders, unexplained physical concerns, dark sexual behaviors, and other issues we have no clear category for within mental health (such as seeing things), all of which used to be outliers in my practice, are now on the rise. Further, my therapists and I also noticed a spike in the number of clients involved in occult activities, New Age practices, and differing types of rituals.

Arguably, the surge in the occurrence of unusual cases might be due to a heightened awareness of mental health; it might just be the result of more people seeking counseling services. While this may be partially true, the abnormal incidents I've noticed go far beyond what most therapists and other professionals are trained to treat. This, combined with a mushrooming interest in spirituality among younger generations and the use of divination (the practice of seeking knowledge for the future or by supernatural means) for certain problems leads me to question other issues.[1] They aren't simply clinical; they're odd, sometimes disturbing, and increasingly difficult for clients to navigate. Often, they are dark, making me wonder whether some supernatural or unseen force is at play.

As I began researching how to treat my clients more effectively, I thought about changing the questions I was asking as a way of helping me better understand some of their struggles. Asking questions and assessing issues is a foundational part of the job as a therapist. One thing we ask is: "What have you tried to help with your concern?" It's frustrating to deal with a client who's continuing to experience difficulties even after trying everything to find relief or freedom. So, I began to ask God to show me and teach me more about the *human struggle*.

Don't just take my observations as fact. Let's look at some of the research I found to support these observations. First, we will discuss some of the previously uncommon symptoms I referred to earlier.

---

1 https://www.washingtontimes.com/news/2025/jun/7/americas-unhealthy-obsession-new-age-spiritualism/

Uncommon Symptoms

As you read through the following, remember they're simply symptoms *my* staff and I have noticed over the past several years. Other mental health professionals may report having seen different symptoms or narratives. We've learned of similar stories and experiences after talking with others in the field and by reading posts in online groups.

Dissociation: Dissociative symptoms are becoming increasingly common. J. R. Maldonado and D. Spiegel define dissociative disorders (DD) as disruptions in the normal integration of identity, memory, perception, emotions, thoughts, or bodily control that significantly impair daily functioning."[2]

Previously referred to as "multiple personality disorder" or "split personality," these conditions were once considered rare and were most often linked to severe trauma such as abuse, war, or natural disasters. However, some clients now display dissociative symptoms relating to things beyond trauma.

This raises questions about other possible influences. While some researchers connect the rise in symptoms to social media—especially TikTok—it may do more than spread awareness. Social media could contribute to or even trigger dissociative symptoms in some individuals. More research is needed, and social media use should likely be included in psychological assessments to better identify its possible impact.

Sleep paralysis: This is another strange symptom that seems to be more prevalent among many clients these days. Sure, people have often discussed sleep problems in therapy, but they haven't specifically said they've had "sleep paralysis." Those who have sleep paralysis (SP) can describe their experiences in detail. They're often fearful and almost always explain what happens as if some type of entity/evil figure is preventing them from moving while they are seemingly awake.

---

2 Maldonado, J. R., and Spiegel, D. (2023). "Dissociative Disorders." In A. Tasman, et al. *Tasman's Psychiatry*. Springer. doi.org/10.1007/978-3-030-42825-9_80-1.

Sleep paralysis is a parasomnia disorder that results in the unpleasant experience of being unable to move after the onset of sleep or upon awakening. It occurs when rapid eye movement (REM) sleep intrudes into the wake state. In REM sleep, there is a muscle "safety lock" that prevents sleepers from acting out their dreams. An episode of SP is sometimes accompanied by vivid hypnagogic (at sleep onset) or hypnopompic (upon awakening) hallucinations that are also REM intrusions into the wake state.[3]

Some studies show that about 20 percent of the population has had sleep paralysis at some point, and some suggest there is a genetic link. As a Christian, I wonder if the genetic link is more like a generational influence instead. Many therapists in mainstream practice don't assess for generational influences that might be connected to sleep paralysis. There isn't much research on an overall increase in sleep paralysis, but from an anecdotal perspective, my staff and I have absolutely seen more reports of it among clients. A man at church who's struggling with sleep paralysis even stopped me to ask what I believe about it.

Gender dysphoria: Reports of gender dysphoria have also multiplied. Of course, the media, social media, and other factors play into this symptom, but I believe there is more behind the proliferating confusion. Each case can't simply be excused as a fad or as a true mental health struggle. One person we've treated discussed her transgender identity as the most important aspect of who she is and where she finds meaning, which many suggest is a religious idea or thought.

Researchers note that "gender dysphoria is defined as a persistent desire to live and be accepted as the opposite sex, usually accompanied by a perceived inconsistency with the sex assigned at birth and a desire to change the body in accordance with the perceived sex." They assert that "the cause is unknown despite attempts of etiological mapping including genetic analyses, hormonal studies, and modern brain

3 Scarpelli, S., et al. (2022). "Sleep Paralysis." sciencedirect.com/science/article/abs/pii/.

imaging techniques." Recent studies have shown a dramatic increase in the number of younger people seeking treatment for gender dysphoria.[4]

Gender dysphoria greatly affects not only individuals but families as well by introducing a struggle that almost always causes frustration, confusion, and dissension. Parents are often told by school officials or legislators they're not allowed to have their own opinions regarding their child's gender, as if it were a choice. Even when parents are somewhat supportive but aren't completely affirming, they're frequently made out to be the enemy by school officials, legislators or the media. Research suggests family members feel judged and unsupported by the child protection system regarding gender-affirming care.[5] The devastating effects of gender dysphoria on families make me question if some type of evil entity is influencing or behind it all.

Unexplained physical or psychosomatic symptoms: Another escalating concern is the number of physical problems that can't be explained. Many medical doctors are referring clients to mental health professionals in the hopes of gaining insight into their clients' physical issues. For example, a young woman may go to her physician's office with intense stomach pain, but all medical reports show nothing is wrong. Referrals from clients like this come to my practice weekly. While anxiety and other mental health concerns can often manifest in physical ways, the number of referrals mental health professionals are receiving seems to suggest there may be another explanation.

"Clinical studies have shown that Medically Unexplained Symptoms (MUS) are related to common mental disorders," one group of researchers reported. "MUS were associated with the highest prevalence rates of mood

4 Frisén, L., Söder, O., and Rydelius, P. A. (2017). "Dramatic Increase of Gender Dysphoria in Youth." Lakartidningen, 114:EFMY. PMID: 28245038.

5 S. Bekaert, E. Paavilainen, H. Schecke, A. Baldacchino, E. Jouet, L. Zabłocka—Żytka, B. Bachi, F. Bartoli, G. Carrà, R. M. Cioni, C. Crocamo, J. V. Appleton, "Family Members' Perspectives of Child Protection Services, a Metasynthesis of the Literature," *Children and Youth Services Review*, Volume 128, 2021, 106094.

and anxiety disorders."[6] While we know this to be the case, could more be going on in a person's life leading to the manifestation of physical symptoms?

In the book *The Body Keeps the Score,* author Dr. Bessel van der Kolk describes many instances when patients' responses to stress aren't noticeable in terms of feelings or emotions but rather are evident through physical ailments such as migraines or asthma attacks. One section in the book discusses a patient who had an asthma attack every time her husband made an insensitive comment. Also, Dr. van der Kolk mentions research showing that children who've been abused often report feeling abdominal pain or other physical sensations with no known physical causes. Thus, the increase in physical symptoms may suggest an increase in trauma or traumatic events. Yet if there is no known history of trauma, what else could explain what's happening?[7]

At times, it may be necessary to look beyond clients' current circumstances if they're experiencing potential psychosomatic symptoms. Mental health professionals often inquire about a person's past—but not necessarily when the symptoms seem to have come on suddenly or physically. Assessing family generational issues may be helpful here, in addition to looking into other, possibly evil, influences on a person's life.

Increase in rates of self-harm and suicide: According to current research, there has been a massive jump in the number of suicides and attempts to self-harm. For example, an article in the *Journal of Policy Analysis and Management* points out that "the suicide rate in the United States has risen nearly 40% since 2000," and notes that "this increase is puzzling because suicide rates had been falling for decades at the end of the 20th century."[8]

---

6 van Eck van der Sluijs, J., et al. (2015). "Medically Unexplained and Explained Physical Symptoms in the General Population." PLOS ONE, 10(4): e0123274. doi.org/10.1371/journal.pone.

7 van der Kolk, B. A. (2014). *The Body Keeps the Score: Brain, Mind, and Body in the Healing of Trauma.* New York, NY: Viking.

8 "Suicide Increase Since 2000." *Journal of Policy Analysis and Management.* onlinelibrary.wiley.com

Here again is another category that might cause us to wonder about the influence of social media. Whereas I agree to a point that platforms such as TikTok, X (formerly Twitter), and Facebook might play a role in the rising number of these disturbing practices again, asking what or who is *behind* the evil influence of any media is worthwhile. We cannot simply say the problem is social media and stop there.

Additionally, there are reports of artificial intelligence (AI) having compelled some people to end their own lives. My staff members constantly discuss the range of activities clients are using AI for. One colleague said a client was using ChatGPT when seeking any type of advice or answers to questions on topics ranging from existential issues to recipes.

Think about that for a moment: An artificially intelligent program provides answers to questions about the meaning of life. This is scary in and of itself, but the fact that artificial intelligence has induced suicide or suicidal ideation should be even more concerning. And that's not to mention that many people believe AI may not merely be an algorithm or algorithmic intelligence providing us with algorithms but rather a form of communicating with a type of transdimensional intelligence—in other words, a being/entity.

Suicide is not just on the rise in the US; in 2024, I was asked alongside my co-counselor and friend, Beth, to help our friends who are missionaries in the Philippines deal with a massive increase in the number of suicides within the past year in the villages where the nation's residents work. We were blessed to lead suicide-prevention rallies in multiple areas during our time there. The sense of darkness those around us felt was real; it was a direct result of so many adolescents having killed themselves. Researchers blame the spike in the suicide rate among young people on social media influence; the rise of cell phone usage because of the 2020 pandemic forced many to transition to online learning. Be that as it may, I ask you to contemplate whether there is something else, something behind the means of media, some evil force behind the effort to cause a precious human to end his or her life, because I'm sure most would agree that suicide and self-harm come from a very dark place… or a very dark *being*.

Dark sexual behaviors: One glance at the headlines likely reveals some form of sexual abuse, human trafficking, pornography, sex work, or otherwise dreadful activity related to sexual behaviors. Bonnie Blue, for example, is a recent "star" from the OnlyFans site who sought to hold a world record for having the most sexual partners in one day. Sean ("P. Diddy") Combs and Jeffrey Epstein also come to mind in terms of widely known stories that fall in this category. There are also terrifying accounts of people who have fallen prey to online scams that require them to submit horrifying sexual images of themselves. Some of these incidents have even resulted in victims taking their own lives. In our practice, we also deal with people who are engaging in vile activities online, such as creating AI child pornography.

Sex trafficking is taking place in many neighborhoods in virtually all major cities in the United States of America. A total of 1,912 people were referred to US attorneys for human trafficking offenses in fiscal year 2022, a 26 percent increase from the 1,519 referred in 2012.[9] My practice partners with two local nonprofit organizations. One helps prevent and intervenes in sex-trafficking activity involving minor girls; another works with adults who have been trafficked. I also serve on my county's Human Trafficking Task Force with local law enforcement leaders and other community members. As a result, I've heard stories that have affected every family type, structure, and socioeconomic status. Sex trafficking is more prevalent than most people want to acknowledge.

Some clients have even reported sexual abuse in satanic ritualistic abuse. This is a harder symptom to review in terms of research, as often survivors are in fear for their lives if they report their experience, or they have extreme dissociation and thus haven't uncovered memories

9 bjs.ojp.gov/library/publications/human-trafficking-data-collection-activities-2024

of what they've gone through. Nonetheless, a 1994 study indicated the following:

> During the past decade in North America, a growing number of mental health professionals have reported that between 25% and 50% of their patients in treatment for multiple personality disorder (MPD) have recovered early childhood traumatic memories of ritual torture, incestuous rape, sexual debauchery, sacrificial murder, infanticide, and cannibalism perpetrated by members of clandestine satanic cults.[10]

This, in addition to the stories we hear in counseling today, leads me to believe sex trafficking has only continued to increase.

Many young people are sending nude pictures of themselves or their private parts to others via text messaging or other messaging apps. One study suggests that 90 percent of teenagers believe their peers are "sexting" or sending sexually explicit images or pictures to others. This indicates that teenagers believe this is normal behavior.[11] We hear these stories weekly, it seems. One client disclosed that her boyfriend required her to send nudes and make sex videos.

Symptoms reported from going missing: Some people believe they were taken by a foreign entity; in other words, they report having experienced something like an alien abduction. Symptoms of these ordeals also appear as dissociations at first, as some state they feel as if they have "lost time," but they're different from dissociations in that the experiencers can give details of what they went through. I've even seen mental health professionals post in Facebook groups to ask for consultation on how to deal with clients who have had these

---

10 Mulhern S. "Satanism, Ritual Abuse, and Multiple Personality Disorder: A Sociohistorical Perspective." *Int J Clin Exp Hypn*. 1994 Oct;42(4):265-88. doi: 10.1080/00207149408409359. PMID: 7960286.

11 brownhealth.org/be-well/what-sexting-and-it-common-among-teens

experiences, suggesting that the number of alien abductions or similar occurrences is also growing.

Limited information is provided for mental health professionals and pastoral or other counselors working with clients who have experienced or reported abductions from paranormal beings. Some who talk about these experiences have greater attraction to paranormal phenomena and are more likely to have a history of post-trauma episodes. Additionally, clients often have hallucinations, sleep disturbances, and the tendency to dissociate.[12]

Whether or not one believes there is a darkness behind these experiences, those of us who help them can't simply dismiss their accounts. Counselors, pastors, and others should be willing and prepared to help those who are struggling. People with the types of symptoms listed above shouldn't be left alone and thought to "just be crazy."

In my practice, because we're dealing with these issues increasingly often, it's not hard to consider that something sinister lies behind these atrocious behaviors. The darkness is often unseen, but it is there—seemingly in the supernatural realm, influencing humans in the realms we can see. On many days as I drive home from work, the darkness weighs on me like a heavy blanket when I pray and think about how to help my clients and staff.

Beyond some of the unusual *personal* symptoms we've looked at, some societal changes are worth considering as well.

12 neuroscigroup.us/articles/APT-4-116

Symptom	Observed Trend	Possible Explanation
Dissociation	Increased cases, including among youth with no known trauma history	Trauma, spiritual influence, social media exposure
Sleep Paralysis	Heightened client reports, often spiritual in nature	REM intrusion, possible generational/spiritual influence
Gender Dysphoria	Significant rise among youth, often without strong prior indicators	Media/social influence, identity confusion, spiritual deception
Psychosomatic Symptoms	Increase in medically unexplained physical issues (stomach pain, migraines)	Trauma manifestation, spiritual oppression, generational patterns
Self-Harm & Suicide	Dramatic increases, especially post-2020, among young people globally	Media influence, spiritual darkness, possible AI involvement
Sexual Deviance & Trafficking	Increased exposure to pornography, trafficking, ritual abuse, and hyper-sexualized content	Cultural normalization of darkness, spiritual corruption, lack of parental boundaries
Alien-abduction Experiences	Rising reports of people describing abductions, "lost time," and paranormal contact	Trauma responses, spiritual deception, fascination with the paranormal

QUESTIONS FOR REFLECTION

1. Have you heard of any uncommon symptoms among people in your church, your practice, or life in general?
2. Which symptom concerns you the most? How has your congregation or practice responded? OR how have you responded personally?
3. How would you explain the increase in atypical symptoms?
4. What do you believe is behind the rise in strange mental health occurrences?

PRACTICAL APPLICATION

Encouragement for pastoral counselors and mental health professionals:

- Be a loving observer as you pay attention to those you serve.
- Note any possible explanations you may have for symptoms you've noticed.
- Pray for discernment about how you can respond in love. This could be as simple as preaching a message on the influences of today (for example, social media and pornography).
- If you're a counselor, contemplate new strategies for dealing with dark influences.

Prayer prompt: *Lord, bring to mind any symptoms you're concerned about among those I serve or have influence over. Allow me to be a gentle observer as you prepare my heart for how to respond.*

SCRIPTURE TO CONSIDER

Romans 1: 22–28 (NET):

> Although they claimed to be wise, they became fools and exchanged the glory of the immortal God for an image resembling mortal human beings or birds or four-footed animals or reptiles. Therefore God gave them over in the desires of their hearts to impurity, to dishonor their bodies among themselves. They exchanged the truth of God for a lie and worshiped and served the creation rather than the Creator, who is blessed forever! Amen. For this reason God gave them over to dishonorable passions. For their women exchanged the natural sexual relations for unnatural ones, and likewise the men also abandoned natural relations with women and were inflamed in their passions for one another. Men committed shameless acts with men and received in themselves the due penalty for their error. And just as they did not see fit to acknowledge God, God gave them over to a depraved mind, to do what should not be done.

Chapter 2

DARK SOCIETAL CHANGES

The world changes according to the way people see it, and if you can alter, even by a millimeter, the way people look at reality, then you can change the world.

JAMES BALDWIN[1]

Disclaimer: These are simply observations; try not to read this information through a personal value lens or political point of view.

Societal changes are worth reviewing, as these influence the overall well-being of a culture. Over the past twenty to thirty years, these types of changes of note in terms of mental health include mass shootings (including school shootings); the rise of the internet and its effect on children and adolescents; increased numbers of abortions; a decrease in the level of social connectedness; a surge in the numbers of participation in cults; mushrooming involvement in the occult; overall social unrest; and exponential growth in the use of artificial intelligence.

Personally, since 2020, my awareness of societal changes has been shaped by the COVID-19 pandemic—a marking point in time, to be sure. The pain of realizing I couldn't physically sit across from my clients who were desperate for help and who needed to be in the presence of a caring human is something I can still remember. I felt at a very deep level the consequences of so much of our daily lives going virtual.

1 idealist.org/en/careers/20-quotes-inspire-and-committ-to-social-change

During that time, I found counseling much more challenging. Of course, members of just about every generation believes things are "getting worse" to a degree, but if we look back over history, the seemingly limitless access to knowledge via the internet alone has arguably created more problems in a shorter amount of time than any other generation has faced. What's behind these dark changes? Is something in an unseen realm influencing society?

Let's look at these dark changes individually.

Surging numbers of mass shootings/school shootings: I graduated from high school in 1999, the year of the Columbine school shooting in Jefferson County, Colorado. Since that horrific event, in which "twelve students and one teacher were killed and twenty-four others were injured, mass shootings in the United States have caused tremendous concern among both the public and policy-makers."[2]

Aside from the horror of the loss of so many lives and the injuries of the survivors, the practical effects of the Columbine tragedy were far-reaching.

My high school graduating class in North Carolina, for example, as did other schools across the nation, had to forego the tradition of holding its commencement on our football field in a stadium that could hold all our friends and family. Instead, we had to move the event to a local college auditorium with only enough seating for us to invite just four of our loved ones. As a middle child with two sisters and two parents, I had to inform my grandmother that she couldn't come. Even now, almost thirty years later, in the county where I live, all high schools hold graduations at indoor arenas instead of local schools and stadiums.

School shootings haven't just pushed graduations into smaller, safer venues, they've also compelled many parents to rethink their children's education altogether by considering homeschooling to be a more secure

2 Schildkraut, J., and Geller, L. B. (2023). "Mass Shootings in the United States: Prevalence, Policy, and a Way Forward." *The ANNALS of the American Academy of Political and Social Science, 704*(1), 181–203. https://doi.org/10.1177/00027162231164484 (Original work published 2022).

option. For example, an article titled "In the Wake of Mass Shootings, Parents Reconsider Mass Schooling," notes that after the Parkland, Florida, shooting in 2018, more parents were considering homeschooling their children.[3]

School shootings changed the way of life on campuses around the country as well. As a school counselor before I became a therapist, I recall always having to carry my keys because, from 1999 on, every outside door remained locked for security. Personnel and students were also required to participate in regular "school shooting" drills. The worst effect of the school shootings I've dealt with, however, has been counseling those who've been a part of one of those horrific incidents. The victims rarely fully recover from this type of trauma. One client who had been involved in a school shooting who is now a teacher still sets up her classroom in a way that she can protect her students and herself should a shooter enter the building.

School shootings are simply one type of mass shootings. We've also seen rampages at family gatherings, nightclubs, malls, and concerts. At times, the violence has made me think twice before taking my family into a crowded place because of the risk of attack. Mass shootings are pure evil. Innocent lives are lost. No explanation ever satisfies.

The terror of mass shootings has only increased in recent years. The number of school shootings has risen drastically since 2020.[4] And a 2015 study that included a review of forty-nine peer-reviewed articles of mass shootings concluded the following:

> Mass shootings are associated with a variety of adverse psychological outcomes in survivors and members of affected communities. Based on our review, we concluded that less is known about the psychological effects of mass shootings on

3 https://fee.org/articles/in-the-wake-of-mass-shootings-parents-reconsider-mass-schooling/

4 Matthews, A. L., O'Kruk, A., and Choi, Annette. "School Shootings in the US: Fast Facts," CNN.

indirectly exposed populations; however, there is evidence that such events lead to at least short-term increases in fears and declines in perceived safety.[5]

Increasingly harmful effects of the internet on children and adolescents: Years ago, I did extensive research for my dissertation on the impact of pornography in the K–12 school setting and how school counselors responded. One of the most disturbing statistics I found was that one-third of the content on the internet was pornography. Let that sink in for a moment. Think about all you do on the internet—pay bills, communicate, research, work…the list goes on. Yet a third of the entire worldwide web is comprised of pornography.[6] This fact alone is dark.

Social media is also a part of the internet that causes mental health struggles among young people and adults for many reasons—and not just suicide, as previously stated. Consider the family feuds, the gossip, the dangerous and unfair comparisons, the online gambling, and other unhealthy activities also engaged in. Of course, social media can serve a good purpose, but often it is negative—especially for children and adolescents, who are often using those platforms and the internet in general longer than adults, which harms their development.

Sleep is vital for adolescent development. Yet many adolescents have come into our practice with sleep issues and anxiety because they stay up all night playing video games. Lengthy internet use can also lead to unhealthy behaviors like spending minimal time outdoors and being seated—thus inactive—for long stretches, which can contribute to weight gain. Further, anxiety and depression can also be triggered by excessive internet use because it increases loneliness and relational

---

5 Lowe, S. R., & Galea, S. (2015). "The Mental Health Consequences of Mass Shootings." *Trauma, Violence, & Abuse, 18*(1), 62–82. doi.org/10.1177/1524838015591572 (Original work published 2017).

6 Atwell, Natalie, "School Counselor Experiences or Perspectives in an Age of Increasing Pornography Use and Sexual Behaviors of Students" (2019). *Doctoral Dissertations and Projects*. 1970. digitalcommons.liberty.edu/doctoral/1970.

problems.[7] Whenever there is a rise in activities that harm children, it isn't difficult to assume a nefarious entity is behind it.

Rising abortion rates: From 2017 to 2020, there was a 45 percent increase in the number of medicated abortions (abortion via a pill). One study even suggests that if the current rate remains the same, around 25 percent of women between the ages of fifteen and forty-four will have had an abortion. Additionally, "In the year(s) prior to the Dobbs [Supreme Court] decision, one-quarter of US women would have been expected to have at least one abortion in their lifetime if abortion rates for those years stayed the same."[8, 9]

Abortion negatively affects mental health, a fact that's been proven in many studies. For example, "a 2016 analysis of data from the National Longitudinal Study of Adolescent to Adult Health (Add Health) has shown that each exposure to abortion increases the risk of mental disorders by 23 percent, even after controlling for 25 other factors, including prior mental health issues."[10]

A true and almost visible darkness presents itself when clients who have had abortions discuss this part of their lives. I can speak from an anecdotal perspective and confidently state that most clients I've counseled who have had abortions have struggled at some level with the issue of forgiveness—mainly of themselves. Many have made comments such as, "I know God forgives me, but I can't forgive myself." It's as if they won't *allow* themselves any self-forgiveness. Yet that's the only way to completely heal from the emotional effects of having an abortion.

Decreasing social connectedness: As we all experienced firsthand, the pandemic of 2020 led to extreme social isolation. According to one

---

7 Du N, Liu L, Zhang L, Yin S. "The Impact of Internet Use on Adolescents' Health: Empirical Evidence from China." *Front Psychiatry*. May 28, 2024;15:1404574. doi: 10.3389/fpsyt.2024.1404574. PMID: 38863618; PMCID: PMC11165346.

8 Guttmacher Institute. doi.org/10.1363/psrh.12215.

9 Jones, R. K. (2024). "Estimate of the Lifetime Incidence of Abortion in the United States." *Contraception*, 135, 110445. doi.org/10.1016/j.contraception.2024.110445.

10 lozierinstitute.org/fact-sheet-abortion-and-mental-health/

study, social isolation had already been increasing, and social engagement with family and friends had been on the decline. The study showed that "household family social engagement and companionship showed signs of progressive decline years prior to the pandemic, at a pace *not* eclipsed by the pandemic."[11]

Conversations at parties or other events often turn to how "the world lost its mind" during 2020. Schools and churches shut down, businesses closed, and even the busiest highways were quiet. Families fought over unprecedented issues such as whether to get vaccines and/or whether to wear masks. School boards were in an uproar as their members tried to decide what was best for children. Parents grappled with balancing work and educating their children from home. Teachers were worried about students with difficult family lives. Medical professionals were pressured to receive vaccines seemingly without having a choice. Mental health professionals, in the meantime, became overwhelmed by the growing list of those needing services.

Many conclusions have been made about COVID-19's social effect on children and adolescents. For example, we know that increased time spent online and engaging in social media—direct consequences of mass shutdowns—negatively affects everyone, but especially those with developing minds. Despite that, not many have discussed the repercussions of the shame and fear techniques that were used to motivate people to remain at home, receive vaccinations, or isolate from loved ones. Shame and fear are terrible motivators; they deplete our energy and make us more susceptible to a variety of problems. Love and compassion are much better motivators. Sadly, many leaders around the world used words such as "love" and "compassion" to disguise their fear and shame messaging. The effects of these tactics will be felt for generations to come.

Humans were created for connection with other humans. The perilous time of 2020 jeopardized that connectedness. The influences in society

---

11 Kannan, V. D., and Veazie, P. V. (2022). *Social Isolation Trends, 2003–2020.* doi.org/10.1016/j.ssmph.2022.101331.

going against our need for interaction makes us wonder what—or who—is behind these influences.

Swelling popularity of cult participation: Although people have been more socially isolated and less interactive in recent years, the desire to have connections remains. This may be one reason for an increasing interest in cults, which tend to look a little different than they have in the past. "The long and the short of it," notes an article in *Teen Vogue*, "is that our cravings for connection, belonging, and purpose have existed since the dawn of humanity, and cultish groups have always popped up during moments of social turbulence when these cravings have gone majorly unsatisfied." The article's writer continued:

> What makes the 21st Century an especially culty time for America's youth is that in this social media-ruled age, when gurus can be godless, when you can "join" a digital "cult" just by clicking "follow" with your fingertip, and when folks who hold alternative beliefs are able to find each other (and radicalize) more easily than ever online, it only makes sense that "cults" of all stripes would start raging like wildfire.[12]

The number of clients who come into our practice who've been involved in cults disguised as churches is almost unbelievable. It's easier to observe cult-like tendencies in people from the outside looking in, so I'm thankful people are coming to counseling when they're harmed by a cult-like church experience. Locally, in my metro area, a major Christian leader has been accused of treating certain girls differently because he said they were "like daughters" to him. Meanwhile, he kissed one and told her that was normal behavior for a church leader. It took the young woman years to disclose this information because she felt shame for what this man would have described as "speaking against a man of God."

---

12 *Teen Vogue.* (2022). "Why Are Young People So Obsessed with Cults?" teenvogue.com/story/why-are-young-people-so-obsessed-with-cults.

People longing for connection are often easily "groomed" into wanting to be accepted into cult-like groups. Grooming often looks like the following to victims:

- A leader notices you, acknowledges something "special" in you, and begins to pay you extra attention.
- You're given a platform through which to "elevate your gifts" (for example, singing or speaking) even though you may have had little to no training, education, and/or mentoring in that area.
- You're given the impression that you are part of an exclusive group.
- Once you've been given more responsibility within the church/group, leaders begin to question your authority figures (folks such as your parents, grandparents, or other pastors who've shepherded you), leading to confusion.
- You begin to ask questions, but answers aren't coming from Scripture in ways you've thought or been taught before.
- At some point, you begin wondering more and more what the leader will say or how the leader will respond...or you worry about your leader's response before you consider what God says.
- If you leave the church/group, you're considered to be disobedient, to have deficient faith, or not called to be a part of the "special movement" happening within the church/group.
- If you've questioned any of the leaders' instructions or practices, or have asked for clarification on any matters, the leaders remind you of their "calling" or special "authority" and reprimand you, possibly harshly.
- You battle confusion between the good you've experienced as a part of the group/church/ministry and the confusion and hurt of being separated from family or friends who have loved you for years.

- You suffer the inner turmoil of feeling good about the kind words spoken to you and the hurtful ones used in times of "correction."
- If you've considered leaving the cult, leaders or members remind you of the times they've blessed you with kind words, gifts, special treatment, or more.

Being groomed by a cult can be a slippery slope; it's important to be aware of how it's carried out. Nothing good is behind this type of manipulation. Have you experienced any of these behaviors or attitudes in a church? Have you noticed them in a family member, coworker, leader, or friend? If so, you're not alone. Good intentions are not behind these red flags—whether you see them or not.

Escalating engagement in the occult: This may seem surprising, but the number of clients in my practice who are engaging in occult practices is alarming. However, many of these folks—of varying faith backgrounds—think these activities are harmless. One client has disclosed that her husband has been participating in New Age practices by speaking to spirits; this is causing problems in the home.

Other clients have described playing video games in which they cast spells and play with a Ouija board. One experienced anxiety after a family member called a psychic to do readings for her. Others say they use crystals to aid in their healing.

When clients put their hope in their horoscope, it can alter their thoughts and plans—not typically a positive step. On certain Facebook groups for mental health professionals, some therapists even promote the use of practices such as using tarot cards in sessions. Other therapists seek advice about how to counter what a psychic told their client. Darkness is associated with these practices, so the increase in engagement should be explored.

"At the turn of the twentieth and twenty-first centuries," notes an article in the *Social Compass* journal, "the landscape of religions and the dynamics of beliefs were reshaped by several movements. On one side, a 'return of magic' in contemporary societies and the rise of a modern witchcraft, and in parallel, and on another side, the rise and expansion of forms of 'spirituality.'"[13] We don't have to watch the media very long to understand the ubiquitous influence of psychics, mediums, astrology, and more.

New Age or occult practices can seemingly have positive effects in the beginning, but they can eventually cause a wide array of mental health struggles, including anxiety and sleep disturbances.

"New Age" emerged as a popular term in the 1980s and can be traced back to the interest in the holistic health movements of prior decades. It is rooted in the appearance of Theosophy (seeking hidden knowledge through practices such as meditation), New Thought (the power of positive thinking or manifesting positive things in your life), and overall spiritualism (interacting with the spiritual realm in general). Overall, it's characterized by a mix of traditions including mysticism, esoteric metaphysics, the occult, and self-actualization concepts.[14]

Heightening societal unrest: It should be no surprise that between politics, racial issues, the pandemic, healthcare costs, wars, and more, many people in societies throughout the world are experiencing unrest. Numerous studies suggest the numbers of those involved in political and cultural turmoil were rising before 2020, and they continue to trend upward. In fact, according to one report, "Since 2017, more than 400 significant anti-government protests have erupted worldwide, according to the Carnegie Global Protest Tracker."[15]

Social unrest is often discussed in the counseling office. My practice's therapists have noted that clients of varying backgrounds have been bringing up racial issues much more frequently in recent years. Police

---

13 Obadia, L. (2023). 'Spiritual' Witchcraft and Magic 2.0 as Weapons of Resistance: Emergence of a New Movement? *Social Compass*, *70*(4), 549–565. doi.org/10.1177/00377686231217194 (Original work published 2023).

14 Levin, J. "New Age Healing: Origins, Definitions, and Implications for Religion and Medicine." *Religions*. 2022; 13(9):777. https://doi.org/10.3390/rel13090777.

15 Carnegie Global Protest Tracker. ajg.com/news-and-insights/features/responding-to-rising-social-unrest.

officers are, thankfully, engaging in counseling more often; yet, because of the pressures of the social unrest, they often don't want to come to sessions in uniform. Professional counseling conferences feature a seemingly endless number of classes on how to combat social unrest of all types.

School board meetings are often places of contention and arguments about books in libraries rather than places where board members discuss what keeps children safe and enhances learning. College campuses used to be places of scholarship, exploration, and fun. Now they seem to be more centered on protests and the agendas of certain groups pushing their ideologies. Cultural wars are being fought in meetings that are available for any viewing audience with access to YouTube.

Once I was asked to speak at a school board meeting about my research on pornography in schools and give my professional recommendations. One person with a political agenda who was campaigning for a position on the board made a nasty post on social media about me being "dangerous." Apparently, I was "dangerous" because I am a Christian who does not hide her faith. My views were based on research and evidence that pornography is harmful to children and that parents should have a right to know what books their children are reading. The superintendent, clearly afraid of this person, asked me to wait so he could further review my information; he said he would have me come back to a later meeting. That was two years ago; the call inviting me to return still hasn't come. I'm certain darkness is behind this situation.

Again, these are just a few aspects of social changes I've noticed. While some allude to these challenges as leading toward social growth of some kind, they feel like more of a breakdown of society led by something or someone pernicious.

Pervasive use of artificial intelligence: Of course, AI refers to the ability of technology to do tasks that typically require humans to perform. While one study suggests that only 55 percent of Americans interact with artificial intelligence daily,[16] we all use it regularly. For

16 https://www.nu.edu/blog/ai-statistics-trends/

example, we recruit help from Siri or Alexa to do everything from playing music to reminding us to go to the gym; we rely on AI tech for speech or facial recognition on our phones and apps; we use it to seek virtual customer service; and we lean on it when we're searching for information or products.

In some instances, AI is used instead of human intelligence. In truth, AI can be a powerful tool when used responsibly, but it's important that we use it with caution.

Multiple studies have found significant negative effects of artificial intelligence on our well-being.[17] Technology can cause us to become dependent on machines, which aren't always equipped to make the best decisions. Our dependence can lead outside to mind control, diminished critical thinking skills, declining relational skills, and decreased mental stimulation. One client has used AI as a "friend," and there is a noticeable difference in the way he relates to AI versus real humans.

In counseling, we see difficulty in relating to other people (rather than AI) often present as "social anxiety" or a social phobia characterized by significant anxiety and fear of being judged by others in a negative way.[18] Many would prefer to have "online friends" over friends in a natural setting. This lack of connection has an adverse effect on their mental health, with special concern about their scarcity of healthy attachments.

Some counselors use AI for treatment planning and note taking. While it's not "wrong" to use AI for this purpose in every circumstance, mental health professionals should approach it with extreme caution. One troubling concern is the potential risk it presents to professional/patient confidentiality.

From a spiritual perspective, there's a legitimate worry that AI might come to be considered as a type of deity to be worshipped. One article even suggests technology worship is a sort of new religion.[19] AI can be

---

17 Yong Zhao, Da Yin, Lili Wang, Yihua Yu. "The Rise of Artificial Intelligence, the Fall of Human Wellbeing?" First published: February 5, 2023, https://doi.org/10.1111/ijsw.12586.

18 mayoclinic.org/diseases-conditions/social-anxiety-disorder/symptoms-causes

19 https://airmail.news/issues/2025-5-24/the-view-from-here

seen as a "genie" that will provide whatever information is needed, or as a vending-machine type of deity; "put the coin in the slot" ("tell AI what you want") and receive something in return—most likely something that's unhealthy. The reality, though, is that we don't always know what we need, and AI is not sovereign. Therein lies the danger. A recent episode of the Theology Pugcast podcast, titled "Emerging Paganism," noted that some of AI's creators have said they felt the knowledge of how it was developed came to them from "unknown sources" or "energies." This in and of itself seems malevolent. At the very least, we must question what or who is behind this knowledge and not just trust it. Some type of intelligent being must be behind it.

I hope by now you can begin to at least question whether there is someone or something behind the changes in society. Something in the supernatural realm seems to be interacting with society in nefarious ways. Undoubtedly it is dark and often unseen, but it is real.

Societal Change	Mental Health Impact	Evidence
Mass/School Shootings	Cause fear, anxiety, trauma, PTSD; long-term psychological effects for victims; increased homeschooling and anxiety about public spaces.	2015 review: Mass shootings cause short-term fear and reduced perceived safety. Increase in school shootings since 2020. Parkland example cited for shift toward homeschooling.
Rise of the Internet	Leads to anxiety, depression, social isolation, body-image issues, developmental delays in children due to overexposure; harmful effects of pornography and media.	One-third of internet is pornography; media encourages gossip, comparison, gambling; internet use linked to loneliness, anxiety, and obesity in children.
Abortion Increase	Increases risk of mental disorders (depression, guilt, inability to forgive one's self); deep emotional and spiritual wounds.	2016 Add Health study: Each abortion increases mental health risk by 23%; 25% of women aged 15-44 expected to have at least one abortion if rates continue.

Societal Change	Mental Health Impact	Evidence
Decline in Social Connectedness	Increase in anxiety, depression, and trauma due to isolation, especially post-2020; shame and fear tactics during pandemic caused deep emotional exhaustion and mistrust.	Research showed social connectedness declined prior to the pandemic; 2020 accelerated it. Shame and fear as motivators leave people depleted and vulnerable.
Cult Participation	Victims experience confusion, spiritual abuse, isolation, grooming, and emotional manipulation leading to psychological damage.	Quotes article about cultish rise in social media era; outlines a multi-point list of grooming tactics within churches, highlighting prevalence and warning signs.
Occult Involvement	Leads to anxiety, spiritual confusion, sleep disturbances, and a false sense of control; replaces hope with superstition.	Traces history of occult/New Age beliefs; rise of spirituality tied to media influence. Occult practices linked with dark mental health effects. Therapists have even used tarot cards and sought to counter psychic input in sessions.
Social Unrest	Causes chronic stress, fear, avoidance, and mistrust (especially around politics), race, education, and health-care systems.	Carnegie reports 400+ significant protests since 2017; social unrest increasingly addressed in counseling; police reluctant to attend therapy in uniform; counselors trained to deal with unrest; cultural tension disrupting education.
Rise of AI	Reduces critical thinking, human connection, and relational development; may contribute to social anxiety and loss of real-world interpersonal skills.	55% of Americans use AI daily; AI dependence may result in mind control, reduced mental stimulation, and lack of social skills. Counselors using AI tools raises concerns about confidentiality breaches.

QUESTIONS FOR REFLECTION

1. What changes in society have you noticed in recent years, and how would you explain them?
2. What changes have you seen lately within your community?
3. Have you noticed changes in society related to mental health?

PRACTICAL APPLICATION

Encouragement for pastoral counselors and mental health professionals:

- Be aware of changes within your community and congregation.
- Speak out against harmful changes and practices. These could be seen in something as simple as a social media post or in something as intentional as a Sunday-morning sermon.
- Encourage those over whom you have influence to pray and fast regarding the growing darkness in society.
- Seek training on how to deal with the negative influences in society.

Prayer Prompt: *Lord, show me how to be a light in the dark in my neighborhood, church, and community. Give me steps and strategies for how to push back the darkness in Jesus' name.*

SCRIPTURE TO CONSIDER

Ecclesiastes 1:9 (NLT):

> What exists now is what will be, and what has been done is what will be done; there is nothing truly new on earth.

2 Timothy 2:15 (NCV):

> Make every effort to give yourself to God as the kind of person he will approve. Be a worker who is not ashamed and who uses the true teaching in the right way.

Philippians 2:12–13 (NIV):

> Therefore, my dear friends, as you have always obeyed—not only in my presence but now much more in my absence—continue to work out your salvation with fear and trembling, for it is God who works in you to will and to act to fulfill his good purpose.

1 Corinthians 2:12 (NIV):

> What we have received is not the spirit of the world, but the Spirit who is from God, so that we may understand what God has freely given us.

1 Corinthians 2:16 (NIV):

> Who has known the mind of the Lord so as to instruct him? But we have the mind of Christ.

Chapter 3

NEFARIOUS CHANGES IN THE CHURCH

Understand that you cannot singlehandedly change an entire system; you are not called to do so. Yet we are to speak truth about our systems. This is difficult to do and sometimes quite risky.

DIANE LANGBERG, *Redeeming Power: Understanding Authority and Abuse in the Church*

According to Pew Research in 2023, the American church has a declining population, especially among young people. In contrast, a growing number of folks in America consider themselves to be atheists, agnostics, or non-religious. Sadly, many of these changes are due to secularization within the church, social issues that are misunderstood, and church-related scandals that lead to mistrust. I considered the enigma of cults or involvement in the occult increasing while churches are decreasing in attendance. What explains the growth in spiritual exploration among young people and the decline in church attendance by the same population? In my practice, we encourage those seeking connection socially to give us examples of types of places they can try. Many times, younger people especially are more excited about looking into a New Age-type group than they are about considering a church group.

The unseen or supernatural realm should not be an uncommon topic in churches. Yet, it's often off-limits, particularly in terms of the darkness. Some churches focus too much on the good aspects of the supernatural while never addressing the darkness and how it can infiltrate the church. Meanwhile, others zero in too much on the darkness outside the church without realizing how it lurks within. The proliferating number of church scandals is just one bit of evidence of the darkness that can infiltrate church administrations and congregations.

Topics that often come up in therapy regarding the church are narcissism of leadership, non-Christian practices, spiritual abuse of members, and a lack of strong relationships amongst members that would lead to healthy discipleship. Let's review these.

Narcissism

One major problem contributing to the declining interest in the church is shared often in the therapy room: narcissistic leadership. In their book, *Let Us Prey: The Plague of Narcissist Pastors*, authors Glenn Ball and Darrell Puls found that 31.2 percent of pastors surveyed met the criteria for narcissistic personality disorder, which is characterized by someone who needs excessive attention, lacks empathy, and has a series of troubled relationships. Narcissistic pastors are not following the biblical example of being a shepherd (see Ezekiel 24).[1]

You may doubt the statistics or find it hard to believe pastors struggle with narcissism. Consider the following characteristics to gauge leaders you know or have heard, all of which are used to describe and at times diagnose narcissistic personality disorder:

- Their language consists of "I," "me," "my," and "mine" often, and they regularly turn conversations back to themselves.
- They share more stories about themselves or their family than others.
- They show a lack of interest in the words, stories, or experiences of others.
- They respond to questions and challenging situations with anger and defensiveness.

1 Ball, G., and Puls, D. (2014). *Let Us Prey: The Plague of Narcissist Pastors.*

- They preach sermons that support their behaviors and/or misuse Scripture to defend the way they act.
- They resist allowing others to help lead.
- They push out or reject ministries that aren't their top priority or interest.
- They manipulate situations and people to benefit their agenda.
- They have a false sense of humility, devaluing themselves or their contributions in a way that draws attention to themselves; they "humbly" brag.
- Their demeanor often makes them seem unapproachable.
- They excuse their bad behaviors by saying it's just "something they struggle with."
- They expect others to sacrifice or serve in ways they will not.
- They surround themselves with people who don't question them. They "oust" or shame those who do challenge them.
- They rarely speak to people they've disagreed with and/or who have left the churches they serve.

Sadly, the list could continue, but these are the main, consistent ways narcissism has been demonstrated by pastors battling this darkness. A pastor I worked with once said, "I know how I handled this situation was wrong, but I'd do it all over again the same way." This man also has a reputation for surrounding himself only with those who agree with him. So, in a sense, he can handle things poorly simply because he is allowed to.

Narcissistic pastors believe subtle, flattering, and destructive lies such as:

- "You're the chosen one."
- "You alone are trustworthy."
- "You don't need permission"

Then, those lies escalate:

- "You're just mentoring her."
- "You're a father figure to her, so a hug like that is fine."
- "People are only fighting you because of the calling on your life."

Before the church leader knows it, he has passed the point of no return.

Most church and ministry leaders today have a board or an accountability structure, but they don't often welcome the board or accountability partners' involvement and feedback. Or, even worse, they hand-select people to serve in these roles who will simply support whatever they say or do. Leaders who just want to build a ministry or lead one without listening to God (and to others God has chosen to walk with them) will experience destruction when they're told no. Just watch the news and you're likely to hear a report about a church leader who has "fallen from grace." These pastors are often reported for their financial or relationship failures.[2] Where did their decline begin? I believe it likely started with the lack of being questioned and not being held accountable. Many have forgotten that if no one ever challenges our thinking, the danger is that we'll always think we're right.

Leaders alone aren't to blame. Some studies suggest that larger churches and/or those with congregants who have less-dominant personalities tolerate narcissism at higher levels in their leaders.[3] At times, the congregants are even a part of the problem as well. When we want the most educated, the most charismatic, the most personable, and the most talented to lead our churches, we often fall prey to a lack of humility in the person we choose. Sadly, I watched a pastor mistreat people for years and I excused it because he delivered good sermons. Only when he mistreated me did I begin looking more closely at his "rotten fruit."

---

2 usatoday.com/story/news/nation/2019/06/17/joel-osteen-kenneth-copeland-10-televangelists

3 Dunaetz, D., Jung, H., and Lambert, S., "Do Larger Churches Tolerate Pastoral Narcissism More Than Smaller Churches?" (October 1, 2018). *Great Commission Research Journal,* 10(1), 69–89, 2018, Available at SSRN: ssrn.com/abstract=3267070.

Asking what's influencing the tolerance of ungodly characteristics such as narcissism in the pulpits leads us to one answer: evil. Sexual abuse scandals alone are disgusting, and it's almost incomprehensible that they're taking place in (and concealed by) the family of God. And that's not to mention the hiding of such cases. This is pure wickedness.

Non-Christian Practices

Another factor contributing to the declining interest in attending Christian churches is non-Christian practices and teachings, including paganism/neo-paganism, modern-day gnosticism/neo-gnosticism, and occult activity.

Paganism is any form of spiritual practice that doesn't look to the Most High God. Pagan practices include using or promoting the enneagram personality test, teaching the prosperity gospel (which correlates financial well-being and good health to the degree of one's faith), and even creating certain types of moods and using specific kinds of music. Yoga and even using essential oils, if we don't guard ourselves against what they may represent, can also be pagan.

Gnosticism is like paganism, yet it's different in that gnostics believe some hidden knowledge ("gnosis") is needed for the path to salvation. Gnosis can come through overt or covert teachings, but we should be aware of any teachings that require the inclusion of extrabiblical or hidden knowledge. We can see a modern-day example of gnosticism in the transgender movement, in which some people suggest the physical body is separate from the true self. They may believe this isn't a concept the Bible covers about identity; thus, one needs extra knowledge to understand who they are.

Enneagrams

The enneagram, briefly mentioned earlier, is a personality test using a nine-pointed star polygon, with points representing numbers associated with personality types.[4] Books about the practice have been written and/or promoted by the likes of pastors and authors Rick Warren, Andy Stanley, and Russell Moore.[5] Many people believe knowing their enneagram number helps them do everything better: from connecting with God to understanding themselves and even helping their marriages.

However, using the enneagram is not a biblical practice; it isn't a legitimate psychological assessment for personality types, either. It is rooted in paganism and thus can be dangerous. "The 'evil' is that the Enneagram presents a modernist, gnostic view of Church teachings," states an article on catholicinsight.com. "The Enneagram is a mix of philosophical and religious ideas that veer away from Christian belief."[6]

One of many pitfalls of the enneagram is when people use it to help them excuse their behavior. For example, a client might come in and say, "Well, I'm a 9 [a number indicating their personality might be accepting and willing to go along with others], so this is just who I am." The principle behind the enneagram also runs contrary to what Scripture teaches us about humans and their personalities and behaviors.

Prosperity Gospel

Further pagan practices in the church are attempts to infiltrate it with the prosperity gospel, which promotes the "god of health and wealth." This is far from the Most High God of the Bible. Although many people are aware of the prosperity gospel and even warn others against following it, I still hear it creep into services in subtle ways. For example, at a church's graduation Sunday I recently attended, the pastor said, "If you follow Jesus, you will succeed in life." This is misleading. I heard it as I was seated by someone who faithfully follows Jesus, yet who was going through a difficult divorce. That was clear evidence that the pastor's words simply weren't true.

4 https://bcworldview.org/the-problem-with-the-enneagram/
5 Ibid.
6 catholicinsight.com/2023/enneagram-spiritual-direction-paganism-modernism-or-valuable-tool

Meanwhile, not many pastors teach congregants about suffering. LifeWay research found in a 2021 poll of pastors that most speak on the topics of God, Jesus, love, power, faith, and glory.[7] Yet Scripture mentions suffering hundreds of times. In just a quick glance at the book of Philippians, we read that the Apostle Paul tells the people to suffer for Christ and the gospel (see Philippians 1:29–30).

Atmospherics, Yoga, Essential Oils, Self-Help

The enemies of God know exactly what to do to deceive us, and they're doing it through a variety of practices. For starters, a focus on creating the "right atmosphere" can become a slippery slope into pagan darkness. One article notes that "creating an engaging worship space" includes taking steps such as building a team for stage design, budgeting for stage design, and using color to establish a certain "mood."[8] In truth, the only atmosphere that matters in a church is the posture of our hearts. Promoting experiences outside of the gospel is pagan.

Yoga is another concerning practice taking place on church campuses more frequently in recent years. It's increasingly accepted in churches as "spiritually and physically beneficial"[9]—and, in and of itself, it isn't necessarily wrong. In fact, I've done it for stretching, but I'm cautious about when I do it, with whom I do it, and most importantly to whom I do it. Did you know that certain poses represent aspects of worship to fallen gods?

Some churches also promote and sell essential oils, which can also be treacherous because some essential oil companies describe their products

---

7 research.lifeway.com/2022/03/31/most-popular-sermon-passages-topics-in-2021

8 shop.ccisolutions.com/StoreFront/category/7-tips-for-creating-an-engaging-worship-space

9 Csala B., Springinsfeld C. M., Köteles F. "The Relationship Between Yoga and Spirituality: A Systematic Review of Empirical Research." *Front Psychol.* August 2021, 2;12:695939. doi: 10.3389/fpsyg.2021.695939. PMID: 34408712; PMCID: PMC8365182.

as being able to help users obtain spiritual awareness.[10] I occasionally use products like this, but I do it knowing fully well that healing comes from God, period. It does not come from oil.

Many churches have bought into the big business of "self-help," a practice that can open the door to gnosticism (a type of knowledge—"gnosis"—leading to freedom) if it leads to thinking that suggests the truth is within the individual self, for example. Even if churches or ministries say they haven't promoted self-help, just Google "Christian self-help books" and you'll get thousands of responses for books, programs, videos, speakers, and more. In 2020, *Publisher's Weekly* reported that religion publishing was a billion-dollar industry, with top books sold on topics in the self-help category.[11] Many of these books are in my personal library, including *Boundaries* by Henry Cloud and John Townsend, a great book I refer to clients regularly. I'm not saying some self-help books aren't beneficial. The point is that often a church's focus is more on self-help than sacrificial love.

Consider this: If a church advertises a childcare-provided event designed to give women a break and during which to take care of themselves, the event sign-up sheet will likely fill up quickly. Conversely, if a church holds a class on the subject of "learning to die to yourself" or provides an opportunity to volunteer at the dirtiest place in town on a Saturday, likely the sign-up sheets won't fill up. Here again, events promoting self-care aren't all bad or wrong; we simply must keep our attitude in check. When we focus more on self-help than on dying to ourselves—our human nature—we can more easily be led to darkness or evil. This is one of the main ways evil can enter and establish an influence: by starting out a positive action that, allowed to become our focus, pushes away the gospel. There are also many other ways paganism is infiltrating our churches slowly—often under the guise of health and wellness. We must be alert for these things and shine light in the darkness.

10 Michael Miller, "Essential Oils: Use Spiritual Discernment," *Samaritan Ministries*, August 1, 2013, https://samaritanministries.org/blog/essential-oils-use-spiritual-discernment.

11 publishersweekly.com/religion/article/how-religion-publishing-became-a-billion-dollar-industry

Lack of Discipleship and Meaningful Attachments

Some churches are growing in size, but they aren't growing in Christ. Research suggests that while larger congregations boast packed pews, members of smaller congregations tend to show a deeper level of commitment, demonstrate a stronger emphasis on giving, and can often be found taking part in others-focused activities such as volunteering.[12] Recently, when one of my practice's therapists asked a client about her relationships with other members of her church's congregation, she answered, "Well, church is okay; we just don't fit into our Sunday school class." According to her description, her class at a well-known church in our area had become a social club instead of a place where people can grow because of healthy interactions with others. There is some level of this lack of a sense of belonging at every church, it seems.

Who we are is shaped by who we love. If we don't have healthy, loving attachments, we will be formed by unhealthy ones…if we haven't been so already. In one of the most powerful books I've read in recent years, *The Other Half of Church,*[13] the authors approach this problem from a neuroscientific and theological perspective. They say the healthy ingredients of a church are seen in evidence such as true joy found through connection, *hesed* (loyal) love among members of securely attached communities, a Christlike group identity, and a culture of uplifting, healthy correction.

When was the last time you experienced these benefits of being involved in a church? Tragically, not many do these days. Isn't it just like the evil enemies of God, combined with the sinful nature of humans, to try to take down the church by redefining it as a social club? Paul told the church at Philippi to "imitate," or "follow," his example (Philippians 3:17). They were only able to do this as they learned to love

---

12 research.lifeway.com/2021/10/20/small-churches-continue-growing-but-in-number-not-size/

13 Wilder, J., & Hendrix, M. (2020). *The Other Half of Church: Christian Community, Brain Science, and Overcoming Spiritual Stagnation*. Chicago, IL: Moody Publishers.

him—because he loved Christ and them. Once love was built as a foundation, they spent time with him to learn how to follow his example. While he was away, he wrote a letter and sent others to help them. Change always happens within the context of a relationship.

Exploration Continued

Beyond the questions and personal contemplation surrounding the symptoms of societal and church changes, I was still pondering the fact that I was experiencing spiritual warfare while treating clients. I wondered whether some of the issues at hand were deeper than mental health within society or even within church structures. Based on much study of the Bible, I firmly believe in spiritual war, but I hadn't honestly questioned what I was seeing in practice with this correlation in mind—until I noticed the increase. What if there is a true spiritual war: Are evil forces trying to destroy humans as described in Scripture? And am I seeing it play out in everyday sessions with clients? What if the symptoms see more and more often are the result of clients somehow being exposed to darkness—even, at times, when they're unaware? These questions became the foundation of my hypothesis.

Research supported my observations and hypothesis, but there weren't enough mental health professionals equipped to assess and treat these new, potentially spiritual situations. In fact, one study suggests only one in five mental health professionals feels comfortable addressing religious and spiritual struggles.[14] That led me to wonder if we, as mental health professionals, are even asking the right questions. Do we understand the true problems with people today? Can we explain what's happening within ourselves, our families, society, and/or the church? To test my new theory that there's a correlation between spirituality and

---

14 Vieten, C., Oxhandler, H. K., Pearce, M., Fry, N., Tanega, C., Pargament, K. "Mental Health Professionals' Perspectives on the Relevance of Religion and Spirituality to Mental Health care." *BMC Psychol.* December 12, 2023;11(1):439. doi: 10.1186/s40359-023-01466-y. PMID: 38087372; PMCID: PMC10717464.

mental health, I began thinking about clients' problems on different levels. No longer was I able to label unusual symptoms or long-standing challenges as simple anxiety. There had to be more to the stories of a massive increase in atypical symptoms, suicide, depression, and the breakdown of society and the church.

With so many possibilities running through my mind, one thing I was convinced of is that there is a spiritual or unseen battle to destroy humans. Suicide, abortion, thoughts of being born in the wrong body, isolation, narcissism, cults, and occult activities are all effective means of destroying humans as we know them…as God created them to be. As my questions turned to further research, finding disturbing facts led to more questions, prompting me to see if the Bible had any answers.

As a disclaimer, I will state that these three categories are influenced by my supernatural worldview, faith, and education. I encourage you to stick with me even if you don't believe the Bible. I challenge you to think critically and consider the battle humans are experiencing and, in turn, how to find true supernatural healing.

QUESTIONS FOR REFLECTION

1. What have you examined as changes within the church or religious communities?
2. How would you explain the changes in the church?
3. Have you noticed changes in the church related to mental health?

PRACTICAL APPLICATION

Encouragement for pastoral counselors and mental health professionals:

- Be prepared to deal with those who have been hurt within the church.
- Guard against narcissism and other potentially harmful attitudes and behaviors in your church by having accountability structures in place.

- Reflect regularly on the health of your church.
- Seek training on how to respond to spiritual abuse.
- Offer support, such as counseling, to those who have been harmed by the church.

Prayer Prompt: *Lord, reveal any concerns within my church. Clean out anything that is not from you. Guide me to help any who've been hurt by the church or religion.*

SCRIPTURE TO CONSIDER

Ephesians 4:1–64:

> As a prisoner for the Lord, then, I urge you to live a life worthy of the calling you have received. Be completely humble and gentle; be patient, bearing with one another in love. Make every effort to keep the unity of the Spirit through the bond of peace. There is one body and one Spirit, just as you were called to one hope when you were called; one Lord, one faith, one baptism; one God and Father of all, who is over all and through all and in all. For just as the body is one and yet has many members, and all the members of the body—though many—are one body, so too is Christ. For in one Spirit we were all baptized into one body. Whether Jews or Greeks or slaves or free, we were all made to drink of the one Spirit. For in fact the body is not a single member, but many. If the foot says, "Since I am not a hand, I am not part of the body," it does not lose its membership in the body because of that. And if the ear says, "Since I am not an eye, I am not part of the body," it does not lose its membership in the body because of that. If the whole body were an eye, what part would do the hearing? If the whole were an ear, what part would exercise the sense of smell? But as a matter of fact, God has placed each of the members in the body just as he decided. If they were all the same member, where would the body be? So now there are many members, but one body. The eye cannot say to the hand, "I do not need you

nor in turn can the head say to the foot, "I do not need you." On the contrary, those members that seem to be weaker are essential, and those members we consider less honorable we clothe with greater honor, and our unpresentable members are clothed with dignity, but our presentable members do not need this. Instead, God has blended together the body, giving greater honor to the lesser member, so that there may be no division in the body, but the members may have mutual concern for one another. If one member suffers, everyone suffers with it. If a member is honored, all rejoice with it.

1 Corinthians 27:

Now you are Christ's body, and each of you is a member of it. And God has placed in the church first apostles, second prophets, third teachers, then miracles, gifts of healing, helps, gifts of leadership, different kinds of tongues. Not all are apostles, are they? Not all are prophets, are they? Not all are teachers, are they? Not all perform miracles, do they? Not all have gifts of healing, do they? Not all speak in tongues, do they? Not all interpret, do they? But you should be eager for the greater gifts.

Matthew 22:39:

Jesus said to him, "Love the Lord your God with all your heart, with all your soul, and with all your mind." This is the first and greatest commandment. The second is like it: "Love your neighbor as yourself."

PART TWO

The Spirituality Behind the Struggle

Chapter 4

WORLDVIEW MATTERS

I'm not one of those guys that has a great worldview. I kind of deal with terror and fear and isolation and abandonment.

David Bowie, English musician and actor

As a believer in the Bible as my foundation for truth, I needed to consider what Scripture teaches about severe mental health problems and the influences that might be involved. I wanted to go beyond typical human trauma that can be treated more easily by the usual methods. Was my suspicion about there being a battle in the unseen realm accurate? If so, what does it mean, and in turn, how do we understand it? My research led me to a book titled *The Unseen Realm: Recovering the Supernatural Worldview of the Bible* by Michael S. Heiser, which details a biblical worldview (the divine council, or Deuteronomy 32, worldview). I'd never heard of this worldview before, especially in the way it is written.

Most historians suggest that the concept of a worldview began as a discussion in the eighteenth and nineteenth centuries as German philosophers discussed their visions for the world. The German word *Weltanschauung* is translated into English as "worldview" and surfaced around the beginning of the twentieth century.[1] But without a doubt, the concept of people having a worldview or a lens through which they

1 Elena Paola Carola Alessiato, "What is a Worldview? Some Suggestions from the History of the Concept." *Negotiation Journal* 2022; 38 (3): 397–404. doi: https://doi.org/10.1111/nejo.12404.

view the world has been around since the first humans. The viewpoints also change; the Bible even discusses this change with the first humans. Adam and Eve's worldview shifted physically when they realized they were naked: "Their eyes were opened" (Genesis 3:7). In counseling, I see worldview come into play when clients who have faith in a higher power and believe they'll be held accountable for their actions. I also see it when clients don't have faith in something greater and think this world is all there is. They reason, "Why not do whatever I want, even if it harms others?" Worldview also plays a big part in how people grieve. Those who believe they'll see their loved ones again in heaven deal with loss much better than those who don't believe in an afterlife.

A worldview is a lens through which people view the world in the hope of answering the existential questions of life. According to an article on worldviewjourneys.com,[2] there are four major worldviews: traditional, modern, postmodern, and integrative:

- **Traditional:** Those who have a traditional worldview hold to a belief in a Creator God. They find truth in Scripture and have a sense of a high purpose, or calling, in life.
- **Modern:** Folks who embrace a modern worldview see the world as an object that is physical and mechanical. They find truth in science and logic and are driven by hedonism and success.
- **Postmodern:** Postmodernists view the world as being subjective and relative; they find truth in ways of knowing, such as through art or morality. They value self-expression and equality.
- **Integrative:** Finally, people with an integrative worldview have a lens of the universe that sees it as evolving, having spiritual meaning. Those who hold to this worldview find truth through the integration of science and spirituality. Driven by

2 worldviewjourneys.com/four-worldviews/

the desire for self-actualization, they search for truth and wisdom as and regard them as principles to collaborate with.

Though most of us don't sit around contemplating worldviews, our views impact everything we do.

In addition to the four leading worldviews cited on the worldviewjourneys.com website, other, perhaps less common, views include naturalism, transcendentalism, and theism:

- **Naturalism** (which includes atheism, humanism, and existentialism): This view suggests that the world can be explored through scientific inquiry and that the material universe is the sum of all reality. Religious or spiritual groups that fit within this view may include humanists, Unitarians, freethinkers, pagans, and Buddhists, among others.[3] Individuals with this worldview often turn to science and human achievement as their source of identity. In this view, there is no concept of God; rather, there is simply randomness and inherent uncertainty related to biochemical reactions.
- **Transcendentalism:** Those who engage in transcendentalism (which includes pantheism, animism, and polytheism) view the world as being material and spiritual. They view "God" as a universal force that we are a part of. Transcendentalists are often Unitarian, a liberal Christian sect that emphasizes rationality, reason, and intellectualism. Those who believe this way may struggle with issues that don't fit into one of these emphases.
- **Theism** (encompassing the Abrahamic religions): Theists view the world with God as the Creator of all things and assert that His creation and created beings are not a part of Him. God is beyond human comprehension. Those with this view

3 https://www.snsociety.org/about-sns/what-is-spiritual-naturalism/

> do believe that human souls are eternal and accountable to the Creator.[4] Theism requires belief in something higher and outside of oneself and the earth, a Sovereign with complete control and love.

Worldviews seemingly change over time, yet in some ways they also stay the same. Typically, one believes in science alone, science *and* spiritual beings, or spiritual beings alone. Humans typically believe in many gods, believe they are a god, or believe there is a God who created us as humans and we're responsible to Him in the end. This may sound like a simple concept, but it's important. What we believe matters!

When was the last time someone asked you about your worldview? Have you ever thought about what lens you view life through? Many of us simply go from one activity to the next, one day to the next, without considering life's purpose: why we're here, why we struggle, or why we succeed. Regularly, people rely on spirituality or religion to help them live out their purpose.

Many begin to raise questions about their worldview as teenagers; I was one of those teens. When I was an inquisitive (and likely annoying, at times) teen asking my dad a million questions about church, God, religion, denominations—you name it—he lovingly encouraged my curiosity. He even showed me the Book of Mormon and the Quran and encouraged me to read them. He wasn't fearful, as some parents might be when their kids question their beliefs and seek answers. My dad believed—and still does—that the truth of the Bible sets us free. He was right, because it did set me free. A child or church member who shows curiosity about other faiths and/or questions your own faith may give you anxiety as a parent or pastor; the key for me was having my godly father guide me through the process.

His encouragement never drove me away from the faith; rather, it compelled me to fall into deeper understanding. Studies show that

4 stevegollmer.people.cedarville.edu/origins/worldview/

parents are more effective they approach these big life topics with their kids in a way that's more transactional than preachy.[5] So, if you're afraid of asking questions or digging deeper, remember that many of the heroes in the Bible, including King David, questioned God. I challenge you to find a loving, respected Christian who can come alongside you to help you seek answers to your deepest questions so you can be confident of what you believe. I know, just as my dad does, that if you truly seek the truth, you'll find it in God's Word, the Bible. There is only one truth!

As I examined the reasons for the increase in the number of strange mental health stories and symptoms, my understanding of my worldview solidified that not all spiritual practices, religions, or beliefs about human struggles lead to the same experience or result. Studies suggest that a biblical worldview positively influences mental health, yet few people take the time to align their behaviors with a healthy worldview, let alone with a biblical one. *Foundational beliefs* are rarely discussed in families or examined deeply among members of faith communities. Beliefs surrounding the definition of a human, for example, are often taken for granted. Many cannot answer the simple question: *What does it mean to be human?* Yet we live in a society where *identity* is discussed daily.[6]

Behavior stems from what we think—our attitudes, beliefs, values, and opinions. Consequently, knowing what we believe and developing a worldview should be of prime importance. The bottom line, again, is worldview matters. Even more so, a *biblical* worldview has been proven to help reduce mental health concerns. Knowing this further solidified my theory that the mental health battle has something to do with the unseen realm.

Let's explore an example of a biblical worldview.

---

5 Dollahite, D. C., & Thatcher, J. Y. (2008). "Talking About Religion: How Highly Religious Youth and Parents Discuss Their Faith." *Journal of Adolescent Research, 23*(5), 611–641. doi.org/10.1177/0743558408322141(Original work published 2008).

6 *Arizona Christian*, Barna Study (2023). arizonachristian.edu/RaisingSpiritualChampions.

Seven Tenets of the Christian Faith

A couple of years ago, I attended a conference where a speaker from the Barna Group, an evangelical Christian polling firm, discussed their recent study on worldview and mental health. According to their research, mental health problems can be mitigated by a biblical worldview. In practice, I've worked with individuals who are new to a biblical worldview and have seen firsthand how believing in the truth of the Bible can reduce anxiety. This stood out to me. As someone with a biblical worldview, I wondered how the organization defined it. Barna's research showed that if a person believes the following "7 Tenants of the Christian Faith," their chance of developing a mental illness decreases to 2 percent. My notes in parentheses follow each point below:

1. Believing that absolute moral truths exist and that such truth is defined by the Bible. (Belief is an unseen concept.)
2. Jesus Christ lived a sinless life. (This was a supernatural occurrence that no other human has ever accomplished.)
3. God is the all-powerful and all-knowing Creator of the universe, and He still rules today. (He is unseen and a part of the supernatural realm.)
4. Salvation is a gift from God and cannot be earned. (This is an unseen or supernatural reality.)
5. Satan is real. (He is also unseen and part of the supernatural realm.)
6. Christians have a responsibility to share their faith in Christ with other people. (Christ, to those living on earth today, is unseen.)
7. The Bible is accurate in all its teachings. (It's a supernatural book.)

Go back and read that list again. Can you believe that if you believe these seven tenets, your risk of developing a mental illness reduces to

2 percent? This is a big deal, and it's why worldview matters. This is the very information mental health professionals should be sharing![7]

Now, let's look at these biblical principles through a mental health lens.

1. **Believing that absolute truth exists and that such truth is defined by the Bible.** Belief is an unseen, yet very real, concept practiced by all humans. What we believe matters. Most people today don't adhere to the truth of Scripture. Many think we can find and adopt or even define our own truth. Some even claim the truths of the Bible are harmful or outdated. Mental health professionals certainly rarely, if ever, promote a biblical worldview to clients. Yet knowing there is an absolute truth provides freedom in our thinking. Following the teachings of the Bible as a standard of truth gives us the ability to not have to "make up" our own system of principles or find one that fits us personally—which may or may not be helpful.
2. **Jesus Christ lived a sinless life.** As a human, it's extremely hard to imagine a perfect human being, yet Jesus Christ was sinless—a supernatural concept, indeed. Why does this concern mental health? Some might think that if Jesus lived a sinless life, then they can do the same. Christians need to remember that Jesus' sinless life was sacrificial; He died in our place since we are unable to live sinlessly. Could it matter that we believe Jesus lived a sinless life simply because, if that is true, it is also true that there is only one human in all of history who was loving enough to do so, making it possible for us to be kind and loving, too? Since Christ forgave, we, too, can forgive; this is a pivotal aspect of healing in mental health.

---

7 Dr. Tracy F. Munsil, March 14, 2023, CRC, *American Worldview Inventory 2023*. From the Cultural Research Center at Arizona Christian University.

3. **God is the all-powerful and all-knowing Creator of the universe, and He still rules it today.** God is unseen but real; He's supernatural. Whoa! Now this may be stepping on some people's toes. Does this mean people have to believe in God, a Creator who is all-knowing and rules today, in order to be mentally healthy? You might ask, "Why can't I figure it out on my own?" Well, if you think you were created by God, wouldn't you also find relief in knowing He is all-powerful and all-knowing? By believing in an all-powerful, all-knowing Creator, we can live in a healthier state of mind than those who have no creation foundation and nowhere to put their faith and hope. Understanding there is a sovereign Creator provides hope for believers not only for today, but also for the future. Hope is essential for good mental health.
4. **Salvation is a gift from God that cannot be earned.** This is the ultimate supernatural reality. This truth is loaded, too; I see how it would be helpful for someone's mental health. Believing God forgives every time we miss the mark is foundational. Realizing and believing that forgiveness and reconciliation with God are freely given, and we can do nothing to earn that gift (we can only accept it), is the cornerstone of a Christian's faith—and freeing to the mind. Choosing not to believe this would cause cognitive dissonance (tension between beliefs/values and actions) because it leaves us striving to attain forgiveness and reconciliation that were never possible to earn. Salvation is also a gift that provides victory over all enemies. The gift of salvation from all evil is crucial to being mentally healthy.
5. **Satan is real.** He is unseen, but he is real indeed. I can almost see readers raising eyebrows on this one! How does knowing there is an evil being called Satan make us less likely to have a mental illness? For those who aren't Christians, knowing

Satan is real may provoke more, not less, anxiety. But for Christians, it clarifies the identity of the true enemy. When we identify the true enemy, we can stop fighting ourselves and one another. This truth provides a foundation for where the journey to mental wellness can begin.

6. **Christians have the responsibility to share their faith in Christ with other people.** We are to share our faith in an unseen (supernatural) Christ, our very real Savior. If sharing our faith is equal to helping someone in need or simply speaking of Jesus' love to others, it's easy to see how mental health can be positively influenced by this tenet. However, do we still see sharing our faith with others as positively affecting our mental health when sharing our faith looks like sacrificial love that causes us discomfort and even leads to loss? We should always see sharing the love of Jesus as a blessing, no matter what it causes us to do. Sharing the gospel is also a way to win the battle against the dark forces of the world.
7. **The Bible is accurate in *all* its teachings.** Wait, what? *All?* As in, I can't cheat on a test, I can't have sex with whomever I want, and I have to care for the poor and lay down my life for others? As a Christian, I see the Bible's teachings as loving and protective. This truth requires a shift in mindset and critical thinking for those who aren't Christians, for sure. This truth is supernatural; it is unseen, but it exists! Ultimately, the teachings in Scripture (even the ones we can't quite understand) are for our own good—physically, spiritually, and mentally. Freedom comes when we trust God's ways over our own feelings, preferences and thoughts.

These principles might sound good to someone who's been raised in church, but many people aren't sure what it all means. As a Christian who is a mental health professional, I place having a biblical worldview as a high priority, but I can't just start drilling these truths into my clients' heads. Worldview matters, so I want to be able to provide good answers, solid explanations, and effective treatments. The desire to be able to do this led me to search for deeper, better answers, ones that present the unseen realm as it relates to mental health and darkness. Thankfully, as I've focused on sharing the importance of a biblical worldview and helping clients learn biblical truths about their circumstances, I've seen positive outcomes such as freedom from anxiety and reduced levels of depression.

QUESTIONS FOR REFLECTION

1. What is your worldview?
2. How do you explain what you believe about the world to others?
3. Why do you believe worldview matters?

PRACTICAL APPLICATION

Encouragement for pastoral counselors and mental health professionals:

- Be able to articulate your biblical worldview.
- Teach a biblical worldview at your church, to your children, and to those you influence.
- Frequently ask those you serve questions about worldview.
- Offer a sermon series on mental health and a biblical worldview.
- Host a training on understanding and articulating a biblical worldview.

Prayer Prompt: *Lord, help me hide your Word in my heart and lead others to do the same. Give me understanding of your Word, the lens through which I view the world.*

SCRIPTURE TO CONSIDER

Colossians 2:8:

> See to it that no one takes you captive by philosophy and empty deceit, according to human tradition, according to the elemental spirits of the world, and not according to Christ.

Proverbs 30:5:

> Every word of God proves true; he is a shield to those who take refuge in him.

Romans 13:1–14:

> Let every person be subject to the governing authorities. For there is no authority except from God, and those that exist have been instituted by God. Therefore, whoever resists the authorities resists what God has appointed, and those who resist will incur judgment. For rulers are not a terror to good conduct, but to bad. Would you have no fear of the one who is in authority? Then do what is good, and you will receive his approval, for he is God's servant for your good. But if you do wrong, be afraid, for he does not bear the sword in vain. For he is the servant of God, an avenger who carries out God's wrath on the wrongdoer. Therefore, one must be in subjection, not only to avoid God's wrath but also for the sake of conscience.

Chapter 5

THE DIVINE COUNCIL WORLDVIEW

Seeing the Bible through the eyes of an ancient reader requires shedding the filters of our traditions and presumptions. They processed life in supernatural terms. Today's Christian processes it by a mixture of creedal statements and modern rationalism.

DR. MICHAEL HEISER, *The Unseen Realm: Recovering the Supernatural Worldview of the Bible*

As my search for better answers began and I was clearly experiencing spiritual warfare on many fronts, a precious friend, Shalawn, gave me a message she believed was from God. She said, "Natalie, it is time to come off the battlefield and into my courts."

During this time, I was figuring out how to navigate interacting with a very difficult personality at work. I was experiencing temptations I'd never felt before. My oldest son was hurling angry words and actions at me daily. My husband was trying to figure out how to help me deal with all the challenges. I found it hard to even attend church at the time because of a lack of personal connections with other members and a feeling of being overwhelmed by the number of people who kept coming up to me asking for help with their mental health problems. Some of my long-term friendships had significantly changed. These are only a few of the battles I was facing at the time.

As I felt the weight of Shalawn's words sink in, I had no idea what they meant. My usual approach to figuring things out is to do some research to ascertain whether they're in line with what the Bible teaches. As I searched online for resources on subjects like "courts of heaven" and "spiritual warfare," one book that kept coming up was the *Unseen Realm* by Dr. Michael Heiser. I ordered it immediately. It was an intense read, but it has been transformative in my life and practice. I highly recommend exploring Dr. Heiser's work on the divine council. There are other books on this topic, but Dr. Heiser has led the way in the twenty-first century among scholars who are trying to lead people back to this lens of viewing Scripture. Therefore, his work will be my focus.

Dr. Heiser's work resonated with me in relation to what my friend had said because he discusses what he calls "the divine council worldview," or the "Deuteronomy 32 worldview." Basically, it is a biblical outlook that "re-enchants" us by the supernatural, so in a sense it could be labeled a "supernatural worldview." I was intrigued—especially when Dr. Heiser's book led me to read Psalm 82. I had read the Psalms many times over the years, but this time God showed me something I had never seen before. The psalmist describes God's council at times as if it were a court scene. God, the Most High, is above all spiritual beings; He is the Judge but allows other divine beings to help Him govern creation.

Dr. Heiser's work also points to other biblical scenes where the courts of heaven and God's council are alluded to or mentioned, such as in 1 Kings 22, which states:

> And Micaiah said, "Therefore hear the word of the LORD: I saw the LORD sitting on his throne, and all the host of heaven standing beside him on his right hand and on his left; and the LORD said, 'Who will entice Ahab, that he may go up and fall at Ramoth-gilead?' And one said one thing, and another said another. Then a spirit came forward and stood before the LORD, saying, 'I will entice him.' And the LORD said to him, 'By what means?' And he said, 'I will go out, and will be a lying spirit in the mouth of all his prophets.' And he said, 'You are to entice

> him, and you shall succeed; go out and do so.' Now therefore behold, the LORD has put a lying spirit in the mouth of all these your prophets; the LORD has declared disaster for you."

The prophet Micaiah was speaking to King Jehosophat about a situation with King Ahab. We see here that the "spirit that came forward" assumed he could help the Lord as possibilities for how to handle a matter were being discussed.

Simply put, the Bible describes God (Yahweh, the Most High) as the ruler of the cosmos. God uses a council of spirit or divine (supernatural) beings He created to serve Him by carrying out His will. They also govern nations under God's authority, meaning these beings are *not* equal to God. Some of the beings remained loyal to God, serving as messengers of light; others rebelled, leading to deception, idolatry, and spiritual warfare against humanity. Humanity was created as God's earthly council and was given dominion over earth (as we read in the book of Genesis). Humans are to be images of God and act as His representatives in ruling creation. Understanding this helps us see that life on earth isn't isolated from the unseen realm; rather, it's the stage on which the effects of this cosmic conflict play out.

The Divine Council Explored

In summary, I learned from Dr. Heiser's book that the concept of the divine council is based on Psalm 82:1, "God has taken his place in the divine council; in the midst of the gods he holds judgment."

Dr. Heiser explains further:

> The term "divine council" is used by Hebrew and Semitic scholars to refer to the heavenly host, the pantheon of divine beings who administer the affairs of the cosmos. All ancient Mediterranean cultures had some conception of a divine council. The

divine council of Israelite religion, known primarily through the psalms, was distinct in important ways.[1]

Whereas other pagan nations had ruling deities (which were created beings) that were not the same as the Most High God, the divine council of the Israelites was ruled by the Most High God, the Creator and ruler of the cosmos.

The Hebrew term for "god" in Scripture is *elohim*. (In the ancient Hebrew language, there were no capital letters, so often we miss the differentiation of the gods). Because humans were made to be earthly council members as we represent the Most High God on earth and take dominion, we have the ability to partner with God—just like the divine council does in the heavens. (I refer to the One True God as the "Most High God"—an important distinction in counseling because people come in with differing views of God, complex beliefs about gods, and confusion around if—or why—it even matters. I've also met many clients who are "spiritual" and may believe in *a* god, but they need to know the preeminence of the Most High. We are not gods. We are not part of God. We reflect His image and are His representatives. When clients learn this, they learn their true purpose. One client expresses learning this truth as a "sigh of relief.")

So, what does this divine council have to do with mental health and spiritual struggles? As I read Dr. Heiser's book further, I learned about the *council members*—their role in ruling the cosmos, how humans were created to rule on earth, and finally, how *fallen beings* were influential in the fall and destruction of humans. The fall and impact of fallen council members are certainly related to mental health. We'll explore more of this in future chapters.

For now, let's look into the council theme a bit more. These may not

1 Michael S. Heiser, *The Lexham Bible Dictionary* (John D. Barry, et al., eds.; Bellingham, WA: Lexham Press, 2013, 2014), 8. Exported from Logos Bible Software, 10:43 AM, May 9, 2015.

seem like "basic" truths. So, let me unpack the subject a bit and help you see what this part of a worldview could have to do with the intersection of spiritual war in the unseen realm and mental health.

The divine council worldview is not new but has given me a sharper focus on and understanding of Scripture. In a study on belief, the writer of an article in *Psychological Review* found that "those who don't update their beliefs based on new information may look like they are being swayed by their desire to believe something else."[2] I tend to agree, partly because the more I study the Bible, the more I update my beliefs. However, it doesn't take away my foundation, nor does it sway my "desire to believe in something else." In fact, it strengthens it.

The divine council worldview is, in a way, an update to my thinking. It's a part of a biblical worldview many people miss altogether. *I believe the Deuteronomy 32 or supernatural worldview is vital in helping us understand who we are, our purpose, and what or who we're up against on earth.* This worldview reminds us that a supernatural Creator rules over all of creation as well as all created beings (divine and human) to help Him rule and to be a part of His family if they choose to obey Him. Ultimately, the divine council worldview is about the Most High God, Yahweh (His name), and His desire to be a family with His created beings. This is foundational not only for good mental health but also for simply being human and interacting with others.

According to Dr. Ronn Johnson, a theologian and friend of Dr. Heiser, six precepts form the basis of a divine council worldview. Again, my notes are in parentheses following each precept.

1. Understand the original writer, his intended audience, and the culture they shared going into any study. (In other words, we must consider the context of each passage. Who was it written to initially? What cultural context was it written in? Why was it written in the first place?)

2 rutgers.edu/news/study-examines-what-drives-belief

2. The Bible presumes a society of divine beings who were created by one deity named Yahweh first named and separated from other *elohim* (translated as "god") in Genesis 2:4. (The Bible talks about many created beings, both human and divine. There is one divine being who was *not* created, but rather is the Creator, and His name is Yahweh/Jehovah—the Most High God.)
3. Yahweh delegated authoritative power to a number of created deities in the physical world (as we know it). (Yahweh [the Most High God] gave authority to other divine beings in the physical world. Some of that authority involved being guardians or "watchers" of the humans.)
4. Jesus Christ presently, by the decree of Yahweh, assumes the highest place of honor and power over all gods and humans. (Jesus is the King of Kings and Lord of Lords over all divine and human beings.)
5. The locus of the gospel message will be the loyalty we show Jesus Christ and Yahweh, His Father, above all other gods. (A central aspect of the gospel message is to have believing loyalty to Jesus above all others.)
6. In the next age, believers will not just go to heaven but will assume the status of a divine council member. (Our believing loyalty in our current lives as humans may allow us status in the next life as a divine council member; see 1 Corinthians 6:3.)

These statements may seem somewhat different than what you've always heard, but I challenge you to do further study for better clarification and understanding. When our boys began to make choices independently from their father and me (their parents), we realized the reality of rebellion and *choice*. God created a family, not puppets. Even divine beings had the freedom to *choose*. The more we understand that we are created beings and there are other created beings (council members, or sons of God) who fell and want to destroy us, the more clearly we can understand the battle of good and evil in the world.

This fight is at various times physical, spiritual, and most certainly mental. Viewing Scripture through a supernatural lens suggests humans have the free will to choose whom they will worship and obey, and it teaches that fallen divine beings also influence humans in negative ways, such as by causing mental health problems, among others. This "update" doesn't change the truth that I believe there is no one like the Most High God. It is not polytheism, which would suggest that other deities have the same powers as He does. Further, it doesn't change the gospel. It only solidifies my faith, as embracing the divine council worldview has helped me more deeply understand who I am, why I'm here, and what my purpose is. When we grasp this biblical worldview, our lens—not only of Scripture, but also of our own lives and struggles—changes. The unseen realm is important to understand or at least acknowledge in terms of our thoughts, emotions, identities, relationships, and more.

In summary, the divine council/Deuteronomy 32, or supernatural worldview of Scripture means the following:

- Yahweh is the Most High God, the uncreated God of all.
- God (Yahweh) created other spiritual or divine beings (the sons of God) to help Him govern creation. He didn't need help; He just allowed them to join in.
- Some of the divine created beings rebelled against God. This converted their authority from just to corrupt.
- Humans were created to be an image of or to represent God on earth.
- Under Yahweh's rule, through Jesus (the incarnate Most High God), all creation is being redeemed.
- The overarching story of the Bible is truly about God's family (divine and human) being created, rebelling (sin), and receiving the hope of redemption and restoration.

As we apply this worldview to mental health, let's learn some important facts.

Understanding the Identity and Purpose of Being Human

As basic as it sounds, it's important, as Dr. Michael Heiser explains, to understand what a "human" is. I recently asked this question to a general audience on Facebook, and many folks either couldn't answer or offered strange responses. Some of the replies I got were along the same lines:

- "Someone who has intellect or the ability to learn."
- "Someone who has emotions and feelings."
- "A thing of value. Something that can grow and change over time."

Interestingly, all the above descriptions are wrong. (For example, even an animal has intellect or the ability to learn, making that first definition not specific to humanity.) The answers fall short of what truly defines a human. Melissa, a client who came to me with depression, had many lies to untangle, such as, "I was never meant to be here." Once she understood the biblical truth of who she is as a human, an imager of God, it became easier for her to see that she had been believing a lie.

Being human isn't about emotions, will, body parts, intellect, or the ability to change, learn, grow or feel. As Dr. Heiser states:

> We are created to image God, to be his imagers. It is what we are by definition. The image is not an ability we have, but a status. We are God's representatives on earth. To be human is to [be the image of] God, and because we are created in the image of God, we have a basic dignity and inherent significance.[3]

3 Michael S. Heiser, "Divine Council," in *Dictionary of the Old Testament: Wisdom, Poetry & Writings* (eds. Tremper Longman III and Peter Enns; Downers Grove, IL; Nottingham, England: IVP Academic; Inter-Varsity Press, 2008), 112.

In Genesis 1:26, the Creator says:

> Let us make man in our image, after our likeness. And let them have dominion over the fish of the sea and over the birds of the heavens and over the livestock and over all the earth and over every creeping thing that creeps on the earth.

It's also important to note that, as Dr. Heiser states:

> Every human, regardless of the stage of development, is an imager of God. There is no incremental or partial of the image via some ability, physical or spiritual. No member of the animal kingdom, regardless of any cognitive ability it might have, is an imager of God. The same goes for any intelligent life form, artificial or the hypothetical extraterrestrial.[4]

The Hebrew word for "shadow," *tsel*, comes from the word *tselem*, which is also the word for "imager." That means we are to be God's "shadow" on earth.

The following Old Testament passages speak of the image of the Most High God:

1. **Genesis 1:26–27:** "Then God said, 'Let us make humankind in our image, according to our likeness; and let them have dominion over the fish of the sea, and over the birds of the air, and over the cattle, and over all the wild animals of the earth, and over every creeping thing that creeps upon the earth.' So God created humankind in his image, in the image of God he created them; male and female he created them" (NRSV).

It's vital to note specific terms here such as "human," "image," "dominion," and "likeness." These are key words to keep in mind as we

4 Ibid.

consider what a human is. It may be worth taking time to reflect on this a bit here:

2. **Genesis 5:1–3:** "This is the book of the generations of Adam. When God created man, he made him in the likeness of God. Male and female he created them, and he blessed them and named them Man when they were created. When Adam had lived 130 years, he fathered a son in his own likeness, after his image, and named him Seth" (NRSV).

Adam, the first human, was made in the "likeness of God." The Most High God *created* humans. The first humans also created children in the same likeness. Again, these are important aspects to stop and reflect on. What do they bring to mind?

3. **Genesis 9:6:** "Whoever sheds the blood of a human, by a human shall that person's blood be shed; for in his own image God made humankind" (NRSV).

Note here the significance of the shedding of blood and the relationship to the image of the Most High God. When I participate in missions abroad, I see the beauty wrapped into other cultures such as that of the Philippines. There are many differences I appreciate and even celebrate, such as their desire to learn more about mental health. Yet, I'm also reminded that we are all human; our blood is all red. By the blood of Jesus, He made a way for us all to be a part of God's family. Reflect on this here:

The image of the Most High God is also mentioned in the New Testament. Consider reading these passages slowly, and pause for reflection by writing down any thoughts or questions you have.

Romans 8:28–29: "And we know that all things work together for good for those who love God, who are called according to his purpose, because those whom he foreknew he also predestined to be conformed to the image of his Son, that his Son would be the firstborn among many brothers and sisters" (NET).

Paul argues that believers are destined to be conformed to the image of Christ. We are to live as the Most High God would, to represent Him and His character. It is something we can conform to.

2 Corinthians 4:1–4: "Therefore, since we have this ministry, just as God has shown us mercy, we do not become discouraged. But we have rejected shameful hidden deeds, not behaving with deceptiveness or distorting the word of God, but by open proclamation of the truth we commend ourselves to everyone's conscience before God. But even if our gospel is veiled, it is veiled only to those who are perishing, among whom the god of this age has blinded the minds of those who do not believe so they would not see the light of the glorious gospel of Christ, who is the image of God" (NET).

Paul elsewhere refers to Jesus as the image of the Most High God. Jesus is our example for imaging the Most High God.

Hebrews 1:1–4: "God, who at various times and in various ways spoke in time past to the fathers by the prophets, has in these last days spoken to us by His Son, whom He has appointed heir of all things, through whom also He made the worlds; who being the brightness of His glory and the express image of His person, and upholding all things by the word of His power, when He had by Himself purged our sins, sat down at the right hand of the Majesty on high, having become so much better than the angels, as He has by inheritance obtained a more excellent name than they" (NKJV).

The writer of Hebrews uses the same verbiage, calling Jesus "the express image of His person." Jesus is the expression of the Most High God's image!

Colossians 1:15: "He is the image of the invisible God, the firstborn over all creation" (NKJV).

As humans gave visible form to God, so Jesus is the image of the invisible God.

Philippians 2:5–11: "Let this mind be in you which was also in Christ Jesus, who, being in the form of God, did not consider it robbery to be equal with God, but made Himself of no reputation, taking the form of a bondservant, and coming in the likeness of men. And being found in appearance as a man, He humbled Himself and became obedient to the point of death, even the death of the cross. Therefore God also has highly exalted Him and given Him the name which is above every name, that at the name of Jesus every knee should bow, of those in heaven, and of those on earth, and of those under the earth, and that every tongue should confess that Jesus Christ is Lord, to the glory of God the Father" (NKJV).

Jesus was truly incarnate, becoming human (in the flesh) to atone for humankind.

1 Peter 2:21–23: "For to this you were called, because Christ also suffered for us, leaving us an example, that you should follow His steps: 'Who committed no sin, Nor was deceit found in His mouth;' who, when He was reviled, did not revile in return; when He suffered, He did not threaten, but committed Himself to Him who judges righteously; who Himself bore our sins in His own body on the tree, that we, having died to sins, might live for righteousness—by whose stripes you were healed" (NKJV).

Jesus was our example to all of humankind.

Understanding what a human is also defines our purpose: to image/represent God on earth. Our example is Jesus. Of course, there were other created beings—the divine council beings, also created by the Most High or Creator God. As Dr. Heiser explains, these represent the "pantheon of gods" that rule the nations.

The divine council members (the created, small-*g* "gods") also represent their Creator God or the Most High God, but in the spiritual/

heavenly world. The Most High God's desire was for all created beings to be in His family. We simply have various roles in the different realms. The divine council members in the heavenly realm were not called to have dominion on earth; they were called to help humans. (Problems arose when the fallen ones negatively influenced humans.)

Studying this worldview makes me think about how the fallen ones have sought to create additional worldviews. Over time, humanity has seemingly shifted from a traditional to modern, postmodern, and now integrative worldviews…or from theism to transcendentalism and naturalism. It's as if the enemies of the Most High God have used weapons like science, hedonism, and even dark forms of spirituality to deceive us, kill us, deprave us, and destroy humanity. The lies of the enemy convincing people to choose worldviews outside of the one prescribed in the Bible result in stories like Melissa's. She came into our office as someone who had experienced deep trauma in relation to witchcraft, and she had a true love of nature. In addition to the lie she was believing that we looked at earlier ("I was never meant to be here"), she wrestled with lies such as, "I will ruin everything. I have to work hard to make everything right." She needed the truth that it is not *her* job; Christ paid it all! She also found peace in nature, so was tempted to worship it over the Creator until she learned what the Bible taught. Earthly creation was for her, and she was to take dominion because she is an image of the Most High.

As I dug deeper into the divine council worldview, I learned more about the Fall of Man in Genesis 1, the corruption before the Flood in Genesis 6, and the destruction of the Tower of Babel in Genesis 11. As I studied these three rebellions in-depth, God showed me that the roots of many mental health problems can be traced back to these three events. As His imager, these events happened to attempt to kill, steal, and destroy His plans and purposes for humanity. Coming off the battlefield into the Most High God's courts (as expressed in the words my friend said) came to mean that it was time for me to learn about His order, His plans, and His purposes. Further, it was time for me to identify the true enemies, and, finally, to understand what Jesus did on the cross and how it allows me to fight from that place of victory! Realizing the battle takes place in the unseen realm is powerful. It changed how I fought and, in turn, how I taught and led others to do the same.

I invite you to reflect on this for a moment through a prayer of gratitude, with a journal entry of thanksgiving, or by taking a walk and reflecting on God's goodness in this truth!

QUESTIONS FOR REFLECTION

1. Can you explain the divine council or Deuteronomy 32 worldview?
2. How is this different from what you've believed in the past?
3. What is your definition of a "human"?
4. Why does defining what a human is matter?

PRACTICAL APPLICATION

Suggestions for pastoral counselors and mental health professionals:

- Challenge yourself to read Scripture through a supernatural lens by using the divine council worldview at least once.
- Learn more about the divine council worldview by reading *The Unseen Realm*, watching Dr. Heiser's videos, and finding others you respect who may be studying this subject, too.
- Preach or teach on what it means to be human and what all it implies to represent the Most High God on earth.
- View and treat those you serve with this worldview in mind.
- Once you've studied the divine council worldview, consider preaching and teaching on these topics and ideas.

Prayer Prompt: *Lord, give me courage to see the supernatural and unseen realm as it has been described throughout Scripture. Challenge me to live as your imager honoring you daily.*

SCRIPTURE TO CONSIDER

Colossians 2:8 (NIV):

> See to it that no one takes you captive through hollow and deceptive philosophy, which depends on human tradition and the elemental spiritual forces of this world rather than on Christ.

Psalm 119: 97–105 (KJV):

> O how love I thy law! It is my meditation all the day. Thou through thy commandments hast made me wiser than mine enemies: for they are ever with me. I have more understanding than all my teachers: for thy testimonies are my meditation. I understand more than the ancients, because I keep thy precepts. I have refrained my feet from every evil way, that I might keep thy word. I have not departed from thy judgments: for thou hast taught me. How sweet are thy words unto my taste! yea, sweeter than honey to my mouth! Through thy precepts I get understanding: therefore I hate every false way. Thy word is a lamp unto my feet, and a light unto my path.

John 1:1–5 (NIV):

> In the beginning was the Word, and the Word was with God, and the Word was God. He was with God in the **beginning**. Through him all things were made; without him nothing was made that has been made. In him was life, and that life was the light of all mankind. The light shines in the darkness, and the darkness has not overcome it.

Psalm 89:6–7 (NIV):

> The heavens praise your wonders, LORD, your faithfulness too, in the assembly of the holy ones. For who in the skies above can compare with the LORD? Who is like the LORD among the heavenly beings? In the council of the holy ones God is greatly feared; he is more awesome than all who surround him.

Chapter 6

THE TRUTH BEHIND THE HUMAN STRUGGLE

I very much believe in things unseen, both of positive and destructive energy, and I have never seen The Exorcist *through from start to finish. I find it too realistic, frankly, and too disturbing for me. I absolutely believe in spiritual warfare and have experienced it in my life. So I respect [the 1973 film's director] Mr. Friedkin's extraordinary success with that, but it's not a picture I'll ever see.*

Ashley Judd, actress

People not only have different worldviews; they also have different ideas about the human struggle. Some believe the battle is "within," and others believe the battle is "without." These are typically the only two options considered. Entire film series have been based on the battle between good and evil. As a boy mom, the superhero movies come to mind. In counseling, many clients tend to blame other people for all their problems. One client, who experienced struggles in his marriage for years, made his wife out to be the "evil one" and himself to be the "good one." As you can imagine, thinking this way never works in improving a marriage. Yet, at times even recognizing our own shortcomings leaves out part of why humans face difficulties.

Basically, most people believe the human struggle is the result of something we've done or something others have done. Some say it's caused by reasons such as selfishness, pride, anger, fear, and circumstances. No one seems to be asking how those characteristics came to be or when they developed. Mental health professionals mostly believe this and treat problems accordingly. Think about it: Most health problems are said to be caused by one's choices, genetic predispositions (the choices of others), the actions of others, or the environment (which most also believe can be harmful because of human actions). In a way, one could view battles as *human vs. human*. As a result, conflicts are often fought against ourselves or others. Yet they often end in devastation such as suicide, wars, family feuds, and political battles.

The Art of War, a book on Chinese warfare written in 401 BC (more than 2,500 years ago), emphasizes strategies involving creating chaos and discord within the enemy's ranks. This book has been widely used for thousands of years for its principles on the battlefield, in politics, inside the boardroom, and in everyday life. At the center of another classic piece of literature, *The Iliad*, the warrior-champion of the Greeks, Achilles, is engaged in a battle with his own leader, Agamemnon. Recently, my friends from the Philippines asked for prayer for their country because they fear the government may fail and the military will take over. The president and vice president in the Philippines, Ferdinand "Bongbong" Marcos Jr., and Sara Duterte are enemies, and each one's supporters are blaming those of the other for corruption resulting from the misuse of money given to contractors for flood relief and rebuilding prior to 2024. Even in the Bible, the story of Jehosophat details how God causes the enemies of His people to fight amongst themselves:

> Early the next morning the army of Judah went out into the wilderness of Tekoa. On the way Jehoshaphat stopped and said, "Listen to me, all you people of Judah and Jerusalem! Believe in the Lord your God, and you will be able to stand firm. Believe in his prophets, and you will succeed." After consulting the people, the king appointed singers to walk ahead of the army, singing to the Lord and praising him for his holy splendor. This is what they sang: "Give thanks to the Lord; his faithful love

> endures forever!" At the very moment they began to sing and give praise, the Lord caused the armies of Ammon, Moab, and Mount Seir to start fighting among themselves. The armies of Moab and Ammon turned against their allies from Mount Seir and killed every one of them. After they had destroyed the army of Seir, they began attacking each other. So when the army of Judah arrived at the lookout point in the wilderness, all they saw were dead bodies lying on the ground as far as they could see. Not a single one of the enemy had escaped. (2 Chronicles 20:20–24, NLT)

Encouraging fighting amongst one another is obviously a strategy that works for the enemy. It's also a tactic we should know and understand in terms of what humans are up against. The enemies of the Most High God and humans, His imagers, use this plan often, if not solely. At some point, we must contemplate the idea that humans have frequently viewed the battle wrongly or incompletely. I believe this is due to the lies of our Creator's enemies. They're sly; they can tempt us to fight against ourselves or one another so we don't recognize the true enemies. The enemies of our Creator God are not a part of humanity but can be viewed as being an influence behind it.

Through the years, I've also noticed that the stronger my commitment to the Lord, as evidenced by obeying His will and not following my own, the more aggressively the enemies of the Most High God attack me. Yes, He is sovereign and allowed these battles to occur, but He used them for my good. He compelled me to follow Him further by revealing struggles in my own life. He asked me to stop "venting" as much, which can mirror gossip. He asked me to let go of relationships that aren't healthy. He asked me to continue to love instead of resorting to anger when I am frustrated. It's a process, but the Most High God has patiently offered me the chance to be shaped into who He wants me to be rather than who *I* think I should be. The process is painful at times, and it can be heart-wrenching, but it's worth it.

As I rooted my shoes of peace (postured myself with the peace of the gospel) into a battle stance and studied the *Unseen Realm* by Dr. Heiser alongside Scripture, I learned what I was really up against. This new understanding brought to light many issues I had wrestled with for years. I began to see things in Scripture, in my life, and in my clients' lives differently.

I had read and believed Ephesians 6:12:

> For we wrestle not against flesh and blood, but against principalities, against powers, against the rulers of the darkness of this world, against spiritual wickedness in high places.

However, it hadn't before occurred to me that, in my profession, we often explain battles as being against the "self"—either oneself or others. Both are "flesh" as defined by Scripture. So, the answer that either oneself (or others) is the problem doesn't always yield effective answers or treatment for mental health concerns. Therefore, it's beneficial to learn *what humans are wrestling against* and *where it all began.*

The Three Rebellions: Where Evil and Its Impact on Mental Health Began

Enter the divine council worldview to offer insight and clarity. One of the major components of this perspective is the three rebellions discussed by Dr. Heiser. Many of us grew up in church being taught to believe all evil in the world was a result of the Fall of Man, when the first humans went from being in a state of innocence and obedience to a state of guilt and separation by choosing to go against the Most High God's instruction (Genesis 3). Yet Dr. Heiser offers much more clarity to the human struggle by looking even beyond that initial devastating transition.

He encourages readers to explore not only the Genesis event, but also to consider the fall of divine beings and their impact on the fall of humans. Genesis 3 tells of the divine being, the serpent, influencing humans to commit the first sin. Later, in Genesis 6, we come to a second "fall." We read about the creation of Nephilim (a hybrid creation springing from a forbidden union of fallen divine beings and humans). Finally, even further into the sixth chapter of Genesis, we find the account of the Tower of Babel and the dispersal of the nations. Let's dive deeper into each rebellion.

The First Rebellion (Genesis 3:3-7)

Genesis 3:3–7 details the first of the three rebellions Dr. Heiser brings up, recounting the story of the serpent (the *nachash*) and the first humans:

> Now the serpent was more crafty than any of the wild animals the Lord God had made. He said to the woman, "Did God really say, 'You must not eat from any tree in the garden'?" The woman said to the serpent, "We may eat fruit from the trees in the garden, but God did say, 'You must not eat fruit from the tree that is in the middle of the garden, and you must not touch it, or you will die.'" "You will not certainly die," the serpent said to the woman. "For God knows that when you eat from it your eyes will be opened, and you will be like God, knowing good and evil." When the woman saw that the fruit of the tree was good for food and pleasing to the eye, and also desirable for gaining wisdom, she took some and ate it. She also gave some to her husband, who was with her, and he ate it. Then the eyes of both of them were opened, and they realized they were naked; so they sewed fig leaves together and made coverings for themselves.
>
> The serpent is Satan or the devil, as stated in Revelation 12:9:
>
> The great dragon was hurled down—that ancient serpent called the devil, or Satan, who leads the whole world astray. He was hurled to the earth, and his angels with him. (NIV)

So, Satan was a divine being who deceived Adam and Eve. The deception began in his language. Notice that Satan switched from referring to the Most High God as "Lord God" to simply "God." This is significant because the name matters. It's as if Satan was trying to suggest something different—maybe less lofty?—about the Most High. This change in his language might suggest that pride is at play for Satan in his deception.

I've often wondered why Satan wanted to deceive Adam and Eve. But the more I study, I've come to believe it simply seems Satan might have been jealous that the humans enjoyed a status he didn't have. Humans were called to be the Most High God's imagers on earth. I'm sure Satan, as Lucifer in the divine council, had a magnificent role in the kingdom of the Most High God, but as the loving Most High God does, He gives free will to all His created beings.

Instead of enjoying his place in the kingdom, Satan chose to let his pride lead him to hate and destroy humans through deception. Satan put himself in the Most High God's place, as mentioned in Isaiah 14:13:

> You said in your heart, "I will ascend to heaven; above the stars of God. I will set my throne on high; I will sit on the mount of assembly in the far reaches of the north."

Satan deceived Adam and Eve into doing the same. They sinned by allowing pride to take over, leading them to think they knew better than the Most High God. The result was death. Many English translations say in Genesis 3:4 "surely die," but the original Hebrew uses a term meaning to "die die." Yes, the repetition is intentional. Think about the significance of repeating that word. Also, note that the text doesn't say Adam wasn't with Eve. It's possible he may have been present when she communicated with the serpent/Satan. Yet, he neglected to protect her. That makes me think about how sin doesn't simply lead to the death of one person; it can lead to multiple deaths—even if it's seemingly just the death of a relationship. Consequently, Satan became ruler of this world (John 12:31) and humans became mortal. Humans would now need a Redeemer to have eternal life again with the Most High God, and Satan's fate would be crushing.

I've heard and read this story many times. Yet it never hit me like it did when I read it while studying the divine council worldview. Recognizing Satan's hatred for humans due to their status on earth as the Most High God's imagers enlightened me to see Satan as the sole reason death comes to all humans—not just "natural deaths," but those including suicide, murder, homicide, accidental killings, and even abortion. Can it be that simple? I believe so. Just think about a person who steals someone's job, award, or wife. The thief took what didn't belong because he was jealous of a status, and the consequences are often grave. As an example, I know of one woman who was envious of her stepdaughter. The younger woman was from the first wife of the man who had passed away. She was so jealous of the daughter's high standing the daughter had with her father that the older woman attempted to push the younger one out of the home. There are massive mental health implications when people steal, kill, and destroy due to hate.

Other ancient stories have a similar narrative. I don't believe this is accidental, but rather related to the third rebellion (which includes the separation of people and creation of languages and diverse cultures; we'll have a closer look later). I'm including these sections to suggest more evidence of the influence divine beings have in the natural world. Many people believed in them for centuries. Ancient humans created temples with the images of their gods on it. See the deception already. We were made in the Most High God's image and didn't need to create temples for other gods. We could call them "small-*g* gods," but remember there were no capital letters in the original language of Scripture. Understanding the difference between the ancient mythologies can help us discern truth or times when the enemies of the Most High God are trying to deceive humans. The differing mythologies also suggest that evil and divine beings are at play in the world, no matter what someone believes.

Ancient Mythology Comparison: The Garden of Hesperides

In Greek mythology, the Garden of Hesperides was guarded by Hesperides nymphs and a frightening dragon named Ladon. This garden, a gift from Gaia (Earth) to Hera (Juno), contained a tree of golden apples. Heracles, the hero of the story, as one of the twelve jobs he was assigned to carry out, was required to overcome the guardians and gain access to the tree in an epic battle. The story involves heroism and temptation, and it illustrates the conflict between good and evil. Like the biblical narrative, the story explores themes of transgression, boundaries, supernatural beings, and powers.[1]

The emphasis in the Greek myth is on heroism versus the biblical narrative's focus on the consequences of sin and the human condition. This is a major difference and why it's important to know the scriptural truth. The ancient narratives, because they often show the enemies of the Most High God, twist the truth. The implication of divine beings being involved in the lives of humans has remained a common belief for centuries.

The Second Rebellion (Genesis 6:6–14)

The second rebellion Dr. Heiser references is described in Genesis 6:6–14:

> When humankind began to multiply on the face of the earth, and daughters were born to them, the sons of God saw that the daughters of humankind were beautiful. Thus they took wives for themselves from any they chose. So the Lord said, "My Spirit will not remain in humankind indefinitely, since they are mortal. They will remain for 120 more years." The Nephilim were

1 *Hesperides, or the Muses' Garden and Its Manuscript History*. Published in: Library, 2009, v. 10, n. 4, p. 372, doi. 10.1093/library/10.4.372 By:Tianhu, Hao.

> on the earth in those days (and also after this) when the sons of God would sleep with the daughters of humankind, who gave birth to their children. They were the mighty heroes of old, the famous men. But the Lord saw that the wickedness of humankind had become great on the earth. Every inclination of the thoughts of their minds was only evil all the time. The Lord regretted that he had made humankind on the earth, and he was highly offended. So the Lord said, "I will wipe humankind, whom I have created, from the face of the earth—everything from humankind to animals, including creatures that move on the ground and birds of the air, for I regret that I have made them." But Noah found favor in the sight of the Lord.

Before I read Dr. Heiser's book, I was familiar enough with this account after having been raised in church and hearing it often in children's classes and programs. "Noah's Ark" was typically taught as a sweet story about the Most High God saving a faithful family and preserving the earth's animals; that was pretty much it. However, reading about Noah's ark at this time in my life was new for me in several ways.

For starters, I had never really looked into what all had happened preceding the Great Flood, nor had I considered what might have led humanity to be so terrible that the Most High God would destroy all except Noah and his family.

Additionally, it's hard to argue about the truth of this story considering how many ancient mythologies include a flood narrative. People believed a flood happened, so it's worth considering why.

Further, after rereading Genesis 6 as an adult, it seemed harsh and confusing. I had simply trusted the Most High God for years when my understanding failed me. Yet I still wondered: If the Most High God had promised humanity a Redeemer from the beginning, then why did He kill everyone except eight people?

Diving deeper into Genesis, we see the "sons of God," "daughters of men," and then the appearance of the Nephilim. This implies that divine beings (sons of God) mated with the daughters of men before the Flood. These fallen sons of God sinned sexually (outside of the Most High God's order), leading to the creation of Nephilim. This much is clear in Genesis 6:1–2.

Dr. Heiser's teachings emboldened me to expand the scope of my research to include extrabiblical writings like the Book of Enoch, which gives much more detail and information about the Genesis 6 account. The Jewish writers of the books of the Bible were addressing people at the time who presumably already knew these details which, many believe, were included in the Book of Enoch. The Book of Enoch is referenced elsewhere in the Bible (2 Peter 2:4–6 and Jude 5–6) and is also mentioned in many other Jewish oral and written traditions outside of the Bible. While it may not be canonical Scripture, if the biblical writers quoted the Book of Enoch, it may be worth our time to read, because it provides a lot of important context.

Enoch 1: The Book of the Watchers states in chapter 6:1:

> And it came to pass when the children of men had multiplied that in those days were born unto them beautiful and comely daughters. And the angels, the children of the heaven, saw and lusted after them, saw and lusted after them and said to one another: "Come let us choose wives from among the children of men and begat us children.... And they were in all two hundred, who descended in the days of Jared on the summit of Mount Hermon."

Chapter 7:1–5 of the same book states:

> And all the others together with them took unto themselves wives, and each chose for himself one, and they began to go in unto them and to defile themselves with theme, and they taught them charms and enchantments, and the cutting of roots, and made them acquainted with plants. And they became pregnant and they bare great giants, whose height was three thousand ells: Who

consumed all the acquisitions of men. And when men could no longer sustain them, the giants turned against them and devoured mankind. And they began to sin against birds, and beasts, and reptiles, and fish, and to devour one another's flesh, and drink the blood. Then the earth laid accusation against the lawless ones.

And in chapter 8:1–4 of that book, we read:

And Azâzêl taught men to make swords, and knives, and shields, and breastplates, and made known to them **the metals** <of the earth> and the art of working them, and bracelets, and ornaments, and the use of antimony, and the beautifying of the eyelids, and all kinds of costly stones, and all colouring tinctures. And there arose much godlessness, and they committed fornication, and they were led astray, and became corrupt in all their ways. Semjâzâ taught enchantments, and root-cuttings, Armârôs the resolving of enchantments, Barâqîjâl, (taught) astrology, Kôkabêl the constellations, Ezêqêêl the knowledge of the clouds, <Araqiêl the signs of the earth, Shamsiêl the signs of the sun,> and Sariêl the course of the moon. And as men perished, they cried, and their cry went up to heaven.

Upon reading Enoch 1, we discover that "fallen" or "rebellious" sons of God (possibly some who were in the divine council originally; see Psalm 82) were interacting with humans in forbidden ways and thus were corrupting them. Pride was also at play, as the fallen sons of god (divine beings) wanted to interact with humans in their own way instead of the Most High God's.

In the ancient source, we also read of divine beings called "Watchers." In Daniel 4:13, that term is translated as "holy ones," further indicating these were divine beings. Even if the Watchers in Daniel 4:13 weren't the fallen ones, they were to "watch" humans and help them, *not* mate with them and produce offspring. Many scholars believe their sin resulted in the creation of the earlier-mentioned hybrids (half human and half nonhuman/divine being) known as the Nephilim. The fallen sons of God, these Watchers, just like Satan, rebelled against the Most High God's ways. The Book of Enoch details sexual sins of all types as well as other actions that harmed humans. In Heiser's 2017 book, *Reversing Hermon: Enoch, the Watchers, and the Forgotten Mission of Jesus Christ,* he explained that the Watchers were the ones whom Jews from the Old Testament to the days of Jesus believed were "part of the explanation for why the world was so profoundly depraved."[2]

Some theologians argue that the Watchers attempted to "have dominion" on earth by mating with humans and producing offspring so they could use their children for control purposes. Others indicate the Watchers hated humans for their status as the Most High God's imagers on earth and jealously wanted to corrupt them with forbidden knowledge. Either of these sins could be at play. Beyond sexual perversion, the fallen Watchers are recorded as being the ones to teach humans all types of forbidden knowledge, including the art of war (making weapons and using humans in their battles); the production of dangerous pharmaceuticals (addictive substances); conjuring spirits (witchcraft); the perversion of astrology; and other information in attempts not to just kill humans but to ruin their bloodline as the Most High God's imagers.

Taking it a few steps further, Nephilim (translated as "giant" or *gibbor*) are also mentioned after the Flood, as stated in Genesis 6:4. Scholars differ in their views of how Nephilim came on the scene after the Flood. Regardless of how they got there, the giant clans showed up in the land of Canaan, where Joshua and those entering it were told to destroy the people living there. To many of us, this instruction seems extreme. Again, why would the Most High God destroy entire populations? In the past, I had to believe and trust that the He was good, even in telling Joshua to wipe out these people. Now, I realize He was telling Joshua to obliterate the *hybrids*, much like the ones mentioned above. These

2 Heiser, *Reversing Hermon.*

giants weren't fully human (they taught child sacrifice, cannibalism, and worship to fallen sons of God); they were partly fallen sons of God and were truly evil beings corrupting humanity.

The fallen sons of God in the days of Noah and afterwards ultimately sought to defile the bloodline of humans with unnatural and harmful sexual practices, addiction, witchcraft, and trauma (from war, et cetera), and through teaching forbidden knowledge. The fallen ones wanted to destroy the human imagers of the Most High God on earth. They did everything to try to destroy humans in their essence. The only ones not compromised were Noah and his family.

As a mental health professional, the clarity came as I realized these fallen ones were the ones who likely introduced all sexual sin, war, witchcraft, New Age practices that lead to harm, addiction, and other aspects of depravity to humans. I also learned that demons, as we know them today, are believed by many scholars to be the disembodied spirits of the Nephilim killed by the Flood. My mind was blown as I realized that the mental health struggles related to sexuality, addiction, witchcraft, the occult, war, and others weren't only a result of sinful human choices but were the casualties of a battle with fallen beings.

Ancient Mythology Comparison: The Epic of Gilgamesh

The most popular flood narrative in mythology is likely the *Epic of Gilgamesh*. In this story there is an assembly of gods. Doesn't that sound like a divine council? The flood in this story is unleashed by the gods, mainly by one named Enil, to destroy all humans as some sort of retribution. It also discusses the goddess Ishtar and her reproach of Enil's lack of thought in leading the assembly's decision. There is no mention of a reason other than just an impulse.

In the Genesis Flood narrative, the deluge was a rational, ethical, and patient choice by Yahweh in response to rebellion. Yahweh also preserved the righteous humans. In contrast, the gods in the *Epic of Gilgamesh* do not act ethically. One book on Genesis describes the gods as "truly pagan in their lies and toleration of lies, in their hunger for the sacrifice, in their behavior, in the caprice with which they deal with people, and in the reversal of their moods."[3] These ancient stories aren't simply fictional. They're perversions of the true narratives. This is a tactic the enemies of the Most High God use often. Whom do you want to serve? As Joshua said, "As for me and my house we will serve the Lord" (Joshua 24:15). Sadly, rebellion continues.

The Rebellion of Genesis 11

Sadly, once the earth was cleansed after the Genesis 6 Flood, the effort to destroy humans was still in motion. Some theologians suggest there may have been another fall among the divine council beings resulting in the third rebellion. Others believe one of Noah's descendants had Nephilim DNA in his bloodline that had not been expressed until the choices of Nimrod (who helped to lead the rebellion). Epigenetics is a possible explanation here, meaning our choices determine how our genes express at times. Many scholars believe a combination of rebellion among divine beings and humans is what Genesis 11 is about. I tend to agree, as this is the case in the first two. While the influence may come from the enemies of the Most High God, the choice to engage in evil was made by both divine beings and humans.

Regardless, we read in Genesis 11:

> Now the whole earth had one language and the same words. And as people migrated from the east, they found a plain in the land of Shinar and settled there. And they said to one another, "Come, let us make bricks, and burn them thoroughly." And they had brick for stone, and bitumen for mortar. Then they said, "Come, let us

3 Holzinger, quoted by Hermann Gunkel in *Genesis*, Mark E. Biddle (Trans.), Mercer University Press, Macon, p. 72, 1997.

> build ourselves a city and a tower with its top in the heavens, and let us make a name for ourselves, lest we be dispersed over the face of the whole earth." And the LORD came down to see the city and the tower, which the children of man had built. And the LORD said, "Behold, they are one people, and they have all one language, and this is only the beginning of what they will do. And nothing that they propose to do will now be impossible for them."

Here again, the fallen sons of God, alongside the rebellious humans they influenced, allowed pride to control them as they sought to put themselves in the place of the Most High God by attempting to build a tower to heaven with a desire to be above the Almighty. The tower was believed to be more of a man-made structure versus one made by the Most High/Creator God. Towers—often called mountains or ziggurats—such as the one at Babel were temple-like structures built to commune with the gods. They are still found all over the world today.

Humans who built the Tower of Babel may have wanted to commune with the Most High on their own terms or they may have been seeking to interact with divine beings without connecting to Him. It's likely humans may have also been trying to find or learn about the hidden/forbidden knowledge they had heard about before the Flood, so they attempted to contact divine beings.

Punishment was two-fold: The fallen sons of God received nations of rebellious humans, *and* the rebellious humans received the authority of the fallen sons of God. The result was devastation and the scattering of fallen sons of God throughout the nations (Psalm 82), along with the confusion of language. This is why we see many nations not serving the Most High God today. They worship other gods or spirits. Thankfully, God then chose one nation to which He would reveal His plan for humanity to the world.

Many theologians and even other mythologies mention the use of forbidden knowledge again here. This rebellion created principalities throughout the world for those who seek to influence nations with power, control, pride, and self-sufficiency. Some organizations or groups, such as the Freemasons, have at times traced their roots back to the Tower of Babel. Groups such as these ultimately promote the idea that they have secret knowledge that gives them power. Knowledge in and of itself is not evil, but if it isn't coming from the Most High God or isn't taught within the right context, it can lead to destruction, such as in Genesis chapters 6 and 11.

The narrative in Genesis 11 is similar to the foundational story of all ancient "mythologies." Nimrod, a great-grandson of Noah, was the founder of the first world empire at Babel (*Bab:* "gateway"; *El:* "god," or the "gate of the gods"), later known as Babylon (Genesis 10:8–12; 11:1–9). Nimrod is believed to have led the people to worship their own gods—and even himself—as king. This is likely the beginning of Baal worship, which can be found in many cultures and religions around the world at all points in history, but at times under differing names. For example, Baal is in Phoenicia-Canaan, but it is known as Enmerkar in Sumeria, Osiris in Egypt, Zeus in Greek, and Jupiter in Rome. Some forms of this worship consider the father/son deity interchangeable. This all lines up with the truth of Scripture. Just as God confused the languages because of the rebellion (Genesis 11), so, of course, the deities or principalities (fallen sons of god) have different names, depending on the culture.

The result of this rebellion is further told in Deuteronomy 32:8–9:

> When the Most High gave to the nations their inheritance, when He divided mankind, He fixed the borders of the peoples according to the number of the sons of God. But the Lord's portion is His people, Jacob His allotted heritage.

God *disinherited the nations because of their rebellion*. Does this mean nations that don't follow God today are under the rule of an evil principality or principalities? I believe it does. Nations that go against the God of the Bible are plagued with destruction, corruption, and all kinds of evil. Nations that seek God and follow Him are blessed. The good news ultimately is that God raised up *one nation* under Abraham that would be His own, and it was through this nation that He planned the redemption of the world.

The Tower of Babel narrative, sadly, continues today. Influences of pagan gods/principalities/demons (i.e., Nimrod, Baal) are still trying to turn people against the Most High God. These evil entities push their own ideas/ideologies, such as governments and cultures that are anti-Most High God. They encourage beliefs such as "choosing your own truth" and incessantly pursue control of government. They foment hatred for traditional families and those who follow the Most High God. Their goal is to drive Him out of cultures entirely. These controlling influences can be found in fraternal orders (which use ritualistic practices), New Age practices, occult practices, and/or powerful groups that can control societies. These influences are evident in the rise of numerous mental health struggles, such as relational problems, racism, trauma, personality disorders, and more. Anytime any being points to anything other than the Most High God, destruction is the result. Who we serve matters.

Ancient Mythology Comparison: The Ziggurats or Pyramids

As mentioned previously, the Tower of Babel is the foundation of many ancient mythological stories and the beginning of many cultures and religions. Ancient Babylonians called the structure a "ziggurat" or "rising building." It is equivalent to the pyramids in Egypt. Although these are said to be tombs, some believe they were shrines to their deities.

In ancient Babylon, the Etemenanki was the largest and most important ziggurat. It was a shrine to the Babylonians' deity. In the story of Enuma Elish, Marduk was their god who defended other gods against the evil Tiamat. The epic continues with Marduk bringing order to the planet and building a tower at the center of the world, known as a line from earth to heaven.

Obviously, there are many diversions from the biblical narrative here. This epic myth, like others, suggests we need a tower to get to heaven. These perversions of truth indicate that we must work our way to heaven. The lie that we must worship created beings instead of the Creator is present throughout these myths.

While visiting Egypt with my family in 2022, we sailed the beautiful Nile River and stopped along the way at one temple and then another, finishing our tour with a stop at the Great Pyramids of Giza. At one point, I said to my husband, "People don't build these massive structures to worship gods they don't believe are real." He agreed. It may seem silly, but today a growing number of people are venerating the ancient Egyptian gods—a practice that leads to darkness.

The three rebellions we've just looked at have massive implications for mental health. In a way, the rebellions of fallen beings fractured heaven, and the attempts of the fallen ones also seek to fracture the minds of humans. Yet, Jesus the Christ came to offer redemption for the minds and hearts of humans. These truths allow us to move from frustration to hope! Once I studied the accounts of these rebellions, I realized we can trace all mental health problems back to Genesis 3, 6, and/or 11. Evil has infiltrated our world and every aspect of it but having a deeper understanding of where it all began can lead us to better treatments and eventually towards healing.

QUESTIONS FOR REFLECTION

1. What do you believe humans are truly battling?
2. What are the three rebellions that have influenced humans?
3. What are your reflections on how the enemies of God are attacking humans concerning mental health?

PRACTICAL APPLICATION

Encouragement for pastoral counselors and mental health professionals:

- Study and view the human struggle with Genesis 3, 6, and 11 in view.
- Review your sermons and/or counseling techniques and look for ways in which you explain the human struggle as

from within or against others instead of against the enemies of the Most High God.

- Make changes in the way you speak, teach, and counsel according to the truth about who humans are up against.
- Offer a sermon series on the three rebellions.

Prayer Prompt: *Lord, teach me your ways. Show me the truth of your Word. Reveal to me the ways in which I've wrongly viewed humans and their struggles.*

SCRIPTURE TO CONSIDER

Genesis 3:8–24:

> And they heard the sound of the LORD God walking in the garden in the cool of the day, and the man and his wife hid themselves from the presence of the LORD God among the trees of the garden. But the LORD God called to the man and said to him, "Where are you?" And he said, "I heard the sound of you in the garden, and I was afraid, because I was naked, and I hid myself." He said, "Who told you that you were naked? Have you eaten of the tree of which I commanded you not to eat?" The man said, "The woman whom you gave to be with me, she gave me fruit of the tree, and I ate." Then the LORD God said to the woman, "What is this that you have done?" The woman said, "The serpent deceived me, and I ate." The LORD God said to the serpent, "Because you have done this, cursed are you above all livestock and above all beasts of the field; on your belly you shall go, and dust you shall eat all the days of your life. I will put enmity between you and the woman, and between your offspring and her offspring; he shall bruise your head, and you shall bruise his heel." To the woman, he said, "I will surely multiply your pain in childbearing; in pain you shall bring forth children. Your desire shall be for your husband, and he shall rule over you." And to Adam, he said, "Because you have listened

to the voice of your wife and have eaten of the tree of which I commanded you, 'You shall not eat of it,' cursed is the ground because of you; in pain you shall eat of it all the days of your life; thorns and thistles it shall bring forth for you; and you shall eat the plants of the field. By the sweat of your face you shall eat bread, till you return to the ground, for out of it you were taken; for you are dust, and to dust you shall return." The man called his wife Eve because she was the mother of all living. And the Lord God made for Adam and his wife garments of skins and clothed them. Then the Lord God said, "Behold, the man has become like one of us in knowing good and evil. Now, lest he reach out his hand and take also of the tree of life and eat, and live forever—" therefore the Lord God sent him out from the garden of Eden to work the ground from which he was taken. He drove out the man, and at the east of the Garden of Eden, he placed the cherubim and a flaming sword that turned every way to guard the way to the Tree of Life.

Genesis 6:9–14:

This is the account of Noah. Noah was a godly man; he was blameless among his contemporaries. He walked with God. Noah had three sons: Shem, Ham, and Japheth. The earth was ruined in the sight of God; the earth was filled with violence. God saw the earth, and indeed it was ruined, for all living creatures on the earth were sinful. So God said to Noah, "I have decided that all living creatures must die, for the earth is filled with violence because of them. Now I am about to destroy them and the earth. Make for yourself an ark of cypress wood. Make rooms in the ark, and cover it with pitch inside and out."

Genesis 11:9–11:

"Come, let us go down and there confuse their language, so that they may not understand one another's speech." So the Lord dispersed them from there over the face of all the earth, and they left off building the city. Therefore, it was called Babel because there the Lord confused the language of all the earth. And from there the Lord dispersed them over the face of all the earth.

PART THREE

Mental Health and Implications of the Unseen Realm

Chapter 7

THE THREE REBELLIONS

You can't have the true peace of Christ's kingdom with lies and pretense.[1]

PETER SCAZZERO, pastor, author and podcaster

Rediscovering biblical truths about the human struggle changed the way I thought about my clients, my family, and myself. Hope increased as I began viewing people and problems differently. My prayer as a mental health counselor has always been that I would have the ability to overflow with hope by the power of the Holy Spirit. One way people often look for hope is by getting answers to their questions. After I explained to one client, John, that the mental battle he was undergoing could have supernatural influences, he expressed feeling a sense of freedom. Understanding that his thoughts seemed to "originate outside of himself," he finally had the desire to fight the darkness. Through the divine council worldview, the Most High God has shown me how to offer comprehensive answers to people about the evil and darkness they're facing.

Clients draw much hope when they learn their struggles aren't only influenced by their own sinful nature, but by spiritual forces of darkness as well. Hope prevails when they know evil has been defeated. Enduring through trials is possible...when hope is present.

---

1 https://www.goodreads.com/work/quotes/241288-emotionally-healthy-spirituality-unleash-a-revolution-in-your-life-in-c

Examining the three rebellions led me to amazing, hope-filled conclusions.

Mental Health Implications of the Rebellions in Genesis 3

Walking with clients in times of grief following a death is challenging, heart-wrenching, and often dark. Death is incomprehensible, and grief after loss is almost impossible to heal from fully. Suicide is one of the darkest forms of death. Considering the complex design of the human body and how the body often naturally heals itself, it isn't hard to realize that our Creator God/the Most High God designed our bodies to *live*, not to *die*.

For example, in the book *The Body: A Guide for Occupants,* author B. Bryson points out some of the body's natural resistance to common attempts at suicide. One of the many scientists and doctors Bryson interviewed discussed the wrist from an orthopedic surgeon's perspective. "You shouldn't ever try to kill yourself by cutting your wrists, by the way," said the surgeon, Ben. "All of those things going in are wrapped in a protective band called a fascial sheath, which makes it really hard to get to the arteries. Most people who cut their wrists fail to kill themselves, which is no doubt a good thing." The surgeon added, "It is also really hard to kill yourself by jumping from a height. The legs become a kind of crumple zone. You can make a real mess of yourself, but you are very likely to survive. Killing yourself is difficult. We are not designed to die."[2]

Years ago, a client in complete despair called me. He didn't sound like himself. I asked him to come into the office, and when he did, he didn't look like himself, either. Turmoil about whether to take his own life was clearly raging. After taking time to remind him of who he was, what he had to live for, and how the Most High God planned to use him in his family and work, he regained peace. He had needed to identify the lies of the enemy to defeat the evil threatening his life. Thankfully, he is alive and well today.

---

2 Bryson, B. (2022). *The Body: A Guide for Occupants*. Doubleday.

If you've ever met someone who is suicidal, you may have noticed you can almost see a dark cloud over the person. There is a heaviness…a darkness…a thickness that is tangible. The family also often feels the oppressive presence, as if the hopelessness is a tsunami overtaking everyone around the person with the fear of destruction and death.

Those who have already lost a family member to suicide know the pain of the one who passed isn't really eradicated; it's simply transferred to close family and friends. It takes a great deal of work in the counseling room to help families heal from the anguish caused by the suicide of a loved one. The despair often falls over them in many ways, including feeling pain when having to whisper to others that the loved one was lost to suicide; it becomes an identifier, in a way, for those left behind.

As a Christian, I know that compelling humans to end their own lives is the work of the enemy. It's the influence of Satan trying to do exactly what he did in Genesis 3: kill a human, an imager of the Most High God on earth.

After years of counseling people who've struggled with suicidal thoughts, I've noticed one common characteristic: They don't believe they're controlling their own thoughts. They're often made to believe the thoughts are theirs, but many times they can't truly buy into the idea. When I can explain to someone that these thoughts are likely coming from the enemies of the Most High God, what they're experiencing makes more sense. The enemy tries to convince them that there's no other way to ease their pain, and there's no other way to release their family from the burden of themselves. They believe suicide is the only answer.

You have to be a really good liar to convince people to go against their natural design and take actions that are contrary to how the body works. Well, a "really good liar" is exactly who we're dealing with: the father of lies.

> You belong to your father, the devil, and you want to carry out your father's desires. He was a murderer from the beginning, not holding to the truth, for there is no truth in him. When he lies,

> he speaks his native language, for he is a liar and the father of lies. (John 8:44, NIV)

When I hear clients bring up listening to "suicide playlists"—music with dark themes related to self-harm—it is obvious who is behind this darkness.

Murder, homicide, accidental killings, and abortion are also often viewed as having their roots in mental health struggles. Murders or homicides usually spring from deep-seated anger. The first recorded murder in Scripture (Genesis 4) involves Adam and Eve's son, Cain, killing his brother, Abel, in a vile act that had its origins in anger and jealousy.

Accidental killings and abortion also lead to a great deal of mental agony. This is by no means a judgment; my heart goes out to women who've had abortions and are living with regret. I've never had one client who's had an abortion who was able to forgive herself or get over it outside of being able to understand the forgiveness of Christ through the power of the Holy Spirit. The grief and remorse plague women in ways that, to me, can only come from the enemies of the Most High God.

One woman specifically fights daily depression that manifests as illnesses such as migraines, stomach issues, and weight struggles. Her relationships have also suffered because of her inability to forgive herself for having had an abortion. The children the Most High God has blessed her with since the abortion can't figure out how to relate to her. Her husband, who has patiently loved her for many years, has had to be hospitalized due to mental illness caused by his ongoing frustration with her. Ultimately, abortion is also like the dark cloud surrounding suicidal people and their families in that the enemy uses the circumstances to continue plaguing women and those around them for years.

When we consider Ephesians 6:12 in light of the truth that killing is not natural, it becomes evident that *Satan, not our own flesh and blood, is the one we are battling when thoughts of suicide or harm enter our minds*. Neither is it the influence of others, but rather of Satan, that causes harm. Satan has always wanted to eliminate humanity—the imagers of the Most High God on earth. I can't help but think when Satan/the Serpent of old said, "die, die" in Genesis 2:17, though it was said as emphasis, the results are the death of someone or something *and* the impact of death on those surrounding the person who dies. It also makes me think about Adam and his failure to protect Eve—which is not unlike our lack of protection at times of those around us.

Considering mental health in light of the rebellion, or Fall, in Genesis 3 led me to connect its influence on humans—via mental health problems such as anxiety (panic, phobias, generalized anxiety disorder), mood disorders (bipolar depression), trauma-related disorders, and disruptive mood dysregulation disorder—to Satan's temptation. Symptoms such as suicidal ideation or self-harm and societal concerns such as mass shootings and abortion also seem to be rooted in the initial influence of the death of humans as recorded in Genesis. We have much to glean from Genesis 3 in terms of its implications for mental health. As the battle rages around us, I pray the truth of where the negative influences of pride and death originated gives you hope concerning yourself and those you love.

Mental Health Implications from Genesis 6

The harm stemming from believing the lies and perversions that began in Genesis 6 are easily seen in sexual struggles, which are reported daily in counseling. My staff and I often discuss the feeling we get in our "gut" when a couple first comes into the office and shares their story—but holds back one very important detail: one of the spouses has cheated. Often the discussion begins with words like: "We love each other. We have wonderful children. We have great jobs. We make a great team. We're here simply with a desire to fix some things because maybe we've grown apart." Trust must be built between the counselor and couple before the truth can surface, but experienced counselors almost always know that one of the partners was unfaithful...even before it's said. Honestly, there have been times I've said in a first session, "That sounds amazing, but tell me what's *really* going on. What happened?" This is when the tears begin to fall and the clients express the truth. In sharing about how they were deceived leading to an affair, the unfaithful spouse almost always says in some form, "I cannot believe I allowed this to happen. I can't believe I fell for the lies."

In addition to unfaithfulness, other sexual problems influence humans negatively as well. The transgender agenda seems to have been a daily headline since 2020. In many Western countries, homosexuals can now marry and are treated the same as heterosexual couples legally and socially. Some argue that this is progress; meanwhile, there are families in disarray due to the fallout of the transgender and homosexual narratives being told, believed, and lived out. Sadly, these folks are often those who've previously struggled with abuse. One client was sexually abused by her father when she was a child, and she never again wanted to be a girl due to the hatred she had for her own body based on that childhood trauma.

A 2021 National Institutes of Health report concluded:

> In a nationwide online sample of US adolescents, transgender adolescents had elevated rates of psychological, physical, and sexual abuse compared with heterosexual cisgender adolescents. Risk for psychological abuse was highest among transgender adolescents assigned female at birth. In the future, researchers should examine how more frequent experiences of abuse during childhood could contribute to disproportionate mental health problems observed within this population.

Other studies suggest that intimate partner violence is worse among LGBTQ+ individuals.[3] The lie of the enemy is that they were "born this way" or have the right to choose their gender. The lies are endless.

3 Hubbell, J. T. (2023). "Elucidating Intimate Partner Violence Rate Disparities Between Same- and Opposite-Sex Couples: A Demographic Approach." *Journal of Interpersonal Violence, 39*(3–4), 651–675. https://doi.org/10.1177/08862605231197781 (Original work published 2024).

Ephesians 4:17–24:

> So I say this, and insist in the Lord, that you no longer live as the Gentiles do, in the futility of their thinking. They are darkened in their understanding, being alienated from the life of God because of the ignorance that is in them due to the hardness of their hearts. Because they are callous, they have given themselves over to indecency for the practice of every kind of impurity with greediness. But you did not learn about Christ like this, if indeed you heard about him and were taught in him, just as the truth is in Jesus. You were taught with reference to your former way of life to lay aside the old man who is being corrupted in accordance with deceitful desires, to be renewed in the spirit of your mind, and to put on the new man who has been created in God's image in righteousness and holiness that comes from truth.

The deception comes from the same liars who corrupted humanity in Genesis 6. Their goal was to deprave humans—and they succeeded with everyone but Noah and his family. These same evil influences are still lying to humans today. They're telling us that it's fine to live outside of the natural order created by the Most High God. The Bible speaks often of these evil influences—not only in Genesis 6, but throughout the Old and New Testaments. In the New Testament, for example, the people of Ephesus were battling the demonic forces of sexuality in the temple of Artemis, a goddess of fertility whose rituals consisted of debauchery. She was also represented by a meteorite, as she was said to have "fallen from the sky." I agree that she fell from the heavens, and it was her choice as a divine being to be evil. Evil influences like her are still trying to debauch humans to this day.

New Testament scholar and author N. T. Wright describes what he observed while visiting the ancient ground of the Temple of Artemis:

> Many of us in the West have lived quite comfortably with all these things in separate compartments, and everything clinically wrapped so that nothing can leak from one compartment to

> another. We are inclined to look at the riot in Ephesus, shudder, and thank God that we don't do things like that any more.... We should think again about the way in which wickedness gets a grip on a society, somewhere down below its polite exterior, and about the way in which, sooner or later, someone needs to take their courage in one hand and their Bible in the other, throw to the winds any caution about their own prospects, and say what needs to be said. And we shouldn't miss, either, the way in which, once again, the gospel functions as a critique of all temples, whether the Parthenon in Athens, the temple of Artemis in Ephesus, or even, as in chapter 7, the Temple in Jerusalem itself. Is that, too, a theme which Luke is gently rubbing in?[4]

I agree with Wright. I've seen Western churches celebrate Pride Month and participate in Pride parades—even in the Bible Belt of the US where I live. How can Christians not think this is like what was happening in Ephesus, even if at a very basic level?

Clients who've struggled with evil or unnatural sexual influences are plagued by the forces of darkness. There are many stories of those struggling. Freedom truly comes when they realize the battle is not within but is the result of evil influences trying to destroy them. As believers in the Most High God, we must lovingly share the truth. We must stop saying things such as, "They are gay and just don't know it." We also need to stop believing lies such as this.

In other efforts to deprave humans, the fallen watchers from Genesis 6 also introduced *pharmakeia* (drugs used in witchcraft or the abuse of drugs/substances), which leads me to believe this is likely the beginning of addictive behaviors related to the use of substances. Addiction plagues society at large in many ways, costing nations billions of dollars annually in medical treatment, legal fees, and many other related costs. Virtually everyone can say they've battled addiction or they know someone who

---

4 ntwrightonline.org/great-was-artemis-of-the-ephesians

has. Addiction is an unhealthy attachment. Addictive substances hit on the same part of the brain as loving attachments, but they don't have the same effect over time; eventually, users need more of the substance to get the same result. Most clients' stories related to addiction are rooted in conflict within one or more family relationships. One man recently told me, "I never felt like my dad wanted to spend time with me." He never blamed his dad for his addiction, but he knew the lack of attachment to his dad was somehow tied to his addictions.

Evil influences from Genesis 6 until today harm humanity with the lie that a substance can provide what we need and can fill the void only the Most High can truly fill. The lies of addiction destroy humans and their families; I've seen the destruction firsthand. Addiction is relational, as those who struggle often leave their families for the next "binger" or "high." It truly does steal, kill, and destroy.

Lies regarding addiction often sound like this: "I can't stop. I don't have a problem. It is just impacting me. Everyone uses something." Treatment centers are full of those influenced by the enemies of the Most High God. We must let them know this influence is from pure evil and darkness, not from within themselves.

In addition to ungodly sexual practices and addictions, other lies of the enemy come in the forms of witchcraft and war. These arts were also taught by the fallen ones in Genesis 6. Some may not think witchcraft is alive and well today, but every week I see clients who talk about playing video games that involve casting spells or using Ouija boards, visiting psychics, and more. And it's not hard to see war as a way to destroy humans; whether one survives it or not, its effects often torment people who have experienced it for the rest of their lives.

It's easy to see the ramifications of the rebellion or fall of Genesis 6 include mental health problems such as anxiety (obsessive compulsive disorder, social anxiety, panic), mood disorders (bipolar, depression, seasonal affective disorder), psychotic disorders (schizophrenia, schizoaffective), and attention-deficiency hyperactive disorder, eating disorders, dissociative identity disorder, gender disorders, and substance abuse.

In addition, symptoms such as dissociation, sleep paralysis, psychosomatic, sexual abuse, gender dysmorphia, and abductions also could have stemmed from Genesis 6. Societal concerns such as the rise of internet abuse, sex trafficking, engagement in occult activities, participation in cults, and disturbing artificial intelligence applications may have originated in the Genesis 6 account. In fact, the origin of the negative influence of so many health challenges began in the days of Noah. Again, this is not a battle against flesh and blood! Finally, we have an answer that provides complete understanding.

Mental Health Implications of Genesis 11

Here is another story that's very different from the way it was told to many of us in children's Sunday school. When I learned about the Tower of Babel as a child, I thought it seemed unjust for the Most High God to disperse people simply because they were trying to build a tower to reach Him. I understood that somehow it was a bad idea, but I wasn't sure why. Now I understand the truth of that narrative: Humans' attempts to worship, gain knowledge from, or commune with any divine being other than the Most High always lead to devastation. Learning that divine beings were influencing humans to try to usurp the authority of the Most High also matters because it's a reason for the effects on humans to this day.

One day at the office, one of our therapists—a skeptic (which I love because she keeps me sharp)—said to me, "I hate it when you're right." She had been dealing with a difficult case involving a client who didn't have the "normal" background for having dissociative symptoms. When I encouraged her to dig deeper, she discovered the client had a close family member who was active in a fraternal order. It may seem to be a stretch, but this ties to Genesis 11. Most fraternal orders, including the Freemasons, trace their roots back to the Tower of Babel.[5] In my opin-

5 heritage-history.com/index.php?c=read&author=webster&book=secret&story=freemasonry

ion, the rituals this client's family member was engaging in as a part of the order's practices were in some way cursing his family. As a result, a family member was having unusual mental health experiences.

A more common mental health implication of Genesis 11 to note is narcissism. Narcissists exhibit behaviors such as having a grandiose sense of self; dreaming of unlimited power and success; needing excessive admiration; believing they can only be understood by others who are important; having a lack of empathy; unreasonably expecting special treatment or favors; exploiting others; and displaying arrogant and envious attitudes. Nimrod exhibited all these characteristics, as did the fallen sons of God. Narcissism is also at the core of all personality disorders. My heart breaks for each client who reports having been harmed by a pastor who has fallen prey to narcissism. Narcissistic behavior often starts with the pastor demonstrating a noticeable need for admiration and affirmation, and it reaches its worst extent when the pastor demands control and engages in manipulation that leads to abusive behaviors.

Personality disorders are among the hardest to treat. This is due to the deeply ingrained, maladaptive patterns of behavior; thinking that is resistant to change; and relational challenges that hinder the development of a trusting relationship, which is needed in effective therapy.[6]

Individuals with personality disorders often lack insight into their problematic behaviors, making them resistant to therapy and unwilling to engage in the necessary changes. Additionally, these disorders frequently lead to interpersonal difficulties, stifling the development of a strong therapeutic alliance, which is crucial for effective treatment.

Beyond personality disorders is the impact of relational struggles because of racism, trauma and more. The events of Genesis 11 and the impact of the fallen ones on the world are vast. The destruction of trying to usurp the Most High God is seen daily in the world of mental health.

Analyzing Genesis 11 alongside mental health disorders directed me to believe issues such as anxiety (obsessive compulsive disorder,

---

6 solmentalhealth.com/2021/10/12/why-personality-disorders-are-so-hard-to-treat

social anxiety, generalized anxiety disorder); psychotic disorders (schizophrenia); trauma-related disorders; personality disorders (narcissism) attention-deficit/hyperactivity disorder; and autism spectrum disorders had their potential beginning at the Genesis 11 story. Societal unrest may also stem from the events described in that narrative. Even church-related issues such as narcissism in leadership, the lack of healthy attachments with other congregants, and paganism could all be traced to the rebellion at the Tower of Babel. I can't emphasize it enough: Evil entities are behind the origin of all mental health disorders.

Comparing the rebellions of divine beings and humans to the mental struggles we face is helpful in planning to battle the darkness. The chart that follows is an attempt to categorize all mental health diagnoses in terms of the original origin of evil influence.

Biblical Rebellion	Resulting Sinful Behaviors/Issues	Related Mental Health Concerns
Genesis 3 *Serpent in the Garden*	Death-related concerns (suicide, homicide, abortion) Anger, irrational thinking, harmful behavior	Anxiety disorders (panic, phobias, GAD) Mood disorders (bipolar, depression) Trauma-related disorders Disruptive mood dysregulation disorder Personality disorders (antisocial/borderline)
Genesis 6 *Watchers & Nephilim*	Sexual sin/perversion Addictions (drugs, hallucinogens) Genetic engineering, transhumanism Witchcraft, occult, astrology Violence, vanity, body modification	Anxiety disorders (OCD, social anxiety, panic) Mood disorders (depression, bipolar, SAD) Psychotic disorders (schizophrenia, schizoaffective) Trauma-related disorders Personality disorders (histrionic, dependent, antisocial) ADHD, eating disorders, dissociative disorders, gender disorders substance-related disorders
Genesis 11 *Tower of Babel*	Anti-God ideologies Control, racism, confusion Pride, self-centeredness, cults Control and manipulation	Anxiety disorders (OCD, social anxiety, GAD) Psychotic disorders (schizophrenia) Trauma-related disorders Personality disorders (narcissism) ADHD Autism spectrum disorder

Understanding why humans experience mental disorders is a powerful weapon for fighting those battles. Discussing the roots of their struggles with clients often leads to reports of a sense of freedom. Also, as a believer in Jesus, the King of Kings and Lord of Lords, the good news is that He has defeated our enemies!

QUESTIONS FOR REFLECTION

1. What mental health implications can clearly be seen as coming from the influence of evil?
2. How do the three rebellions provide clarity to the root of evil?
3. When have you seen the enemies of God attack you, and in what ways?

PRACTICAL APPLICATION

Encouragement for pastoral counselors and mental health professionals:

- Be able to explain the origin of human struggles and the impacts on mental health.
- Modify your language as you discuss challenges, referring to the right enemy as the influencer of darkness.
- Offer a sermon series on mental health and the three Genesis rebellions.
- Provide treatment that falls in line with scriptural teachings for the influences of the forces of darkness.

Prayer Prompt: *Lord, guard me and those I serve from the negative influences of your enemies. Remind me to put on the full armor as I reflect your image daily.*

SCRIPTURE TO CONSIDER

Jeremiah 17:9–10:

The heart is deceitful above all things and beyond cure. Who can understand it? "I the Lord search the heart and examine the mind, to reward each person according to their conduct, according to what their deeds deserve."

Jeremiah 29:13:

You will seek me and find me when you seek me with all your heart.

Proverbs 3:1–2:

My son, do not forget my teaching, but keep my commands in your heart, for they will prolong your life for many years and bring you peace and prosperity.

Romans 5:3–4:

Not only so, but we also glory in our sufferings, because we know that suffering produces perseverance; perseverance, character; and character, hope.

Romans 15:13:

May the God of hope fill you with all joy and peace as you trust in him, so that you may overflow with hope by the power of the Holy Spirit.

Chapter 8

HOW EVIL INFLUENCES HUMANS TODAY

You can believe in whatsoever you like, but the truth remains the truth, no matter how sweet the lie may taste.

MICHAEL BASSEY JOHNSON

At this point, you may be wondering how the good news of Jesus intersects with mental health. If you hold to a biblical worldview or can at least consider it as you read, I hope you're beginning to put the puzzle together with me. We've now gained clarity as to where the battles humans face originated and, ultimately, how they are still at play today. Satan, the powers of darkness, principalities, and spiritual forces of wickedness in heavenly places (Ephesians 6:12) are at war against humans to steal, kill, and destroy—preventing them from being who and what God has called them to be.

As I worked with clients while I was learning all God was showing me, I felt as if I had been given many new tools to help them—beginning with the understanding of what they were up against.

Satan and the powers of darkness are the ones enticing humans toward suicide, wars, abortion, addiction, sexual sins, murder, narcissism, corrupt governments/systems, and all forms of evil in the world. Today the darkness may be evident in transhumanism, transgender issues, homosexuality, sexual perversion, pornography, sexual abuse, sex trafficking, genetic engineering, alien abduction, sexual forms of control/manipulation, satanic ritual abuse, and spiritual abuse—or in any effort to kill humans, pervert or deprave their bloodline, and/or lead people away from the One True God. Every client story at some level involves an evil force seeking to turn them away from the goodness of God. Whether it's Ella, who was trafficked by a family member, or Keith, who was sexually abused by a neighbor, evil is absolutely involved in addition to human sinfulness and depravity. Knowledge is power, so knowing the root of our problems is powerful.

Dark issues are being dealt with daily in the counseling space. This revelation that the origin of many mental health conditions is connected to the three rebellions required me to change how I counsel and approach others. I pray it leads others to change as well.

Changes in the Therapy Session

As I've said, studying Michael Hesier's *Unseen Realm* has changed how I view the problems my clients face. I now consider them in light of the potential evil influence of fallen beings over a person. This shift in perspective has led me to adjust the way I conceptualize problems, the way I discuss issues with clients, and the way I treat certain challenges. One client, Jennifer, tried for a time to understand why she was having depression; it didn't seem to make sense because she had been raised in a loving home. Once I explained my updated views, Jennifer said she understood what she was facing for the first time since she had been diagnosed.

Conceptualizing clients' problems involves learning about the similarities and differences among spiritual manifestation of evil, spiritual warfare, and mental health. The way counselors understand an individual's troubles influences how we administer treatment.

When counseling clients with anxiety, I help them fight their own thoughts and invite them to become aware that evil might also be using anxiety to try to defeat them. My renewed approach also compelled to pray differently for clients than I had previously; for example, I now ask God to help them defeat their *enemies*, not simply their anxiety.

This approach has even changed my language. For example, now I can say to a client, "It may not be you; there may be an evil influence behind your suicidal thoughts." Or I can challenge a client to consider that thoughts of gender dysphoria might be rooted in more than just their own flesh; they might be attributed to an evil force. That transforms the nature of the battle: Clients no longer feel at war solely within themselves. After sharing this perspective with one client, Kelly, she reported feeling relieved to finally have the right words to explain what she felt and to know the problem wasn't simply from within her. Many clients find hope in considering the origin of their feelings and thoughts, and how in turn how to properly confront them.

Implications and Considerations of Evil on the Brain

While I now have better answers about why humans struggle, I still acknowledge the power of human choice with my clients. We may be influenced by evil forces of darkness, but one thing the Most High God gave us all was free will. Romans 10:9–10 states:

> If you declare with your mouth, "Jesus is Lord," and believe in your heart that God raised him from the dead, you will be saved. For it is with your heart that you believe and are justified, and it is with your mouth that you profess your faith and are saved.

We often neglect to realize the power of our choices and/or the choices of others. We don't have to remain victims. We can be overcomers and survivors. Many days, stories like Tom's keep me going. He has fought marital problems for years, but with each time he chooses to obey Christ and love his wife the way Christ loves the Church, he proves he is an overcomer. He is still married after many years of therapy.

Thoughts and Choices: Neuroplasticity

Mind control is a fascinating topic; it's been the subject of countless movies, television series, and books. The science behind the control of a brain is called "neuroscience," and the process of the brain being able to adapt and function is called "neuroplasticity." This term originated in 1948 by Jerzy Konorski, a Polish neurophysiologist, and was popularized by Canadian neurophysiologist Donald Hebb in 1949. Neuroplasticity is "the ability of the nervous system to change its activity in response to intrinsic or extrinsic stimuli by reorganizing its structure, functions, or connections."[1] It can involve negative changes after injuries or positive results after restorative efforts. Neuroplasticity has been observed to be suppressed after exposure to stress, which can change behavioral performance and memory.[2]

The human brain is very malleable. The hope embedded in this truth is that although we can't change what's happened, we can change our *responses* to those circumstances and events. That, in turn, can influence how things play out in our lives. Positive changes come through activities such as positive mind management and self-regulation. Reconceptualizing what's happened to us is one way to deal with emotional distress that, in the past, may have been keeping our brains from readjusting. Ultimately, true change involves applying positive techniques to help rewire our brains, creating useful, sustainable, and automatized actions and attitudes that form better habits.[3]

"Epigenetics" is a term that explains the power of choice and describes when certain choices turn on or off genes. Dr. Caroline Leaf, neuroscientist, describes epigenetics this way:

> Epigenetics shows us that our thoughts are a predominant factor controlling genetic expression; our mind controls what we think, eat, exercise, respond to and so on—it controls how we

1 Puderbaugh, M., Emmady, P. D. "Neuroplasticity." May 1, 2023. In: StatPearls [Internet]. Treasure Island (FL): StatPearls Publishing; January 2025. PMID: 32491743.

2 Duman, R. S. "Neural Plasticity: Consequences of Stress and Actions of Antidepressant Treatment." *Dialogues Clin Neurosci.* June 2004; 6(2):157–69. doi: 10.31887/DCNS.2004.6.2/rduman. PMID: 22034207; PMCID: PMC3181800.

3 drleaf.com/blogs/news/neuroplasticity-what-it-is-how-to-harness-its-power-for-your-benefit

> live our lives. Epigenetics shows us that how we think, feel and choose (our mind-in-action) will influence the behavior of our genes and our subsequent mental and physical wellbeing.[4]

Think about this for a moment. Our thoughts and choices can determine how our genes are expressed. This is a powerful truth.

I believe our Creator designed us this way. We've been saying this in culture for a while. We say, "I think, therefore I am" (in Latin, *Cogito, ergo sum*), words attributed to French philosopher René Descartes. How about the statement, "You are what you eat"? This, too, implies that our choices determine our actions or characteristics. Many people don't believe they can control their thoughts, but we can—and should—control them. We are designed to take our thoughts "captive" (2 Corinthians 10:5). We've simply bought into the lies of the enemies of God that either we can't control them or that all thoughts originate from within.

One strategy I use in therapy often is what I call the "email inbox technique." In helping clients understand how to take every thought captive, I use an analogy of an email inbox. I begin by asking clients to reflect on what messages come into their email or any messaging format (for younger audiences). We may get legitimate messages from family or friends, I explain. But we often find spam or junk messages in our inboxes as well. At times, we may even receive nefarious messages from unknown senders. Sure, at times we can control incoming mail by subscribing or unsubscribing to certain senders, but we can't always do that. We always seem to find at least some messages we never signed up for.

Then, I explain that our thoughts are similar. The identity of the sender of those thoughts may not always be clear. Though we can't always control where the thoughts or messages come from, just like with our inboxes, we can control what we *do* with those messages. We can delete them, respond to them, report them as "junk," or save them for

---

4 Leaf, Caroline (2021). "Break Cycles & Heal Generational Trauma." drleaf.com/use-neurocycle-to-break-cycles-heal-generational-trauma.

later. This is a great way to review our thoughts! We need to act on some by deleting them. We can "unsubscribe" from others by ceasing to engage in the activities that are causing those thoughts (for example, these might be watching unwholesome movies or spending time with friends who gossip). We also receive some thoughts that we should save and process later, in a safe place or at a better time. And some thoughts simply need to be moved to the trash folder. The point is we decide what to do with our thoughts. This is where our power lies as humans. It is truly a supernatural power. Romans 12:2 tells us:

> Do not conform to the pattern of this world but be transformed by the renewing of your mind. Then you will be able to test and approve what God's will is—his good, pleasing and perfect will.

Generational or Familial influences

A ton of research has been conducted in this area generational or familial influences, from how parents' addictions affect children to how eating dinner together as a family enhances school performance.[5] It's common sense: We are affected by the actions and attitudes of the generations that came before us.

We must also understand that certain things we and/or our parents, grandparents, and great-grandparents have done may have opened us up to the influence of evil. These behaviors may have given Satan and the fallen ones access to "accuse" us, "lie" to us, "deceive" us, "kill us, and "destroy" us (see Exodus 20:5, 34:7; Numbers 14:18; Deuteronomy 5:9). The lies may be as simple as clients labeling themselves as "the child of an alcoholic" as their identity. The deception may sound like an incitement to cheat if they watched their parents seemingly get away with cheating. A suicide in the family may compel a client to have similar thoughts of

5 Brown, C. L., Kay, M. C., Thompson, L. A. "Eating Family Meals Together at Home." *JAMA Pediatr.* 2024;178(5):510. doi:10.1001/jamapediatrics.2023.6669.

destruction. The good news is that there is a cure. Certain decisions (i.e., deciding to abuse substances) may have "turned on" certain genes, but deciding to repent has the power to "turn off" those genes!

The cure for generational influences has always been repenting of any bad decisions we've agreed with or partnered in that have carried over from past generations. When Israel turned from idols to serve the Living God, the "curse" was broken and God saved them (Judges 3:9, 15; 1 Samuel 12:10–11). Yes, God promised to visit Israel's sin upon the third and fourth generations, but in the very next verse, He promised He would show "love to a thousand [generations] of those who love me and keep my commandments" (Exodus 20:6). Let this sink in!

Generations influence one another, which makes it harder to fight against generational issues than many other issues, but it can be done. Jesus said:

> These things I have spoken to you while being present with you. But the Helper, the Holy Spirit, whom the Father will send in My name, He will teach you all things, and bring to your remembrance all things that I said to you. (John 14:25–26).

Neuroplasticity and epigenetics here again confirm what Scripture teaches. Our brains can be rewired. We can reconceptualize memories. In other words, we don't have to allow generational issues to influence us forever, but we must put in the work to be able to walk in freedom. We can combat the enemies of God as we fight against their efforts to steal, kill, and destroy.

Other Nefarious Influences: Substances and Parasites

Many people believe their actions or those of others cause mental health problems, but few realize mental health can also be affected by parasites or substances. For example, Cornell researchers found that "manipulations have surfaced in human studies linking *T. gondii* [parasitic] infections to behavioral and personality shifts, schizophrenia and population variations, including cultural differences and skewed sex ratios."[6] In essence, these parasites can control or hijack the mind. Learning this has given me another way to help clients; I encourage them to consult a physician to investigate what could be affecting their mental health. If the cause can in fact be traced to a physical issue, clients often become more hopeful as they work with doctors on treatment for what they once believed was a mental and behavioral issue only.

Substances such as dangerous illegal—or sometimes even legal—drugs can alter thinking as well. Hallucinogens are gaining popularity as a way of seeking an alternate reality. In 2019, more than five million people reported having used a hallucinogen in the United States.[7] Of course, the consequences of using these drugs such as cannabis, alcohol, opioids, methamphetamine, and others have been plaguing humanity for centuries. While some forms of these drugs (i.e., oxycodone prescribed after surgery) may help if closely monitored by medical professionals, they can also alter thoughts and "hijack" the mind. I would never recommend many of these substances due to their potential long-term effects.

Psychedelics are an increasing trend in the mental health field, although studies neglect to report the adverse or long-term effects of substances such as ayahuasca. These can be extremely dangerous even if they indicate help with post-traumatic stress disorder. One must consider the intense emotional and psychological experiences resulting from use.

Abusing substances that alter the way we think and act isn't a new concept—nor is the influence of parasites. Even so, when is the last time someone asked you if you've taken a hallucinogen or had any of the following experiences (related to parasites) lately?

---

6 news.cornell.edu/stories/2011/09/promiscuous-parasites-hijack-host-immune-cell.

7 publichealth.columbia.edu/new-study-estimates-over-55-million-u-s-adults-use-hallucinogens

- Traveled outside of the country
- Been exposed to contaminated drinking water
- Eaten undercooked meats
- Eaten contaminated foods
- Had bug bites from mosquitoes, ticks, flies or other insects carrying parasites
- Contacted contaminated surfaces
- Had unprotected sex
- Contacted contaminated dirt or soil[8]

These are some of the ways humans can be infected with parasites. Homosexuality, cannibalism, and/or a disrupted perception of reality and control of behaviors have all been associated with parasites. Some research also suggests parasites can be used in social engineering.[9]

We should mindfully consider the potential evil behind the lack of conversation about parasites in the field of mental health. I was disgusted when I learned of the extent of their possible impact—and of the failure of most medical professionals to question patients about possible exposure. And that's not to mention the dearth of treatment options there are in this area. Since then, my family and I have regularly gone through parasite cleanses, which can be carried out with the help of a functional integrative medicine doctor. Parasitic cleanses typically involve using products containing ingredients such as wormwood. The enemies of the Most High will use anything to destroy humans—even substances or parasites, which aren't often evaluated as problems.

Many biblical characters were afflicted with mental illness. Let's have a look at a few below.

---

8 my.clevelandclinic.org/health/diseases/24885-parasitic-infection

9 preventionandhealing.com/blog/parasites-and-mind-control/

Biblical Accounts of Mental Illness

Since the days of Genesis 3, 6, and 11, humans have struggled with evil that presents as mental illness. For example, Nebuchadnezzar could have been diagnosed with a schizoaffective disorder or as having psychosis. King Saul displayed symptoms of bipolar disorder. And King David experienced depression and anxiety. Let's look a little more closely at each of these examples.

Nebuchadnezzar is reported in Daniel 4 to have shown symptoms of schizoaffective disorder. He had delusions, disorganized thoughts and speech, negative or no affection for his family, and a depressive episode. The Most High God allowed mental illness in his life as a form of discipline, but I believe it was originally influenced by God's enemies because Nebuchadnezzar sought to harm His people and destroy their temple. In a way, he was just like the leaders in Genesis 11 who thought they knew better than God.

King Saul was chosen by the God when the people of Israel rejected Him as their King and demanded a human king. On many occasions, Saul could have been viewed as having manic episodes characterized by prophetic frenzies, euphoria, homicidal rages, paranoia, and an obsessive pursuit to kill David (See 1 Samuel 18, 19, 15, and 23). In 1 Samuel 16, 13, and 15 we see King Saul's depressive episodes; he is described as filled with fear and a lack of order, and his mental anguish compelled him to engage with the witch of Endor. His homicidal pursuit of David alone suggests the evil that began in Genesis 6.

King David, the man explicitly described as being after the Most High God's heart, failed miserably many times. His battle with depression is evident throughout the Psalms (for example, see chapters 6, 13, 31, 38, and 13). Additionally, David suffered anxious thoughts, as reported in Psalm 55. He clearly felt anguish, experienced trembling, and endured terror of death. Further, we can't forget his sexual sin with Bathsheba, another example of a Genesis 6 influence.

Mental illness, again, is not new—and even those considered at one point or another to be faithful to the Most High God underwent struggles. At times, those who seem to have the most potential for doing good or being holy are often the ones who are attacked by evil forces more frequently.

A man named Michael reached out to me after hearing me on a podcast and was encouraged by hearing what I just shared. Since then, he has chosen to walk in the freedom of Christ as he combats anger towards his parents. Thankfully, we have the good news of the gospel.

QUESTIONS FOR REFLECTION

1. How does sharing the gospel impact principalities of darkness?
2. What are the influences on the thoughts of humans?
3. Does learning about people in the Bible struggling with mental health change the way I view my own health?

PRACTICAL APPLICATION

Encouragement for pastoral counselors and mental health professionals:

- Challenge yourself to review your language in discussing mental health problems.
- Learn more about how you can change your thoughts by studying neuroplasticity.
- Preach or teach on how to take thoughts captive with clinically proven strategies that align with Scripture.
- Preach, teach, and offer training on a biblical understanding of the heart (mind, will, and emotions) and how to allow God to create a clean one in humans.

Prayer Prompt: *Lord, create a clean heart in me. Align my thoughts, feelings, and emotions with your will. Help me to lead others to do the same.*

SCRIPTURE TO CONSIDER

Romans 1:16:

I am not ashamed of the gospel, because it is the power of God for the salvation of everyone who believes.

Luke 2:8–11:

And there were shepherds living out in the fields nearby, keeping watch over their flocks at night. An angel of the Lord appeared to them, and the glory of the Lord shone around them, and they were terrified. But the angel said to them, "Do not be afraid. I bring you good news of great joy that will be for all the people. Today in the town of David a Savior has been born to you; he is Christ the Lord."

Romans 10:15:

How can they preach unless they are sent? As it is written, "How beautiful are the feet of those who bring good news!"

2 Thessalonians 3:1:

Pray for us that the message of the Lord may spread rapidly and be honored, just as it was with you.

Philippians 1:4–5:

In all my prayers for all of you, I always pray with joy because of your partnership in the gospel from the first day until now.

Acts 14:21–22:

They preached the good news in that city and won a large number of disciples. Then they returned…strengthening the disciples and encouraging them to remain true to the faith.

Luke 4:43:

But [Jesus] said, "I must preach the good news of the kingdom of God to the other towns also, because that is why I was sent."

Chapter 9

THE GOOD NEWS: VICTORY OVER DARKNESS

It's always good news when you're closer to the truth.

FABIOLA GIANOTTI, Italian physicist[1]

Let me share the best part of what I discovered using the divine council worldview. It's so good that you won't likely ever think of or celebrate the Resurrection of Christ the same again; I know I didn't!

In the past, I was thankful that Jesus died for my sin, that I had the hope of the Resurrection, and that I could look forward to a new heaven and new earth. This was enough to compel me to praise the Most High God. While this is amazing, it isn't the entire story—just like we've learned that the Fall, or rebellion, in the Garden of Eden wasn't the entire story.

Since studying Michael Heiser's work and the divine council worldview of the Bible, I also discovered that every aspect of Jesus' ministry was intentional—from the places He went and the miracles He performed to the ways He acted in defeating the powers of darkness. Many of the places Jesus went were a way of relaying specific messages to evil entities about the past and His work in overcoming evil for all of humanity. When He walked on water (Matthew 12:22–33), for example, His action demonstrated to the evil entities in the abyss that He was sovereign over all.

1 brainyquote.com/topics/good-news-quotes

Jesus' rebuke of the wind (Mark 4:39) may have been an announcement that *He*—not the wind or storm god—was the Most High God. We often miss these references because we see Scripture through our modern cultural lens, not through the one by which it was written.

Consider the temptations Satan used to thwart the ministry of Christ (Matthew 4:1–11 and Luke 4:1–13). The first temptation, when Satan urged Jesus to turn a stone into bread, sounds like aspects of Genesis 3, 6, and 11, where we see forbidden use or misuse of knowledge and authority at play. Jesus responded by pointing out that we live by the Most High God's words alone, not by the words of any other. The second temptation, when Satan told Jesus to throw Himself down from the pinnacle of the temple and summon the help of angels for His rescue, could be viewed as a way of compelling Jesus to kill Himself, to interact with angels in the wrong ways, and/or to misuse His power. All these aspects are rooted in Genesis 3, 6, and 11. The final temptation, wherein Satan presents Jesus with the prospect of having authority over the nations, is clearly like the Genesis 11 story at the very least (if not like all the rebellions). Jesus "passing" these three tests or resisting these temptations shows us how to overcome temptation and evil. This also commenced His ministry.

Every step Jesus took, every person He interacted with, and every seed He sowed was intentional. His actions culminated in His ultimate victory when He died and rose again. He didn't just save us from our sin and provide a way for us to be with Him in heaven; He defeated *all* our enemies and reversed *all* their curses!

- **Revelation 1:18 (kjv):** "I am he that liveth, and was dead; and, behold, I am alive for evermore, Amen; and have the keys of hell and of death."
- **Colossians 1:13–14:** "For he has rescued us from the dominion of darkness and brought us into the kingdom of the Son he loves, in whom we have redemption, the forgiveness of sins."

- **Colossians 2:12–15 (net):** "Having been buried with him in baptism, you also have been raised with him through your faith in the power of God who raised him from the dead. And even though you were dead in your transgressions and in the uncircumcision of your flesh, he nevertheless made you alive with him, having forgiven all your transgressions. He has destroyed what was against us, a certificate of indebtedness expressed in decrees opposed to us. He has taken it away by nailing it to the cross. Disarming the rulers and authorities, he has made a public disgrace of them, triumphing over them by the cross."

I love these verses, which especially highlight that Jesus holds the keys to death and hell, He rescued us from the dominion of darkness; baptism represents our being raised from the dead; and He disarmed and defeated the rulers and authorities!

First, on the cross, Jesus defeated *death* that had been caused by Satan (powers of darkness) in Genesis 3. First Corinthians 15:55–58 says, "O death, where is your sting? For sin is the sting that results in death, and the law gives sin its power." But thank the Most High God; He gives us victory over sin and death through our Lord Jesus Christ. This means He has defeated the enemy who is behind suicide, murder, abortion, war, accidental killings, and all the problems associated with death.

Of course, our battles may be ongoing in our present understanding of time, but we can have victory in Jesus knowing the war has been won. He can offer forgiveness for our sin in all these issues as well, because Jesus defeated our enemies. We can look to the death of Jesus as the point when all mental health problems associated with death were defeated! Anxiety, grief, guilt, shame, loss, depression, mood disorder, and trauma, if viewed considering the cross, can be overcome! The enemies, regardless of their names (Satan, the serpent), were crushed.

Second, Jesus defeated the fallen sons of God or the fallen council members (spiritual forces of wickedness in heavenly places) by shedding His blood for us. In other words, He fixed the *bloodline* problem these fallen sons created. Jesus' blood covers us! Ephesians 2:11–12 says, "But now in Christ Jesus you who once were far away have been brought near by the blood of Christ." This means the issues related to the depravity of humans from Genesis 6 were able to be reversed or cured. The generational (bloodline) issues or influences can no longer have a hold on us… unless we allow them to. One client, Riley, disclosed her concerns related to bloodline in counseling one day. She asked what it would mean if she had a certain type of dark or evil bloodline. "So what if you do?" I asked her. "The remedy is the same," I explained. "You confess Jesus as Lord and are saved!" She told me later this was so important to her once she realized the human status in her was redeemable…no matter what.

The blood Jesus shed offers the remission of sin. Hebrews 9:22 says, "Indeed, under the law almost everything is purified with blood, and without the shedding of blood there is no forgiveness of sins." Blood represents the life of an animal or human, but it also indicates whose family one is in. It contains identifying markers such as DNA and is often used in genetic testing. We use this idea often when we say things such as, "She is my sister by blood." When Jesus shed His blood for ours, we were placed in the direct bloodline, or family, of the Most High God. Jesus' blood reversed the curse of Genesis 6 for all who choose Him.

Third, Jesus defeated the principalities or the evil influences that separated us from God and His people in Genesis 11. Now *all nations* can be co-heirs with Christ. Matthew 28:18–20 says:

> And Jesus came and said to them, "All authority in heaven and on earth has been given to me. Go therefore and make disciples of all nations, baptizing them in the name of the Father and of the Son and of the Holy Spirit, teaching them to observe all that I have commanded you. And behold, I am with you always, to the end of the age."

This means all issues related to racism, anti-God ideologies, narcissism, and any attempt of people or nations to usurp the His opportunity for us all to be a part of His nation are defeated.

The fallen ones over the nations who are against the Most High were defeated on the cross! Now nations that seek Him can be blessed by Him. They can be ruled justly and compassionately and can treat the poor well. All races, tribes, and tongues can worship the same God. Revelation 7:9 refers to this happening one day:

> After these things I looked, and here was an enormous crowd that no one could count, made up of persons from every nation, tribe, people, and language, standing before the throne and before the Lamb dressed in long white robes, and with palm branches in their hands.

People can view and treat each other the right way when they realize the curse of Genesis 11 was reversed!

Salvation Comes to Those Who Believe

If you want the enemies of God to be defeated in your life and you've never trusted Jesus as your Savior and chosen to loyally follow the Most High God, you can do that now! The Bible says in John 3:16 (KJV): "For God so loved the world that He gave His only begotten son that Whosoever believes in Him will not perish but have everlasting life." Simply believe in Jesus as your Savior and decide to live faithfully for the Most High God.

Yes, it involves recognizing that you're a sinner, a human who is weak or frail and in need of a Savior from sin and the enemies of the Most High God: "All have sinned and fallen short of the glory of God" (Romans 3:23). Therefore, confession is necessary, as stated in Romans 10:9: "If you confess with your mouth Jesus as Lord, and believe in your heart that God raised Him from the dead, you will be saved." Once you have confessed and believed, you are reconciled with the Father, our Creator, the Most High God.

My dad was radically changed once he confessed Jesus as Lord. His testimony clearly reveals that the enemy tried to prevent him from getting saved and becoming a Christ-follower. In the early years of my parents' marriage, they had twin girls who, sadly, died within twenty-four hours of their birth. During my mom's pregnancy, a relative had asked to read my mom's palms during a family gathering. The woman had told my mom she would have twins, but that they would die.

Being pregnant in the 1970s—before technology made it possible to know much about the babies until they were delivered—Mom had no idea she was having twins. Regardless, she told my dad she didn't believe in "palm readings" and that she wanted to leave the family gathering. God miraculously helped her forget what the woman had told her until after the twins died. This, to me, shows God's grace.

Because of my studies over the past few years, I've realized the palm reader was partnered with darkness, because these deaths could have destroyed my parents. But amazingly, the outcome was quite the opposite. A year after the twins died, my dad went to church with my mom and felt the Holy Spirit say, "If you don't give your life to me, you'll never see your daughters again." He was miraculously saved that day and was radically changed forever.

Reconciliation comes from the Greek work *katallage,* which literally means "an exchange" and then "a profit from exchange." *Katallage* pictures the reestablishment of an interrupted or broken relationship. The sin and influence of evil can no longer prevent you from a relationship with the Most High God! Colossians 1:21–23 says it this way:

> And you were at one time strangers and enemies in your minds as expressed through your evil deeds, but now he has reconciled you by his physical body through death to present you holy, without blemish, and blameless before him—if indeed you remain in the faith, established and firm, without shifting from the hope of the gospel that you heard.

Now, if you choose Jesus as your King, your life should show it faithfully. Then you will be a co-heir with Jesus the Christ:

> The Spirit himself bears witness to our spirit that we are God's children. And if children, then heirs (namely, heirs of God and also fellow heirs with Christ)—if indeed we suffer with him so we may also be glorified with him. (Romans 8:16–17)

This also means we will be members of God's council one day: "Now you are the body of Christ and individually members of it" (1 Corinthians 12:27). At that time we will be in God's council ruling and judging angels. Hebrews 2:5 states, "God did not choose the angels to be rulers of the new world that was coming," and we read in 1 Corinthians 6:3: "Do you not know that we will judge angels?" Further, Revelation 2:26 says: "The one who conquers and who keeps my works until the end, to him I will give authority over the nations." We will replace the old gods. If this doesn't make you want to shout and sing, make your heart leap, or at the very least make you smile, go back and reread this chapter!

The good news is a victory call from the cross! The manifold wisdom of the Most High God involved the Church—us!

> To me—less than the least of all the saints—this grace was given, to proclaim to the Gentiles the unfathomable riches of Christ and to enlighten everyone about God's secret plan—the mystery that has been hidden for ages in God who has created all things. The purpose of this enlightenment is that through the church the multifaceted wisdom of God should now be disclosed to the rulers and the authorities in the heavenly realms. (Ephesians 3:8–10, NET)

The enemies never saw it coming. "None of the rulers of this age understood it, for if they had, they would not have crucified the Lord of glory" (1 Corinthians 2:7). They knew who Jesus was, more than some preachers do today, but they had no idea that He would defeat death, hell, and the grave for all humans! Jesus is the Redeemer and the Way for humans to be back in relationship with the Father, the One True God who sent His Son, Jesus, to earth to take on flesh and be our Emmanuel, the Most High God with us, to save us.

If you've accepted Jesus as your Savior, I hope you're now convinced He has the power to help you overcome all the evil, the influence of evil, and the deeds of evil you've ever done or that have ever been done to you. If you haven't accepted him as the Most High, remember, you simply have to believe, ask Jesus to be your Savior, and loyally follow Him. John 3:16 says, "For God so loved the world that He gave his only son that *whosoever* would believe in him will have everlasting life" (emphasis added).

If you've done this, you also should experience what the Apostle Paul said to the Ephesians:

> Since the eyes of your heart have been enlightened—so that you can know what is the hope of his calling, what is the wealth of his glorious inheritance in the saints, and what is the incomparable greatness of his power toward us who believe, as displayed in the exercise of his immense strength. This power he exercised in Christ when he raised him from the dead and seated him at his right hand in the heavenly realms far above every rule and authority and power and dominion and every name that is named, not only in this age but also in the one to come. And God put all things under Christ's feet, and gave him to the church as head over all things" (1:18–22)

This is how we align with the Most High God. We cannot align with His enemies, which can be called other, lesser gods. We are called to die to these spirits (Colossians 2:20).

The Importance of Sharing the Gospel

With this understanding of the power we have, we must proclaim it to the world:

> We proclaim him by instructing and teaching all people with all wisdom so that we may present every person mature in Christ. Toward this goal I also labor, struggling according to his power that powerfully works in me. (Colossians 1:28).

Sharing the gospel is how we displace the enemies of the world. Because of that, baptism and partaking of the Lord's Supper are acts of spiritual war. We should view these practices as our victory cries.

Dr. Heiser states in his book, *The Unseen Realm:*

> The jurisdictional authority of these sons of God has been nullified by the resurrection and ascension of Christ. That reality is what frames the Great Commission—the call to reclaim the nations ("go into all the world and make disciples"). The kingdom of darkness will lose what is essentially a spiritual war of attrition, for the gates of hell will not be able to withstand the Church. This is why believers are never commanded to rebuke.... Believers are in turn commanded to reclaim their territory by recruiting the citizens in those territories for the kingdom of God.[2]

Timothy Chester, author of *The Message of Prayer*, says it this way:

> Spiritual warfare is not about naming territorial spirits, claiming the ground, or binding demons. It is all about the gospel. It is to live a gospel life, to preserve gospel unity and to proclaim gospel truth. It is to do this in the face of a hostile world, a deceptive enemy and our sinful natures. And it is to pray to a sovereign God for gospel opportunities. Advance comes through godliness, unity, proclamation and prayer.[3]

---

2 Heiser, *Unseen Realm.*

3 https://spreadingthefame.com/tag/timothy-chester/

While the good news of the gospel is that we've been rescued from our enemies, according to Colossians 1:13—"He has rescued us from the dominion of darkness and brought us into the kingdom of the Son he loves, in whom we have redemption, the forgiveness of sins" (NET)—we may still experience battles from time to time as we faithfully follow our Savior and await our eternal home. These battles require mental health professionals, pastors, and all who believe in Jesus to accept the unseen realm and embrace the freedom of having a supernatural lens of truth. It matters if we want to know how we overcome our true enemies amid these daily, seasonal, or lifelong battles.

QUESTIONS FOR REFLECTION

1. What do you believe influences your thoughts?
2. Who has influenced you or is influencing you?
3. Do you understand the good news about the defeat of our enemies?
4. Have you trusted Jesus as Savior and Lord of your life?

PRACTICAL APPLICATION

Encouragement for pastoral counselors and mental health professionals:

- Study the gospel in light of Jesus defeating our enemies.
- Offer a sermon series on the enemies Jesus defeated on the cross and why.
- Include the gospel message in your treatment of evil influences.

Prayer Prompt: *Lord, I praise you for defeating all the enemies of darkness. Help me each day to live victorious over evil!*

SCRIPTURE TO CONSIDER

Deuteronomy 28:7:

> The LORD will cause your enemies who rise against you to be defeated before you. They shall come out against you one way and flee before you seven ways.

Isaiah 54:17:

> No weapon that is fashioned against you shall succeed, and you shall refute every tongue that rises against you in judgment. This is the heritage of the servants of the LORD and their vindication from me, declares the LORD.

Romans 12:19:

> Beloved, never avenge yourselves, but leave it to the wrath of God, for it is written, "Vengeance is mine, I will repay, says the Lord."

Luke 10:19:

> Behold, I have given you authority to tread on serpents and scorpions, and over all the power of the enemy, and nothing shall hurt you.

Colossians 1:19–20:

> For God was pleased to have all his fullness dwell in him, and through him to reconcile to himself all things, whether things on earth or things in heaven, by making peace through his blood, shed on the cross.

Colossians 2:15:

> He disarmed the rulers and authorities and put them to open shame, by triumphing over them in him.

John 16:33:

> I have said these things to you, that in me you may have peace. In the world you will have tribulation. But take heart; I have overcome the world.

Hebrews 2:14:

> Since therefore the children share in flesh and blood, he himself likewise partook of the same things, that through death he

might destroy the one who has the power of death, that is, the devil.

Revelation 20:3:

And threw him into the pit, and shut it and sealed it over him, so that he might not deceive the nations any longer, until the thousand years were ended. After that he must be released for a little while.

Matthew 25:41:

Then he will say to those on his left, "Depart from me, you cursed, into the eternal fire prepared for the devil and his angels."

Hebrews 2:14–15:

Since therefore the children share in flesh and blood, he himself likewise partook of the same things, that through death he might destroy the one who has the power of death, that is, the devil, and deliver all those who through fear of death were subject to lifelong slavery.

Hebrews 2:2:

For since the message declared by angels proved to be reliable, and every transgression or disobedience received a just retribution.

Daniel 7:9–14:

As I looked, thrones were set in place, and the Ancient of Days took his seat. His clothing was as white as snow; the hair of his head was white like wool. His throne was flaming with fire, and its wheels were all ablaze. A river of fire was flowing, coming out from before him. Thousands upon thousands attended him; ten thousand times ten thousand stood before him. The court was seated, and the books were opened. Then I continued to watch because of the boastful words the horn was speaking. I kept looking until the beast was slain and its body destroyed and thrown into the blazing fire. (The other beasts had been stripped of their authority but were allowed to live for a period of time.) In my vision at night, I looked, and there before me was one like a son of man, coming with the clouds of heaven. He approached the Ancient of Days and was led into his presence. He was given authority, glory and sovereign power; all nations and peoples of every language worshiped him. His dominion is an everlasting dominion that will not pass away, and his kingdom is one that will never be destroyed.

Chapter 10

TREATMENT CONCERNS

When pain is to be born, a little courage helps more than much knowledge, a little human sympathy more than much courage, and the least tincture of the love of God more than all.

C. S. Lewis, *The Problem of Pain*

Disappointingly, in today's mental health and church communities, there aren't enough practitioners who feel comfortable using effective types of treatment related to spiritual darkness. Research suggests most mental health professionals have little to no training in addressing religion and spirituality in therapy.[1] Some churches don't want to bother with the problems and simply refer those seeking health to mental health professionals or "deliverance ministers." However, some mental health professionals use methods that unintentionally push people who are struggling farther into the darkness that enslaves them. Likewise, others within a church or ministry context provide "deliverance ministries," offering practices at times that worsen the problem. (A "deliverance ministry" is a Christian practice in which prayer, confession, and spiritual authority are used to help people find freedom from demonic influence, oppression, and/or bondage that affects their overall well-being). Amid these extremes, the divine council worldview offers a balanced, biblically grounded perspective so we can prepare for what truly works—and what doesn't—when confronting spiritual darkness with wisdom and effectiveness.

1 apa.org/monitor/2023/11/incorporating-religion-spirituality-therapy

Problems within the Church

Recently, I asked a pastor, "What would you do if someone in your congregation said, 'I was abducted by aliens?'" He replied, "I'd refer them to you." While I'm thankful for referrals to my practice, this simply cannot always be the answer for people who are seemingly at war with darkness. Another pastor states he doesn't refer patients to professionals, preferring instead to handle all problems related to mental health "in house," as he believes all issues can be taken care of by the pastoral staff. Others indicate they believe all people struggling with mental health need "deliverance."

I'm honestly not sure how many pastors today know what to do with congregants who are struggling. Many simply don't have the time or won't make the time to shepherd their church family members effectively. And that's not to mention that many pastors are battling darkness personally yet are unaware of it—or they're unwilling to change. For example, a 2024 study indicated that two out of every three pastors reported struggling with pornography at some point in their lives.[2]

Most churches today are simply unprepared to respond when someone shows signs or symptoms of mental illness, which at times (of course, not always) can resemble demonic possession or oppression. In my experience, most pastors refer folks who need help to counseling agencies they trust within their area. While making referrals like this can be a great practice, pastors can't always do this, because there aren't enough professionals specifically trained to handle issues relating to spiritual and mental health. In fact, there's a current and projected shortage of mental health professionals in general.[3] While some well-meaning pastors or ministries do try to help, they can at times cause more harm than good. Pastors who over-spiritualize mental health can be the type to cause more harm. For example, those who tell someone it's wrong

---

2 barna.com/research/pastors-pornography-use

3 bhw.hrsa.gov/sites/bureau-health-workforce/state-of-the-behavioral-health-workforce-report

to take medicine for their mental health may be causing the person's problems to get worse. They may need to refer the person to a trained professional.

Don't get me wrong; I know of individuals who sought counseling for years with little to no relief and, in turn, went to a church ministry—possibly a deliverance ministry— and found relief from a spirit they felt had tormented them. Conversely, I've heard heartbreaking stories of people seeking help from deliverance ministries but who left with more pain, shame, and trauma than they started with. Some have then gone to mental health professionals for help and found a safe space to find healing. Yet, for many who are battling darkness linked to past traumas, true freedom and healing are elusive when not handled with care, discernment, biblical truth, and sound practice.

We hear lots of horrifying stories in our office. For example, one female client shared that her pastor said she should have sex with her husband "out of duty," even though he had raped (forced her to have sex when she said "no") and abused her in recent weeks. Another client spoke of a pastor who told her she hadn't been "good enough" in the bedroom; otherwise, her husband wouldn't have "needed" to view pornography. One man ended up in our office after his pastor had fallen asleep as the man was pouring out his heart about how his wife had betrayed him. Sadly, these are just a few tragic accounts among many we hear.

Of course, some pastors also preach unbiblical principles about suicide, depression, and anxiety, which can also be harmful. Many pastors and church leaders teach that those who commit suicide go to hell. When I hear this, my response is, "Show me the evidence of this in Scripture." I've studied this subject, and I don't see taking one's own life as the unpardonable sin. It is not blasphemy. We truthfully don't know the state of mind of the person battling the darkness of suicide. We don't know about any last-minute decisions they may have made. Some say teaching that those who die by their own hand go to hell is helpful because it prevents people from attempting to take their own life, but I disagree. Those struggling with suicidal thoughts have reported feeling as if there is no way out of the darkness, and they believe suicide will help their friends and families. They often don't even think of heaven or hell. Others make impulsive decisions—out of anger or frustration—without thinking about the consequences. It is better to teach the biblical truth that suicide is an influence from the powers of darkness.

Another unbiblical truth some pastors have taught is that taking medication for mental health is a sin. This always puzzles me, especially if the pastor is wearing glasses (a form of medication, in my view). Most Christians are divided regarding this issue.[4] Many people with mental illness who are harming their families hold this view. Medication isn't the complete answer, but it can be helpful at times, in seasons. Jesus Himself used substances such as dirt and saliva to heal people. I know of people who are struggling with the kind of mental illness that leads them to abuse others simply because they're not willing to take medication… based on their pastor's words.

Teaching unbiblical truths about identity is another harm sometimes caused by pastors who, in some instances, assume they are mental health experts. Often, they take Scripture out of context and say harmful things based on their personal experiences rather than biblical truth. For example, they might say something like, "I am the anointed one, the prophet, the man of God, so you are to not question me. If I say you have a spirit of ________, it is so." These words and this attitude can be extremely dangerous. In my practice, I met someone who was told she had a "Jezebel spirit." This alarmed me even more when I learned she thought it meant she could never change, as if the "spirit" was who she was. The powers of darkness are after the identity of believers, so any effort to categorize humans is a direct attempt to create an identity apart from who we are as defined by the Most High God. Remember, our identity is "human," meaning we are imagers of God…period. We must begin viewing those we go to church with in this way and not, for example, as "someone who is mentally ill."

---

4 christianity.com/wiki/christian-life/should-christians-take-medication-for-mental-illness

Interviews of the people who protect sexual abusers from a ministry platform create more harm to those who are abused due to their lack of understanding of principles such as traumatic bonding:

> Traumatic bonding (TB) is a strong emotional attachment between an abused person and his or her abuser and is often formed because of the repeated cycle of violence. TB is developed as the result of ongoing cycles of abuse in which the intermittent reinforcement of reward and punishment creates powerful emotional bonds that are resistant to change.[5]

Recently, I've learned of pastors sharing unbiblical and harmful views regarding counseling in general. One pastor encourages women to only see a male counselor because he doesn't believe females can give sound biblical advice. (I would love to ask him about the story of Deborah in the Bible!) I've also heard pastors say a woman should only see a woman, and a man should only see a man. While I can certainly see the benefits of doing this in some cases, at times clients don't have a choice; it all depends on counselors' availability. The best practice in choosing a good counselor should always be wisdom and prayer rather than gender preferences.

I'm thankful to know many wonderful, godly pastors who truly want to help those they shepherd—and some do a great job. I've even had the opportunity to train local lay leaders and pastors on a counseling model designed to help their congregation before they make any referrals. Yet the reality remains: Many in the church aren't helping the downtrodden effectively, if at all. Additionally, many church leaders are battling their own darkness without help or without even knowing they have a problem.

---

5 Effiong, J. E., Ibeagha, P. N., & Iorfa, S. K. (2022). "Traumatic Bonding in Victims of Intimate Partner Violence Is Intensified via Empathy." *Journal of Social and Personal Relationships*, *39*(12), 3619–3637. https://doi.org/10.1177/02654075221106237 (Original work published 2022).

I could go on about some of the horrors in the church I'm seeing today related to my work, but I pray that church leaders and members will open their eyes to how narcissism, paganism, and overall bad theology has been allowed into their congregations. I've shared some of the most basic situations; I haven't included some of the darker ones. But we must raise awareness of how evil ideologies and practices can infiltrate churches. Understanding the divine council worldview can be foundational for pastors trying to help people figure out where their difficulties originate. While interest in learning the divine council worldview is growing, many prefer to keep people with complex issues at a distance.

I hope things will soon change and many will learn that the answers in Scripture are simple and effective for helping people find freedom from mental health problems related to spiritual darkness.

Problems within Deliverance Ministries

On the other end of the spectrum of churches not wanting to deal with mental health issues or being harmful in that regard is deliverance ministries. These are usually run by churches and individuals who may truly want to help. At times, they base practices on "the assumption that both mental and physical ills result from possession of the sufferer by demons and are to be treated by the expulsion of those demons."[6] This line of thinking often leads to creating or increasing toxic shame.

Toxic shame is a chronic or constant feeling of worthlessness. Shame ordinarily is felt in response to doing or thinking something that's wrong.[7] Ordinary shame can be healthy at times, but toxic shame can be detrimental. If you tell a person evil resides within them, it will likely lead to toxic shame or ongoing feelings of being worth nothing. Not all mental health or physical ailments are the direct result of possession by

6 Mercer, J. (2012). "Deliverance, Demonic Possession, and Mental Illness: Some Considerations for Mental Health Professionals." *Mental Health, Religion & Culture, 16*(6), 595–611. https://doi.org/10.1080/13674676.2012.706272

7 psychcentral.com/lib/what-is-toxic-shame

or oppression of demons, although they may be the original influencer. Scripture simply doesn't back this us. Consider Paul having a "thorn in his side" that the Lord used (see 2 Corinthians 12:7–10). His struggle wasn't due to demonic oppression; it was a physical ailment God used in the apostle's spiritual life.

Referrals often come into my office from churches. Some people with mental health problems have reported going through deliverance ministries before eventually being referred to us. I'm very thankful for referrals from anywhere. Also, I'm not against deliverance ministries… but when someone comes in and starts our meeting with, "I went to a special treatment or deliverance session at church and wasn't healed completely," I must ask deeper questions. Some involve the process; often, well-meaning people can unintentionally cause more harm than good. One client told me she had been in a group of six people who were trying to help deliver her from many struggles and sin she was battling that they deemed demonic. This may not be the best method for some who are having troubles, because there is seemingly an imbalance of power at the very least due to the number of people in the room. This client said the people trying to help her would pass notes to one another as she was speaking, which could cause someone to feel paranoid.

While I'm not saying all deliverance ministries are harmful, I suggest careful practice and consideration when using this approach to healing. Surprisingly, many people prefer to seek spiritual remedies over mental health practices. For example, religions such as Buddhism have a form of exorcism or spirit-healing.[8] Of course, I believe they're calling on the wrong spirits or are potentially replacing one evil spirit with another. This is more proof that anyone seeking to displace evil spirits needs to proceed with caution, knowledge, and discernment.

---

8 Nguyen, H. (2014). "Buddhism-based Exorcism and Spirit-calling as a Form of Healing for Mental Problems: Stories from Vietnam." *Journal of Religion & Spirituality in Social Work: Social Thought, 33*(1), 33–48. https://doi.org/10.1080/15426432.2014.873648

Within the Christian faith, the Catholic Church is likely the best known for performing exorcisms. They believe exorcising demons is part of a biblical witness and of Catholic history. They recommend having a basic knowledge of psychology and mental health so those being called on for help don't overlook or dismiss the problems as a demon.[9] In addition, the Catholic Church follows specific assessments and processes for each case. While this sounds like a wise approach, understanding the divine council worldview can provide additional insight for those who practice Catholic exorcisms, as most priests are not documented as being prepared to handle such cases.

Deliverance ministries are, in a sense, a Protestant version of Catholic exorcism. Problems with deliverance ministries are that, at times, the blame can be shifted from sin, addiction, and mental health to demonic entities. While I agree that evil entities (Ephesians 6:12) influence certain sinful behaviors and struggles, I don't think the answer is shifting blame for choices made, which allows doors to be opened to evil influences. There must be a clinical (professional evaluation and treatment of mental problems by trained professionals) aspect to the process. I also agree with Mark 7:20–23:

> And he said, "That which cometh out of the man, that defileth the man." For from within, out of the heart of men, proceed evil thoughts, adulteries, fornications, murders, Thefts, covetousness, wickedness, deceit, lasciviousness, an evil eye, blasphemy, pride, foolishness: All these evil things come from within, and defile the man." (KJV)

Deliverance ministries also often struggle with follow-up care of the person seeking help by not putting enough emphasis on continuing discipleship. If we leave vulnerable people alone after an evil influence has

9 *National Catholic Bioethics Quarterly* 18.4 (Winter 2018): 595–602. Coleman, G. D. (2018). "Separating Exorcism from Superstition." *The National Catholic Bioethics Quarterly, 18*(4), 595–602. https://doi.org/10.5840/ncbq201818463

been rebuked and repentance has occurred, the risk of more oppression returning is even higher (Matthew 12:43–45). Discipleship involves walking alongside people and sharing the love of Christ, which conquers all and defeats evil. We must teach those who are struggling how to fight from the place of victory Jesus won on the cross.

At times, deliverance ministers try to "cast out" spirits, ideas, beliefs, hurts, habits, or behaviors that might be a part of their souls. At times, a person's belief or habit that may be viewed as negative is often how that person has learned to protect himself or herself in times of trauma. This is the case for many who have dissociative identity disorder. Casting out, in my experience, isn't always instantaneous; complete recovery often takes a long time of lovingly walking alongside someone.

How deliverance ministers talk to those they're attempting to help can re-traumatize them. For example, screaming for a "demon" in someone to come out won't help someone who has been abused. Instead, listening, speaking in love, and acting with patience is far more effective. The polyvagal theory provides a more sophisticated understanding of safety and danger from a biological perspective. It explains how a soothing tone of voice or kind facial expression can make us feel calm and safe. Conversely, if we're ignored, dismissed, or reacted to negatively, we can mentally collapse.[10] Some individuals come to mental health professionals after "deliverance sessions" because they were traumatized by the tone of the minister's voice and by the feeling of being pushed to share their stories of abuse. This reminds me of the Scripture passage: "The Lord bless you and keep you; The Lord make His face shine upon you, And be gracious to you; The Lord lift up His countenance upon you, And give you peace" (Numbers 6:24–26, NKJV)

Another example of deliverance ministries causing further trauma would be when survivors of abuse are encouraged to share parts of their story they're not ready to discuss with others. Psychologist Sigmund Freud also believed in a form of "reenactment" as a way of gaining

---

10 van der Kolk, *Body Keeps the Score.*

control over a painful situation. However, the theory of repetition often only leads people to further pain and self-hatred.[11] It isn't healthy to push clients too fast. They need time to build trust with the person trying to help them as a safe space is created.

Re-traumatization can also occur if individuals aren't prepared to handle triggers—reminders of the trauma. Deliverance ministers often aren't trained to help people cope with triggers. Lastly, people being treated in a deliverance ministry need to be able to set boundaries and feel safe enough to say, "That's enough for today," or, "Stop," without being pushed. At the very least, deliverance ministers need to seek training and use trauma -informed practices shown to be effective in intervention and treatment.[12]

Treatment often involves a long journey with those who have been harmed. Success rests on building a loving, healthy attachment—a very slow process most of the time.

Deliverance ministries often encompass a limited number of sessions or are offered over a weekend. That brevity is problematic since the trauma or introduction to evil likely didn't happen just once or in a moment, but rather included years of influence or exposure. Therefore, it typically takes years for a person to heal. Patience and compassion are required when helping those who have been victimized by dark evils. Establishing trust—foundational in true deliverance from evil—takes time and cannot be rushed. Timelines aren't always feasible. In fact, the idea that healing can always be rushed or instantaneous might itself be a lie from the enemies of the Most High God.

Problems within the Mental Health Profession

In addition to ministers, others who play a major role in helping those with what appears to be spiritual suffering in the form of demonic

11 Ibid.

12 Fernández, V., Gausereide-Corral, M., Valiente, C., & Sánchez-Iglesias, I. (2023). "Effectiveness of Trauma-informed Care Interventions at the Organizational Level: A Systematic Review." *Psychological Services*, *20*(4), 849–862. doi.org/10.1037/ser0000737

oppression or possession are mental health professionals. In an article in *Psychology Today*, one author proposed that spirituality is being discussed in 60 percent of his cases.[13] Some even suggest that modern psychotherapy is a form of exorcism, as it seeks to work against what humans are up against mentally. Often, clients even call their difficulties "demons" within. Meanwhile, others believe the battle is "in your head." If this were true, even the influences of marketing wouldn't work. We are influenced by outside messages that aren't simply explained as being "in our heads." We regularly encounter clients with mental health issues such as sleep paralysis and dissociative symptoms related to issues causing spiritual manifestation.

Undoubtedly, most mental health professionals are ill-prepared to deal with such situations with clients. Symptoms of evil influence can mirror some symptoms of mental illness; therefore, mental health professionals often treat people without realizing what could be at play. Training often simply suggests that therapists work within the patient's belief system without considering whether those beliefs are harmful.

Yet many therapists have little to no training within the context of various religious belief systems, leaving them to learn from the clients, as it can be beneficial to incorporate beliefs.[14] Therapists must be willing to ask the right questions when considering spirituality and its impact on clients in therapeutic and other settings. We must be open to learning not only about a person's beliefs but also about how those views can, at times, have a negative influence.

Mental health professionals also need to understand the harm of introducing spiritual practices that are becoming increasingly popular in the health community. Tarot cards, psychedelic drugs, and other divination or dangerous practices forbidden within the biblical worldview are now being marketed as helpful to those with mental illness.

---

13 psychologytoday.com/us/blog/spirit-in-session/how-often-is-spirituality-part-psychotherapy

14 apa.org/monitor/2023/11/incorporating-religion-spirituality-therapy

These methods are also advertised as ways to help one find a "deeper understanding" of oneself. Some suggest tarot cards can help people understand thoughts and emotions.[15] However, I believe—again, because I have a biblical worldview—that tarot cards are a form of divination that can bring about encounters with evil spiritual beings. This practice and other forms of divination can seem to bring about positive results at first. However, over time, they can prove harmful (by, for example, creating an unhealthy dependence upon the cards) and ineffective.[16] One client came to me mentioning that she used tarot cards, and she disclosed that she felt as if she needed to do more to achieve certain results, which caused her additional anxiety.

Without a doubt, many therapists are simply trying to help people. Yet many "spiritual therapists" are introducing harmful and ineffective practices, and although they may not realize it, they're introducing or producing more darkness in people's lives. In my opinion, these practices are inspired by powers of darkness. All practices should always be used with research, caution, and much consideration.

The Solution: Divine Council Worldview

As the human struggle with mental illness is increasing, the church and mental health professionals aren't quite taking the right approaches. So, you may be asking where to go from here. Most agree that religion or spirituality can be helpful, but more education and training are necessary to bring the mental health and spiritual communities together.[17]

In my experience, research, and use of the divine council worldview over the past several years, I believe a combination of trauma-informed,

---

15 Low, Sarah May Poh, 2021. "The Impact of Tarot Card Practice on Teenage Mental Health." ResearchBerg Review of Science and Technology, (online) 1(1), pp.50–66.

16 pmc.ncbi.nlm.nih.gov/articles/PMC4394851/

17 Stanford, M. S. (2007). "Demon or Disorder: A Survey of Attitudes toward Mental Illness in the Christian Church. *Mental Health, Religion & Culture, 10*(5), 445–449. doi.org/10.1080/13674670600903049

evidence-based practices and good theology can be effective in helping people find true freedom and healing from evil. Good theology helps us understand the existence of evil entities trying to steal, kill, and destroy humans. Good theology also helps us learn the evil entities' goals. Then we can focus on their strategies and how doors are opened to evil influences. Ultimately, we can learn how to close the doors of evil influences and rid ourselves and others of them so we can reflect the image of the Most High God in the best ways possible. Closing doors and getting rid of evil influences (or not allowing them in to begin with) can be helped with good mental health practices.

While the church and the mental health community haven't always gotten helping others right because of using harmful practices, ignorance, or refusing to treat/counsel certain individuals, I hope the church and mental health professionals can work together to help people overcome. I believe we can work together, learn together, and allow God to use us as we represent Him by helping people find freedom, relief, answers, understanding, and purpose.

A great first step is learning the differences between mental health, spiritual warfare, and spiritual manifestations. Pinpointing the causes of each one is foundational to understanding. Finally, it's important to learn and recognize the symptoms of each mental illness, spiritual warfare, and spiritual manifestation. Then the battle of treatment both clinically and spiritually can begin with victory and freedom in sight!

QUESTIONS FOR REFLECTION

1. How have you experienced churches responding to spiritual darkness?
2. What have you heard about how mental health professionals deal with issues that may be related to the supernatural?
3. Is your therapist or minister equipped to help you battle spiritual darkness?

PRACTICAL APPLICATION

Encouragement for pastoral counselors and mental health professionals:

- Reflect on your referral practices and consider why you are referring people, and to whom.
- Confront your fear of dealing with darkness among those you serve.
- Preach or teach on trauma, mental health, and the influence of the enemies of God.
- Seek out training on how to effectively help those battling spiritual darkness.

Prayer Prompt: *Lord, forgive me for times in which I mishandled someone you love and their struggles. Strengthen me as I walk alongside them while they're suffering.*

SCRIPTURE TO CONSIDER

John 10:10 (NIV):

> The thief comes only to steal and kill and destroy; I have come that they may have life and have it to the full.

Proverbs 2: 1–6:

> My son, if you accept my words and store up my commands within you, turning your ear to wisdom and applying your heart to understanding—indeed, if you call out for insight and cry aloud for understanding, and if you look for it as for silver and search for it as for hidden treasure, then you will understand the fear of the LORD and find the knowledge of God. For the LORD gives wisdom; from his mouth come knowledge and understanding.

Proverbs 1:7:

> The fear of the LORD is the beginning of knowledge, but fools despise wisdom and instruction.

Proverbs 18:15:

> The heart of the discerning acquires knowledge, for the ears of the wise seek it out.

Proverbs 11:14:

> Where there is no guidance, a people falls, but in an abundance of counselors there is safety.

Proverbs 15:22:

> Without counsel plans fail, but with many advisers they succeed.

Proverbs 24:6:

> For by wise guidance you can wage your war, and in abundance of counselors there is victory.

Mark 16:16–18:

> Whoever believes and is baptized will be saved, but whoever does not believe will be condemned. And these signs will accompany those who believe: in my name they will cast out demons; they will speak in new tongues; they will pick up serpents with their hands; and if they drink any deadly poison, it will not hurt them; they will lay their hands on the sick, and they will recover.

PART FOUR

Spiritual Warfare and the Manifestation of Darkness

Chapter 11

THE HUMAN STRUGGLE: DEFINING MENTAL HEALTH

Mental pain is less dramatic than physical pain, but it is more common and also more hard to bear. The frequent attempt to conceal mental pain increases the burden: it is easier to say "My tooth is aching" than to say "My heart is broken."

C. S. Lewis, *The Problem of Pain*

On any given day, you can watch or read the news through a supernatural lens and see darkness on a large scale. I recently read a news story about four Texas sheriff's deputies (former and current) from the same office who all died by suicide weeks apart. I can't help but ask if there is a fallen son of God, a principality, or some sort of darkness at play.[1]

On a recent trip to a baseball tournament, my youngest son told me about an incident involving him and my husband, his father, while I was out of town. He said on the interstate near where we live, a strange man ran them off the road, stopped as if he was going to get out and kill them based on the look on his face in the rearview mirror, and then drove off. When I asked my husband for his version of the story, he explained that the man was driving crazy and had already almost run into one poor woman before the guy engaged with my husband and son. My husband drives a big truck and is also a big, muscular man;

1 Mion, Landon. foxnews.com/us/4-texas-deputies-from-sheriffs-office-die-suicide-weeks-apart

arguably, at first glance, most men wouldn't want to engage in a fight with him. Yet the man in a smaller sedan literally ran my husband off the road on a busy interstate and pulled over to start a fight. Not one to back down from a fight or from protecting his family, my husband instructed our son to call the police and report the man's license plate number. As he was calling, the man drove away. This wasn't an instance of intoxication; it seemed as if he intended to run people off the roads versus simply swerving. My family didn't know this man nor did they provoke him, yet evil incited him to jeopardize the lives of a father and son. After reading many reports about horrific incidents springing from road rage, I'm grateful for the protection of the Most High God and His angel army when this happened.

Not long after that, multiple reports in our area stated that certain drivers had caused the deaths of innocent people. One told of a man who drove two women off the road, causing them to lose control of the car; both women died.[2] While the news reported that the man was intoxicated, a witness reported feeling an evil spirit surrounding him before the accident occurred. Many described the perpetrators as having an "evil look" in their eyes in times of road rage. My husband disclosed seeing nothing but black and evil in the eyes of the man who ran him and my son off the road. He also knows the difference between someone just being rude and someone who seems to be pure evil. As the darkness continues in people who present symptoms of mental health issues, we must try to better understand what we're dealing with.

In the field of mental health, there are diagnostic manuals, tests, and other means to help professionals find solutions for people's problems.[3] In the context of the church, the Bible and other religious texts provide ways to further understand negative human experiences. But how

2 wcnc.com/article/news/local/i-77-crash-claims-2-lives-man-charged/

3 Jensen-Doss, A., Hawley, K. M. "Understanding Clinicians' Diagnostic Practices: Attitudes toward the Utility of Diagnosis and Standardized Diagnostic Tools. *Adm Policy Ment Health*. 2011 Nov;38(6):476-85. doi: 10.1007/s10488-011-0334-3. PMID: 21279679; PMCID: PMC6114089.

can an everyday individual figure these things out? How can a mental health provider counsel with integrity on the right types of spiritual matters? How can a pastor understand the spiritual influences as well as the mental health issues? Diving deep into topics of mental health and spirituality can be intimidating and confusing without first defining terms, learning symptoms, and exploring causes.

A Basic Understanding

When people come into therapy, they often want to know what's going on within themselves. If they receive a diagnosis, they want to learn more about what it means and how it affects their lives. One of the first things providers can do is explain what a mental health disorder is, what a diagnosis means, and/or what the problem is and how it is or could be affecting someone. A proper diagnosis is increasingly important in improving the quality of services using evidence-based practices.[4]

When clients first come in, I conduct a thorough assessment to understand and then explain in clear terms what I believe they're struggling with. One of my main goals is to inform them that the diagnosis is not their identity. Too often, they internalize labels: "My anxiety...," or "My depression...". Therefore, it's essential to remind people that their identity isn't found in a diagnosis. Period. Their identity should be rooted in being human—in being an imager of God. Once they register this, they can more easily perceive that the forces of darkness are trying to sabotage their sense of who they are. An important part of the process begins with teaching them about what mental health is—and what it is not.

Let's look at the basic definitions of some pertinent terms and review the causes and symptoms of the following three categories: mental health, spiritual warfare, and spiritual manifestation. Separating these categories into definitions, symptoms, and causes helps me and others understand how to discern what's really going on and, in turn, how to

---

4 Ibid.

treat the clients accordingly. I realize some may think breaking the whole scope of human challenges into just three categories might be a bit simplistic, but stay with me: These categories can help with problems that in the past seemed to have no clear answers.

Mental Health Defined

Mental health is defined as "a person's condition with regard to their psychological and emotional well-being."[5] Mental health—or brain health, as I prefer to call it (we should view the brain as the organ it is, like the heart or liver, which needs to be kept healthy)—is when one's mind, will, and emotions are regulated and functioning properly as daily and life stressors are dealt with positively. Mentally healthy individuals have a state of well-being that enables them to cope with the stresses of life, recognize their abilities, continue to grow in learning, and work well with others while contributing to their community.

These are likely not new definitions, but let me share my favorite. Scott Peck, MD, in his book *The Road Less Traveled*, defines mental health as "a dedication to reality at all costs."[6] Think about this for a moment: How many people do you know who try to escape their reality? Consider all the behaviors, substances, hobbies, bad habits, and medications people use to simply escape their reality because that reality includes mentally unhealthy situations.

Biblical definitions must be reviewed in the context of the cultures in which they were written. In ancient biblical times, mental illness was thought of as madness or insanity, and we see twenty-seven mentions of this type of malady in the Bible—nineteen in the Old Testament and eight in the New Testament. Mental health disorders, or "madness," described in the Bible include symptoms such as debilitating moods, thoughts, and behaviors. People we read about in the Bible, like people

---

5 Dictionary.com; dictionary.com/MentalHealth

6 Peck, Scott. capacity-building.com/excerpts/the-road-less-traveled-by-m-scott-peck/

today, didn't always understand the spiritual aspects of mental health. Most believed the "madness" came from God as a form of punishment or for other reasons. Be that as it may, modern research indicates that Christians develop mental illness at the same rate as the general population, and I imagine this was the same even in biblical times.[7]

Some examples of mental health problems are anxiety, depression, bipolar disorder, schizophrenia, adjustment disorder, obsessive-compulsive disorder, and attention-deficit hyperactivity disorder. Inarguably, all of us have at one point or another known someone with a mental health problem. In fact, according to the National Institute for Mental Health, about 23 percent of people in the United States suffer from mental health disorders.[8]

We all face mental health concerns during our lifetimes. Periods of depression or anxiety from the loss of a loved one, for example, is a difficulty every person likely goes through at some point. A struggle doesn't specifically mean a disorder, but people can struggle to the point of having a disorder. Conversely, having a disorder doesn't mean it's a permanent condition. Additionally, disorders don't always remain the same; symptoms can morph over time.

Causes of Mental Health Challenges

A variety of factors can lead to mental health problems. Some believe one's state of mental health is solely based on heredity. Others believe it's completely related to spirituality. Academic sources overall indicate that mental illness stems from genetics, environment, stressful events, childhood trauma, negative thoughts, substances, and brain chemistry.[9] The causes of mental health troubles can be broken down into four categories: genetic predisposition, life circumstances, relational struggles,

7 Stanford, M. S. (2017). *Grace for the Afflicted: A Clinical and Biblical Perspective on Mental Illness* (2nd ed.). Downers Grove, IL: IVP Academic.

8 National Institute of Mental Health, nimh.nih.gov/health/statistics/mental-illness

9 screening.mhanational.org/content/what-causes-mental-illness/

and bodily health. Arguably, all mental health problems fit into at least one of these groups.

Genetic predisposition involves the genes and DNA we were born with and the way we're innately inclined to be or do. Having a genetic predisposition for mental illness doesn't necessarily mean we are guaranteed to run into problems; it simply suggests the potential of a struggle being present. Discovering our genetic predispositions can be essential in responding to mental health difficulties.

Years ago in my school counseling days, I was working with a student who disclosed that she was hearing voices of classmates saying things to her every time she was in the cafeteria. After investigating the situation, we found that not one of her classmates had been saying the things she was hearing. After she talked with her father, he told her she had a grandmother who had been diagnosed with schizophrenia. This is an example of a genetic predisposition. Thankfully, the father was able to get the student help and treatment. As the student and her father engaged in treatment, they saw positive changes. In virtually every initial counseling intake or assessment, a good counselor should ask if there is a history of mental illness in the client's family. Many times, people don't disclose this information until we ask them deeper questions.

Epigenetics (the study of how our behaviors and environment can cause changes to our genetics) is a term that is useful in helping us understand genetic predisposition. As mentioned previously, epigenetics shows us that how we think, feel, and choose (our mind-in-action) influences the behavior of our genes and our subsequent mental and physical well-being. In other words, by changing our thoughts, we can change our genetic expression. In her book *Switch On Your Brain,* Dr. Caroline Leaf explains that we rewire our brain through neuroplasticity, which then impacts our biology. "We switch genes on and off with every thought we have," she says, "and every thought we have is a response to how we perceive our life and the world around us." Therefore, it's important to realize that while our choices and thoughts can change our

DNA's expression, genetic predisposition can be altered to more healthy behaviors by changing what we think and how we behave.

Hence, some people have genetics that may be predisposed to the potential for mental health problems. Subsequently, individual choices can condition them either to experience mental challenges or to prevent predisposed genetic mental health conditions. The good news is there is hope, no matter what's in our bloodline!

Life circumstances include influences involving substance use (whether it's by the person or others), homelessness, abuse of any kind, and any other type of life-altering trauma. This category also encompasses natural disasters, terrorism, and major accidents. Life circumstances aren't always situations that could have been prevented; rather, they're terrible circumstances or events that can take place in a fallen or imperfect world. These can lead to mental health issues, but not necessarily, as often many other factors are at play.

Presumably, most of us have undergone some type of experience that could be categorized as traumatic. Yet not all of us suffer from mental health struggles as a result. For years, researchers have tried to determine what makes us more susceptible to developing a mental health disorder as a result of life circumstances. Studies show variability related to factors such as age, gender, ethnicity, income, co-existing conditions, personality factors, and sociability.[10]

The development of a mental health disorder due to life circumstances is mitigated by resiliency factors, including healthy social, cultural, and familial relationships and contexts.[11] For example, someone who experiences trauma who has a strong, supportive family may be

10 Saunders, R., Buckman, J. E. J., Fonagy, P., Fancourt, D. "Understanding Different Trajectories of Mental Health across the General Population During the COVID-19 Pandemic." *Psychological Medicine*. 2022;52(16):4049–4057. doi:10.1017/S0033291721000957.

11 Mesman, Esther; Vreeker, Annabel; Hillegers, Manon. "Resilience and Mental Health in Children and Adolescents: An Update of the Recent Literature and Future Directions." *Current Opinion in Psychiatry* 34(6): 586–592, November 2021. DOI: 10.1097/YCO.0000000000000741.

less likely to develop a mental health disorder than someone who doesn't have a solid system of support.

On a personal note, I've noticed that life circumstances can affect people from a mental health standpoint in various ways as I've watched the differences between how my parents versus other family members handled situations of abuse. My parents provided a safe place for my sisters and me to share our hurts when a certain incident happened. As a result, my sisters and I haven't struggled mentally in the same ways as others in our family who have battled mental illness for years. This is by no means placing blame; they just didn't have the kind of support during their childhood as we did. I am forever grateful for the gift of presence and safety in my parents.

Relationships or relational struggles refer to family issues such as abuse, ongoing fighting, divorce, abandonment, lack of healthy attachments, enmeshment (when people in relationships are so emotionally connected that they struggle to have their own independent thoughts, feelings, and identities), and more, all of which can influence mental health. In addition, any other areas where close relationships are present can potentially affect people either positively or negatively. Examples could be work, church, and faith communities, friend groups, schools, clubs, and other organizations.

Relationships are vital in forming who we are. In other words, who we are is shaped by who we love. When there is harm in our relationships, it can greatly affect our mental health. Harm can come in the form of physical, sexual, or emotional abuse from a family member or close friend. It can also come in the form of bullying at school. Marital problems such as adultery and divorce, and even financial problems, can lead to mental health complications as well—not only for the couple but for others around them, including their children.

In fact, most of the dilemmas clients are dealing with in my counseling practice are relational. I help children process the changes within their home when parents separate. Couples come in for marriage counseling after the fallout of an extramarital affair. Adolescents seek counseling for troubles they're experiencing because their parents aren't emotionally or even physically available. Older parents are at times on a quest for answers regarding how to deal with adult children who refuse to leave home. And senior adults look for answers regarding end-of-life issues and how those issues affect their families. These matters are all common, yet some battle anxiety and depression as they go through these types of relational challenges.

Beyond more normal occurrences, my colleagues and I have seen a great number of stressors related to spiritual abuse and/or hurt within the context of church relationships. Arguably, if you've been a part of a church long enough, you've experienced some form of church-related hurt. I certainly have. In fact, the wounds I've received from people I've served with have been some of my deepest. When someone you've looked up to verbally assaults you, it challenges not only your opinion about that person, but your belief that you at one point thought you aligned. Heartbreaking stories of church-related distress come into our practice weekly. While we should never expect perfection of anyone we love, we must also take on the attitude of realizing our failures, seeking forgiveness, receiving forgiveness, and, if possible, reconciling. Nevertheless, this is rarely the case.

Relational conflicts that most often lead to mental health problems lack healthy attachments, joy, and the ability to positively navigate the situation. These may include but are not limited to clinical disorders such as anxiety, depression, mood disorders, and substance abuse disorders. Relational problems in addition to clinical disorders can also lead to personality disorders.

Clinical syndromes tend to present later in a person's life than personality disorders. These disorders are also more easily treated with medication and therapy. Traditionally, clinical disorders are also believed to have an underlying biomedical cause, which is likely the reason they're more easily treated. Anyone can at one point or another be diagnosed with a clinical disorder, but the diagnosis may be temporary versus ongoing.

Personality disorders, on the other hand, are thought to develop early in life and are viewed as dysfunctions in personality rather than a matter of biological changes. Deeply ingrained, enduring behavior patterns that lead to a lack of flexibility and difficulty in social interactions characterize most personality disorders. People with personality disorders often deviate greatly from how those without them think, feel, and act. These types of mental health struggles are most often lifelong battles.[12]

Counseling, at the core, is about building healthy relationships defined by healthy attachments. Change happens within the context of relationships. Often the change involves mental health counselors teaching clients what healthy relationships consist of; clients are often only familiar with unhealthy behaviors and patterns. Studies show that people with stable, close relationships report higher levels of psychological well-being.[13] Relational struggles can be mitigated by relationships that are positive. While most of our hurts spring from relationships, healing also comes within the context of relationships.

Bodily health issues: Serious medical issues, biological considerations, and chemical factors or imbalances are included in this category, as are parasites and dietary issues that result in mind-altering and behavioral changes. In addition, traumatic brain injuries fall into this group.

Chemical imbalances are bodily issues that cause mental health problems. Years ago, I did an in-home assessment of a teenager who as a child had witnessed a family member killing other family members. Later, it was found that the family member charged with murder had an extremely low level of serotonin (a brain chemical that helps regulate mood and emotional balance). In fact, many studies have suggested an

12 *American Diagnostic and Statistical Manual of Mental Disorders* (DSM-IV).

13 Sagone, E., Commodari, E., Indiana, M. L., La Rosa, V. L. "Exploring the Association between Attachment Style, Psychological Well-Being, and Relationship Status in Young Adults and Adults-A Cross-Sectional Study." *Eur J Investig Health Psychol Educ.* 2023 Feb 24;13(3):525-539. doi: 10.3390/ejihpe13030040. PMID: 36975392; PMCID: PMC10047625.

association of serotonin system-related genes with homicidal behavior and criminal aggression.[14]

Parasites' impact on the body has already been mentioned, so here I'd like to bring attention to the link between diet and mental health. Dietary changes in general can be mind-altering. For example, some studies have found correlations between refined sugar and depression,[15] as well as between attention and hyperactivity to food dyes.[16] This does not include the mental aspects of eating disorders and the relationship to food.

Interestingly, a couple of years ago, after my niece received a diagnosis of epilepsy, I remembered that the keto diet had been designed more than a century earlier as treatment for epilepsy. So, as I began seeking solutions for my niece, I came across psychiatrist Dr. Chris Palmer's transformative and fascinating work[17] on the ketogenic diet and mental illness. Dr. Palmer reports having patients diagnosed with bipolar disorder and schizophrenia experience "remission" without medication by using a ketogenic diet treatment program. He explores the idea that mental disorders are metabolic in nature, meaning mental health disorders are related to how the body and brain process energy, chemicals, or nutrients.

Bodily issues are certainly worth exploring as potential causes for those suffering with mental illness. That's actually the point where I advise clinicians to begin, because they can occasionally be the simplest causes to treat.

Traumatic brain injuries (TBIs) have been the focus of much media attention, especially surrounding athletes (although TBIs can be caused by physical encounters outside of sports as well) whose stories are ubiquitous

14 Qadeer, M. I., Amar, A., Huang, Y. Y., *et al.* "Association of Serotonin System-related Genes with Homicidal Behavior and Criminal Aggression in a Prison Population of Pakistani Origin." *Sci Rep* 11, 1670 (2021). https://doi.org/10.1038/s41598-021-81198-4.

15 health.harvard.edu/blog/nutritional-psychiatry-your-brain-on-food

16 publichealth.berkeley.edu/new-report-shows-artificial-food-coloring-causes-hyperactivity-in-some-kids

17 brainenergy.com

on sports news channels. In the 1980s, we called traumatic brain injuries "concussions," and they often went untreated. Generation Xers sometimes joke about how athletes today simply aren't as tough as earlier generations. Despite the teasing, TBIs are serious and can cause cognitive, emotional, and sleep changes. Undiagnosed TBIs often show up in accounts of abuse, anger, divorce, depression, and a variety of other problems related to mental health.

My practice has treated people of all ages with TBIs, and we've also counseled family members who have lost loved ones due to complications from these injuries. Research shows that TBI is a leading cause of death—especially in older populations.

Symptoms of Mental Health Struggles

It is important for everyone to know the symptoms of mental illness so we can seek help or identify when we need to encourage others to do so. Below are the most common symptoms to be aware of:

- **Personality changes:** It's normal for people to change over time as we age, mature, and experience life. This type of change, however, is more dramatic in that it happens suddenly or within a short period. Behaviors to note include extreme mood changes, including uncontrollable "highs" or feelings of euphoria. It may also include odd or peculiar behavior that is not characteristic of the person.
- **Emotional changes:** These symptoms often surface as prolonged or strong feelings of irritability or anger; lingering feelings of sadness, hopelessness, or overwhelm; and/or apathy about activities things once enjoyed. Look for changes outside the norm when assessing emotional changes.
- **Increased isolation:** If someone is withdrawing from or showing apathy towards people they love and activities they enjoy, something could be wrong.

- **Sudden decline in self-care:** Diminishing attention to hygiene can be a symptom of mental illness. For example, if someone stops fixing their hair, taking showers or bathing, or dressing as nicely as before, they may be experiencing mental health problems.
- **Excessive worrying or fear:** Signs of this may be evident in nervousness, suspicion of others, or focusing on events that could happen—but may not be likely.
- **Confused thinking:** This shows up as having problems concentrating and learning, displaying illogical thinking, and having memory problems, unusual thoughts, or questioning of beliefs and abilities. Confused thinking may be evident in changes in speech.
- **Increased sensitivity:** Changes in how someone experiences sight, sound, smell, and touch may indicate struggles in the brain and can include a desire to avoid overstimulating situations.
- **Changes in functioning:** This behavior might include decreased performance in work, school, or sports; frustrations in relationships with coworkers or peers; difficulty completing tasks; or failing in subjects. These changes may be evident in work or school attendance or in a struggle to do chores at home.
- **Feeling disconnected from or out of touch with reality:** Those who experience vague feelings of connection with self, others, and their environment may be in denial or reality or feel disconnected from truth.
- **Changes in sleep patterns:** This could come in the form of a decrease in sleep, intermittent sleep, or excessive sleep. Changes to note here are those outside of physical concerns and that are changes in normal patterns.
- **Changes in eating:** Watch for a decrease or increase in eating or changes in the types of food desired. Someone may stop

or slow down eating, binge, or want unhealthy foods such as those high in sugar. Attempts to control eating obsessively may also be a concern.

- **Self-harm/suicidal ideation:** This includes thoughts, talk, or behavior that reflects self-harm. If someone is talking about no longer wanting to be alive, not wanting to "be here" anymore, or reflecting on how much of a burden they are, action should be taken. Any attempt at self-harm is a serious mental health concern.

This list covers most mental health symptoms to be aware of. However, how these manifest varies from person to person. Paying attention to changes within yourself, family, friends, coworkers, and others you interact with is important. If you notice changes, speak up for someone or ask for help for yourself or others, regardless of the reason for the change—whether known or not.

QUESTIONS FOR REFLECTION

1. Consider a relational struggle (family conflict, church-related hurt, friendship breakdown). How did that relationship influence your mental health? What steps could you take to find healing within that context?
2. When you think about the concept of "mental health as brain health," how does that align with (or challenge) your understanding of being made in God's image?
3. In what practical ways might you steward your brain (for example, think about nutrition, rest, your community, and prayer) differently?

PRACTICAL APPLICATION

Encouragement for pastoral counselors and mental health professionals:

- Define "mental health" in your own words and have a conversation with someone discussing what you've learned.
- Assess the mental health struggles of those you serve with the proper definition of mental health by reviewing the symptoms and potential causes.
- Offer a sermon series on mental health and how we can help ourselves and others. Discuss symptoms, causes, and definitions properly alongside Scripture.

Prayer Prompt: *Lord, provide me with opportunities to share how you conceptualize the problem of mental health. As I see symptoms that cause concern for myself or others, guide me in the right ways to respond.*

SCRIPTURE TO CONSIDER

Romans 12:2:

> Do not be confirmed to this world, but be transformed by the renewal of your mind, that by testing you may discern what is the will of God, what is good and acceptable and perfect.

2 Corinthians 10:5 (NIV):

> We demolish arguments and every pretension that sets itself up against the knowledge of God, and we take captive every thought to make it obedient to Christ.

Psalm 139:13–14:

> For you formed my inward parts; you knitted me together in my mother's womb. I praise you, for I am fearfully and wonderfully made.

Ephesians 6:12 (NIV):

> For our struggle is not against flesh and blood, but against the rulers, against the authorities, against the powers of this dark world and against the spiritual forces of evil in the heavenly realms.

Philippians 4:6–7:

> Do not be anxious about anything, but in everything by prayer and supplication with thanksgiving let your requests be made known to God. And the peace of God, which surpasses all understanding, will guard your hearts and your minds in Christ Jesus.

1 Corinthians 6:19–20 (NIV):

> Do you not know your bodies are temples of the Holy Spirit, who is in you, whom you have received from God? You are not your own; you were bought at a price. Therefore honor God with your bodies.

Proverbs 4:23:

> Keep your heart with all vigilance, for from it flow the springs of life.

Chapter 12

THE HUMAN STRUGGLE: DEFINING SPIRITUAL WARFARE

The trumpet still plays the notes of war. You cannot sit down and put the victory wreath on your head. You do not have a crown. You still must wear the helmet and carry the sword. You must watch, pray, and fight. Expect your last battle to be the most difficult, for the enemy's fiercest charge is reserved for the end of the day.

CHARLES SPURGEON

No doubt, understanding the root causes of mental health problems can be complicated, as there are often several avenues to take to find answers. Many people don't know how to find the answers and continue to be plagued by defeat. Certain concerns appear to be physical, yet a diagnosis cannot be found even after multiple medical tests. Others seem to be mental health-related, yet after years of treatment, they remain unresolved. I've worked with a number of young girls—especially those who are in the fourth or fifth grade—who've gone through extensive testing for stomach issues that turned out to be caused by anxiety. While the church or other spiritual communities offer answers for individuals' challenges, their strategies sometimes leave people traumatized and worse off than before.

As I reflect over my life since I started studying spiritual warfare more intently, I can identify some specific markers of periods of warfare I've experienced over the years. Most notably were times of spiritual hurt, which may have been attempts to make me leave my faith or the church. Others included a time when I began my career as a young school counselor and felt the darkness of vicarious trauma (the emotional stress or trauma someone develops after repeatedly hearing about or witnessing the trauma of others). I don't believe these instances were simply a part of life; I'm certain they were battles taking place in the supernatural realm.

When I was nineteen, a challenging time in my faith involved me realizing that some of the spiritual people I had looked up to my entire life were failing me. I later realized this was an attempt by the enemies of the Most High God to cause me to stop serving Him. My faith, however, was sincere, and I learned that loyalty to Him doesn't always mean loyalty to certain churches or people. Taking a peek into the past, I'm amazed I wasn't led astray. This is because of the faithfulness of the Most High, for sure.

As a school counselor in my early twenties, saying I was beginning the job with the enthusiasm and mindset of changing the world is an understatement. I had ideas to share, a love of people to express, and energy for days. The naivety of how emotionally difficult the job could be wasn't on my mind. So, when an adolescent girl came in to tell me she was being molested by her father, I was shocked at how her experience affected me emotionally. I was the first person she told. No education, no person—and, at times, no experience—can prepare you for the first time you hear about pure evil harming a child. During the season when I was helping this girl, I was driving to work one day, and an overwhelming, unprovoked thought came into my head: I should run my car off a bridge and end my life. I had never had this kind of thought before. It was pervasive and real, but I knew it wasn't from me. Even in my immature faith, I knew it was a part of spiritual warfare. I'm overwhelmed with gratitude for those who prayed with me and for me during that time.

I could share many other instances from my own experiences with spiritual warfare surfacing as a mental struggle. Be that as it may, I've also undergone times of anxiety or feeling overwhelmed while I was amid circumstances that didn't exactly feel spiritual. While I argue that all spiritual forces of darkness are influencing mental health at some point of entry, it's necessary and beneficial to define exactly what spiritual warfare is.

Spiritual Warfare Defined

The better part of humanity would likely agree that some type of battle between good and evil is being waged in the world. While it can be defined in varying ways, as a Christ- follower, a loyal believer in the Most High God, I believe what His word says about spiritual war: It is real. We have enemies. We can be and are victorious. Spiritual warfare is real. Consider British theologian and author C. S. Lewis' words:

> Enemy-occupied territory—that is what this world is. Christianity is the story of how the rightful king has landed, you might say landed in disguise and is calling us all to take part in a great campaign of sabotage.

Humans aren't just physical beings; we're spiritual beings—physical beings with a spirit. Genesis 1:26–27 says:

> Then God said, "Let us make mankind in our image, in our likeness, so that they may rule over the fish in the sea and the birds in the sky, over the livestock and all the wild animals, and over all the creatures that move along the ground. So, God created mankind in his own image, in the image of God he created them; male and female he created them. (NIV)

The Most High God is spirit, so if we're made in His image, it follows that we're also, at some level, spirit. The spirit within each human is the part that connects to the divine or spiritual world. God breathed into humans as He formed them out of dirt, and that breath allowed the spirit to become alive in humans. This spirit does not end, although the body does.

Scripture also teaches that there is a difference in the soul and spirit. Consider Hebrews 4:12:

> For the word of God is alive and active. Sharper than any double-edged sword, it penetrates even to dividing soul and spirit, joints and marrow; it judges the thoughts and attitudes of the heart. (NIV)

The soul represents the life principle of the body, including the mind, heart, will, and imagination. In other words, the soul is the entirety of a person's conscious experience or the essence of a personality. The spirit, on the other hand, is a deeper part of the human, the immaterial part of a person that connects to God. It includes the innermost part that can be reborn or transformed spiritually. I like to call it the "spark" of the Creator, given to us from the time we're formed in our mothers' womb. After the body or soul dies, the spirit either goes to be with the Most High God or is eternally damned.

Realizing we are spiritual beings means we also need to understand that a spiritual war is raging all around us. The enemies of God are trying to stop or prevent those who aren't Christians from following the One True God (Father, Son, and Holy Spirit). In other words, the enemy and his forces attempt to hinder salvation:

> This is the meaning of the parable: The seed is the word of God. Those along the path are the ones who hear, and then the devil comes and takes away the word from their hearts, so that they may not believe and be saved. (Luke 8:11–12)

The anti-God legion also encourages sin:

> As for you, you were dead in your transgressions and sins, in which you used to live when you followed the ways of this world

> and of the ruler of the kingdom of the air, the spirit who is now at work in those who are disobedient. All of us also lived among them at one time, gratifying the cravings of our flesh and following its desires and thoughts. Like the rest, we were by nature deserving of wrath. (Ephesians 2:1–3)

For those of us who are Christians, the enemies of the Most High God are trying to fight against His plans and purposes for us. If they can't have our spirits serving them, they will try to make us ineffective for His kingdom! They do this by lying to us and tempting us to sin. Additionally, they seek to hinder our discipleship of others and prevent us from sharing the gospel.

Thus, spiritual warfare is a war between the goodness of the Most High God (His promises, purposes, and plans for us) and all evil (anything that opposes His goodness). Our mental health is most often engaged in an inner battle, but it can become evident in the outer battle as well. The plans of the Most High God, including His ways and will for us, are for good. The plans of His enemies are for evil and consist of attempts to steal from us, kill us, and destroy us. The causes of spiritual warfare can be explained simply, and they're vital in understanding the battle.

Causes of Spiritual Warfare

People often suggest spiritual warfare is solely caused by our sin or the choices we or our parents (or others) have made. I propose that the enemies of the Most High fight against us because we are human—a status they despise and are jealous of. Further, they attempt to destroy us when we choose to loyally follow the Most High God instead of one of them. Therefore, it isn't so much about *what we've done* but rather about *who we are.*

I strongly believe the causes of spiritual warfare can be narrowed down into four categories: being made in the image of the Most High God, becoming a loyal Christ-follower, obeying God's commands, and allowing deception to enter. Each of these or a combination of them invokes the forces of darkness to fight against the good or potential good in our lives. Let me explain.

First, *being made in God's image* is a valuable high status given us at the moment of conception: "So God created mankind in his own image, in the image of God he created them; male and female he created them" (Genesis 1:27). Satan and the forces of darkness *hate* this. Maybe they were jealous; who knows their reasoning? One thing we know for sure is that they hated that humans reflect the image of/represent the Most High God on earth. Genesis 3:15 states: "I will put enmity between you and the woman, and between your offspring and her offspring; he shall bruise your head, and you shall bruise his heel." The warfare involves any attempt to cause us not to be the honorable imager or representative of the Most High God we were created to be.

Second, *becoming a Christ follower* takes the spiritual battle to another level. In 1 Peter 5:8, the apostle says to believers:

> Be self-controlled and alert. Your enemy the devil prowls around like a roaring lion looking for someone to devour. Resist him, standing firm in the faith, because you know that your brothers throughout the world are undergoing the same kind of sufferings.

Satan and the forces of darkness know they can't have us in their kingdom once we become loyal followers of Jesus, so they fight to render us ineffective in our work for the kingdom of God. Their main goals seem to be centered on not wanting us to share the good news with others, which they view as an attempt to take over their territories. They don't want us to love and disciple others.

Third, beyond being a human and deciding to follow Jesus, *actively obeying the commands* and *engaging in God's plan and purposes* provoke war in the spiritual realm. The forces of darkness tried to kill Jesus as a small child via King Herod (Matthew 2:13–23). Be that as it may, when Jesus began His ministry, Satan fought Him from that moment, which is clearly seen in the Matthew 4 temptation. In addition, later in Matthew, we read that Jesus turned and said to Peter, "Get behind me, Satan! You are a hindrance to me. For you are not setting your mind on the things of God, but on the things of man" (16:23). Jesus called Peter "Satan." This shouldn't scare Christ-followers; rather, it should make us aware that as we loyally serve our Lord and Savior, battles will ensue. But we have no reason to fear, because the Lord is with us, and although warfare may be a part of the sacrifice, it is worth every step of obedience.

Finally, spiritual warfare can occur when we *allow deception to enter*. Second Thessalonians 2:1–4 states:

> Now concerning the coming of our Lord Jesus Christ and our being gathered together to him, we ask you, brothers, not to be quickly shaken in mind or alarmed, either by a spirit or a spoken word, or a letter seeming to be from us to the effect that the day of the Lord has come. Let no one deceive you in any way. For that day will not come, unless the rebellion comes first, and the man of lawlessness is revealed, the son of destruction, who opposes and exalts himself against every so-called god or object of worship, so that he takes his seat in the temple of God, proclaiming himself to be God.

We can be deceived through lawlessness, rebellion against God, and engagement in idolatry. Don't think idols merely look like a new car. Idolatry can look like visiting a psychic, participating in rituals, using tarot cards, or utilizing New Age practices or other forms of "spirituality" that fall outside of the teachings of Scripture. These practices prevent us from sharing the gospel, which is a vital warfare strategy! If we allow deception to enter, warfare will ensue. Free will is a gift from the Most High God. He may not want us to be deceived, but He may encourage us to return to Him.

Over the many years I've sat with people in counseling rooms, I've found that some of the most kind, loving, hard-working, smart, talented, and precious people are the ones who've been in some of the most intense battles between good and evil. I believe this is because Satan and the forces of darkness (principalities, powers of darkness, and spiritual forces of wickedness in heavenly places) go *hard* after those with the most potential for holiness. Regardless of our beliefs in the causes of spiritual warfare, we must not make the mistake of thinking warfare doesn't exist. In the *Screwtape Letters,* British theologian C. S. Lewis wrote:

> There are two equal and opposite errors into which our race can fall about the devils. One is to disbelieve in their existence. The other is to believe, and to feel an excessive and unhealthy interest in them. They themselves (the devils) are equally pleased by both errors and hail a materialist or a magician with the same delight.

And Chinese military strategist Sun Tzu, in *The Art of War* wrote:

> If you know the enemy and know yourself, you need not fear the result of a hundred battles. If you know yourself but not the enemy, for every victory gained you will also suffer a defeat. If you know neither the enemy nor yourself, you will succumb in every battle.

We must embrace the truth of why spiritual warfare exists, value our status as imagers of the Most High God, and take dominion by sharing the gospel…no matter what the cost. Finally, we need to know our enemy, know ourselves, and be honest about our struggles to prevent deception from entering our lives.

> The Spirit of the Sovereign LORD is on me, because the LORD has anointed me to proclaim good news to the poor. He has sent me to bind up the brokenhearted, to proclaim freedom for the captives and release from darkness for the prisoners, to proclaim

the year of the Lord's favor and the day of vengeance of our God, to comfort all who mourn, and provide for those who grieve in Zion—to bestow on them a crown of beauty instead of ashes, the oil of joy instead of mourning, and a garment of praise instead of a spirit of despair. They will be called oaks of righteousness, a planting of the Lord for the display of his splendor. (Isaiah 61:1–3)

Categories of Spiritual Warfare Symptoms

In the area of spiritual warfare, it's helpful to first explore the way Scripture teaches us the enemies of the Most High God and His imagers attack. Their main goal in battle is to turn humans away from the Most High God and towards evil. The enemies' strategies most often involve:

1. Temptation
2. Deception
3. Accusation
4. Infirmity
5. Oppression

Let's examine these tactics in more detail.

Temptation: The enemies study us so they'll learn exactly how to tempt us. For example, if we struggle with lust, they may use a beautiful person or an internet search as a temptation. They also infiltrate culture to entice all humanity in every way possible, as they currently rule in this world (Psalm 82). Consider the media as one way the enemies have infiltrated culture with evil. Therefore, it's vital to know our areas of weakness better than the enemies do. This involves being honest with ourselves. For example, one day a client, Joe, told me he was very attracted to a woman at work. He had felt tempted in ways like never before, and he was confused. We discussed how the urge could be coming from supernatural forces to try to destroy his marriage and career. Joe was grateful for this explanation and wanted to learn more about how to battle the temptation.

Deception: The enemies are "professional" liars. They know precisely how to lie in a way that makes people believe the lies are truth. The lies may even be presented in the form of a question, as did Satan's lie in the Garden of Eden:

> Now the serpent was more crafty than any of the wild animals the LORD God had made. He said to the woman, "Did God really say, 'You must not eat from any tree in the garden'?" (Genesis 3:1, NIV)

He knew what God had said, but asking if God had really said it was a deliberate way to cast doubts about the truth of God's words. He may say to some of us today things like:

- "Did your boss really say you can't leave early?"
- "You'd be better off dead."
- "You can't afford to have a child."
- "Your body is shutting down from this illness even if a doctor can't confirm it."

Knowing the truth is essential. We hear the lies of the enemy in the form of deception in therapy daily.

Accusation: Satan stands before the Lord in His courts (this is a divine council scene!) and accuses those who love the Most High God. We find the biblical account of this in the first and second chapters of the book of Job. Like Job, we may experience direct attacks but we're more likely to encounter this type of attack through messages of unhealthy shame. The accusations might be phrased like: "You are not good enough; you'll never escape your past," or "You're unworthy." The enemies also love to remind us of our painful past: "You are a loser and you always will be." They want us to forget who we are in Christ and what He did for us in advocating for us before the Father. Knowing who we are, understanding our purpose, and being aware of all other aspects of our identity are crucial in combatting the accusations of the enemy. Dan, one of my clients, felt the accusation of the enemy telling him his wife had left because he hadn't been a good enough husband. He benefitted from learning where this lie was coming from, because he knew he had tried everything he could think of beyond his imperfections.

Infirmity: Scripture clearly teaches us—from Job and others in the Old Testament to those Jesus encountered and healed in the New Testament—that the enemies of the Most High God can attack humans by inflicting physical sickness. There is no magical formula for figuring out whether an infirmity is caused by an enemy attack. However, we can and should ask the Most High God to show us if an attack from the enemy is at play; if He confirms it is, we should seek healing. Stan, a church-planting pastor with a zeal for sharing the gospel, received a brain tumor diagnosis three months after selling his home and entering the mission field. He lost his memory for a season, and it felt like a setback caused by the enemy.

Healing can come in many forms, which is also why it's necessary to seek guidance from the Holy Spirit. Restoration to health may come through prayer, physical changes, medication, and/or obedience to the Most High God's commands. At times, our struggles—like the thorn in Paul's side—may be intended for our good, so healing while we're still on earth may not be in God's plan. The important thing is to pick up our shield of faith in the only One who can truly sustain us in the meantime.

Oppression: Some folks in theological or church circles consider "oppression" a synonym of "possession." Biblically speaking, the likely best translation is "demonized," which refers to affliction rather than differentiating between possession and oppression. Anyone not in relationship with Christ is technically owned by the enemy. However, to help people understand the difference using the possession/oppression language, in this discussion, I'll use the term "oppression"—but suggest that it may look like possession. Typically, oppression causes people to lose control of their mental wits or faculties, and it can also manifest as sleep paralysis. An evil spirit controls the person in these intermittent times of loss of control or sleep paralysis, yet it may not be ongoing. Individuals experiencing oppression should seek biblical guidance for treatment, which will likely involve some form of deliverance in a healthy, clinically sound way —with healing as the goal.

A spectrum of beliefs concerning oppression range from the thinking that Christians don't experience it to the assertion that it always looks like demon possession. In truth, the demonic or evil may be involved in all struggles at some level, but this doesn't change the fact that people need healing. Christian psychiatrist Matthew Stafford, MD, states, "Demons are involved at many levels of our existence, and it certainly isn't necessary for demonic powers to purposefully cause a given mental illness in a person for us to be able to say that they were involved in the disorder."[1]

Mental Symptoms Caused by Spiritual Warfare

Mental health struggles are often evident in spiritual warfare attacks. At times, symptoms are the first things we notice when we're under siege by the enemy. Symptoms can range from changes in mood or physical struggles such as sleep issues to an increase in temptations.

- **Unexplained mood/emotional struggles:** These include feelings of unusually heavy sadness, hopelessness, and overwhelm, and can also be expressed by intense anger, extreme frustration, decreased motivation, or euphoria even in negative circumstances. In times of spiritual warfare, these mood swings or emotional changes seem to come out of nowhere. Deceptions in these struggles can cause those suffering to seek answers outside of spiritual resources and often lead them into long battles while they're looking for help. For

1 Stanford, *Grace for the Afflicted.*

example, one woman, Susa, entered a season of walking with the Lord more closely; then, about a month later, she felt an intense depression that seemingly came out of nowhere.

- **Abnormal thoughts:** These can include unfamiliar anxiety, fear, thoughts of self-harm, unusual difficulty in focus/attention, and unhealthy thoughts about others. Abnormal thoughts often come in the form of temptations and accusations, with thoughts that can be overwhelming and evasive. If somconc is obcdicnt to the Lord and isn't typically fearful, yet is suddenly overcome with fear, warfare could be at play.
- **Abnormal or escalated relational struggles:** These can come in varying forms and can be isolated or in combination with other symptoms. Examples include family arguments, betrayal of friendships, frustration with church situations, disgust with the community, or the negative effects of a loved one's troubles. Accusations are often prevalent in these situations from both sides. During the COVID-19 pandemic, churches reported exponential levels of relational struggles.
- **Abnormal or increased temptations:** This includes an increase in temptations previously encountered, or temptation in an area of life that previously had not brought any unhealthy temptations. For example, some people may have never thought about sinning sexually, but for some reason, they may have felt tempted in a certain season. Remember, the enemy is great at lying to tempt us in varying degrees and ways.

Physical Symptoms Caused by Spiritual Warfare

Physical issues that don't seem to have an explanation: These can show up as stomach pains/digestive problems, excessive sleep or sleeplessness, headaches, backaches, and shoulder pain. Stomach problems are very common in this category, but as Scripture teaches, attacks on the demonic or evil level can come in all shapes and sizes.

Mental Symptoms
Unexplained mood and/or emotional struggles, such as feeling sad or low, hopeless, overwhelmed, or angry.
Abnormal or anxious thoughts, fear, desire to self-harm; lack of focus, unhealthy thoughts about relationships.
Lack of enjoyment of normal things that brought you pleasure in the past; Depressed feelings instead of joy with certain activities.
Bodily Symptoms *other than the brain*
Unexplained physical struggles, such as stomach pains or digestive problems, excessive sleep, excessive lack of sleep, headaches, or backaches.
Abnormal or increase in relational struggles with family (arguing at home more often), friends, church community.
An increase in temptations you've struggled with or an experience of temptation in an area in which you've never struggled before. Such as you've never thought about cheating on your spouse, but someone has come along that is tempting you.

If you're experiencing these symptoms, seek discernment in your time with the Lord. Pray and ask God to show you what you are battling and why. Enlist prayer warriors. Tune into your five senses (watch, feel, listen, taste, and smell). Let Psalm 34:8 be your guide: "Taste and see that the Lord is good." If something isn't good, seek the Lord and let His word illuminate what is off in your life.

QUESTIONS FOR REFLECTION

1. Have you ever considered a mental struggle to be caused by an unknown nefarious force or spirit?
2. How do you define spiritual warfare?
3. Can you reflect over your life and contemplate times spiritual warfare may have been at play?

4. Have you ever sensed a spiritual cause behind someone's mental distress? How did that awareness (or lack of it) shape the way you offered help, prayer, or counseling?

PRACTICAL APPLICATION

Encouragement for pastoral counselors and mental health professionals:

- Write reflections on your own times of spiritual warfare and contemplate how these times have affected your walk with the Lord, your view of others, and ways you help or avoid helping others.
- Preach or teach about spiritual warfare, including the causes and symptoms—not just how to armor up.
- Adapt assessments and treatment to include questions regarding spiritual warfare.

Prayer Prompt: *Lord, thank you for walking with me through the toughest battles in life. As I continue, guard my heart as I teach and treat others who are also encountering spiritual forces of darkness as we seek to follow you.*

SCRIPTURE TO CONSIDER

2 Thessalonians 3:3:

> But the Lord is faithful, and he will strengthen you and protect you from the evil one.

John 16:33:

> I [Jesus] have told you these things, so that in me you may have peace. In this world you will have trouble. But take heart! I have overcome the world.

1 Corinthians 10:13:

> No temptation has overtaken you except what is common to mankind. And God is faithful; he will not let you be tempted

beyond what you can bear. But when you are tempted, he will also provide a way out so that you can endure it.

2 Corinthians 2:11:

In order that Satan might not outwit us. For we are not unaware of his schemes.

Chapter 13

THE UNBELIEVER'S STRUGGLE: DEFINING SPIRITUAL MANIFESTATION

We are constantly being fed harmful ideas that we adopt and learn to believe in, thinking they are all right, and so we ignorantly follow. This is done without our knowing that a keen, sharp, unscrupulous mind is seeking to control us.

A. W. Tozer, American missionary, pastor, and author

The devil divides the world between atheism and superstition.

George Herbert, Anglican priest and poet

I remember walking into a church one day and seeing a woman wearing a T-shirt that said something about having faith in her zodiac sign. This perplexed me. Most people in churches today—arguably, most adults in general—deny that there's darkness surrounding some spiritual practices. For example, let's say I asked parents sitting beside me at a ballgame, "Do you want a crystal to hang around your neck to help encourage good energy for the team?" Most would likely see no harm in doing so and say yes. Realizing this may be a very elementary example and there may be no direct harm in superstitions or items, the truth remains that the use of items used for divination is increasing. People are overwhelmingly believing the lie that darkness is not tied to these items or that people are using them in growing numbers. The research speaks otherwise.[1] Increasing numbers of people are engaging in practices that involve manifesting evil—whether they know it or not.

Engaging in malevolent practices is common. It may include social media, online gaming, being exposed to items of darkness at a friend's house, or simply visiting a haunted area. It can involve physical or sexual abuse, the introduction to a cult, or a family member's involvement in a nefarious organization. There are many entry points for darkness today, and children are often the most vulnerable. A current study suggests 83 percent of children ages five through twelve regularly play video games, many of which are violent and dark.[2] Young children playing dark video games is something we deal with constantly in my counseling offices.

Parents often don't want to hear or learn about dark behaviors or practices children are engaging in because we want to deny their existence. Take the fact that young people are trafficked daily in virtually every country, for example. I've warned countless numbers of parents about the dangers of not setting up filters, time limits, and other protections on their children's devices. Yet most walk away from the conversation either outright saying or at least thinking, "Yeah right, that would never happen to *my* child." While trafficking doesn't always involve children who are actively engaging in dark activities, many times it does. Some believe activities involving witchcraft, for example, are fun and can even provide some type of control over life, but taking part in those dark practices can make participants susceptible to being controlled or manipulated—which is exactly what traffickers do.

Today, most generally don't believe that rituals, playing dark games, joining fraternal orders, being hypnotized, engaging in New Age practices, or consulting psychics will bring about harm. The deception is that these are merely forms of entertainment or mental stimulation. Few see these practices or behaviors as malevolent.

---

1 campaignlive.co.uk/article/dark-arts-creative-magic-rise-gaming/1593085

2 https://www.theesa.com/annual-esa-study-reveals-video-games-universal-appeal-across-generations/

For sure, not many folks believe in or want to consider the reality of satanic cults or ritualistic abuse. They tend to view people discussing these topics as conspiratorial or, at the very least, unrealistic. One therapist (not in my practice) told me she doesn't believe the practices are real because she's never seen evidence of them in her office. There are many things I haven't seen in my office, but I still believe they happen. I've never seen heart surgery performed, but I know it happens.

Most evil activities come in deceptive, tempting packages labeled as "entertainment," "health and wellness," "fame-boosting," or "pleasure." Others materialize in the search for meaning and purpose. Friends or family members can also introduce or force people into participating in darkness directly or indirectly.

As a result, increasing numbers are experiencing spiritual manifestations of evil; my colleagues and I see it in my practice daily. Clients are coming in with struggles that stem from evil.

Spiritual Manifestation Defined

Some would argue that "spiritual manifestation" can also be defined as "spiritual warfare," but I want to clearly differentiate between the terms. Due to the rise in "nones," or people who identify as "spiritual but not religious," and because of the clear biblical distinctions, it is necessary to separate the two.[3] "Spiritual manifestation" is a term I use to describe what unbelievers (non-Christians) experience as they engage in rituals or other practices designed to bring about encounters with spiritual beings. As discussed earlier, many people today are seeking encounters with spiritual beings. If they seek any god other than the Most High God, they will experience manifestations of evil, even though they may not see it as evil in the beginning. Once the involvement with evil has occurred, the manifestations may ensue randomly.

3 Simmons, J. A. "Religious, but Not Spiritual: A Constructive Proposal." *Religions*. 2021; 12(6):433. https://doi.org/10.3390/rel12060433.

"Manifesting" means to make evident or certain by showing, displaying, or practicing rituals to bring about a desired result in life through belief. Spiritual manifestation of evil occurs when people who are seeking spirituality do so from evil beings—whether they know it or not—and they don't seek that spirituality from the Most High God.

There are many ways people practice manifesting today such as aligning their thoughts, emotions, and actions with their desires to bring them into reality, often using techniques like visualization, journaling, and positive affirmations. There are also unintentional ways people can initiate manifestations of evil, such as using divination materials (like tarot cards, pendulums, spirit boards, charms/objects with assigned meanings, and crystal balls); taking hallucinogens or mind-altering substances; becoming obsessed with dark movies/music; being ritualistically abused; living in dark or haunted places; and more. Often, people think certain activities are games or just entertainment, thus are harmless. Let me offer a loving warning: Nothing is farther from the truth. The forces of darkness set out to deceive us in these ways.

In addition, family members may have made choices to engage in evil practices, such as joining fraternal orders or secret societies and engaging in rituals. Abuse that continues from one generation to the next has the potential to continue influencing future generations even if the abuse stops with one generation. Generations of ongoing or ritualistic abuse also have effects that go beyond those who were abused.

Although you may see some of what I call "entry points" as similar causes of mental health concerns, there can be distinct differences. This is concerning, considering that most mental health providers or pastoral counselors aren't asking questions surrounding dark experiences or practices. It can be difficult to discern the differences, but reviewing causes and symptoms can be helpful.

Causes of Spiritual Manifestation

The phrase "open doors" has been used in recent years as a super-spiritual term in both good and bad ways. People might say things like, "This is the year of the open door," or "I'm praying for 'open doors'." While I don't disagree with using this term at times, I encourage you to think about another concept of an "open door"—one that is rarely talked about but definitely should be.

Spiritual manifestation of evil can be defined as "opening doors" to evil influences. Using the analogy of open doors is accurate in explaining this concept, as one can either open a door or a door can be opened for someone.

Further conceptualization of spiritual manifestation involves splitting it into two categories: prisoners and captives. These are biblical terms used to explain the concept I find interestingly related to war. Spiritual forces of darkness are at war with humanity. They want to kill and destroy humans. The warfare in spiritual manifestation is different than it is in the spiritual warfare category, as spiritual manifestations involve humans who haven't yet decided to follow the Most High God. This distinction is important in understanding and treatment.

Prisoners: Imprisoned by Actions

Prisoners comprise the first category of spiritual manifestations. This involves what someone has done to be put into a prison, of sorts. It might also be considered the acceptance of a prison sentence based on one's actions. For example, if you choose to murder someone, you will receive a prison sentence based on that decision to act. Sure, some believe they aren't guilty and have been unfairly imprisoned, but for this analogy, consider the choices made as holding someone prisoner to darkness.

Choices made to be put into a prison of darkness include the following:

- **Agreement with lies (Acts 5:3–4):** This may include holding ungodly beliefs, choosing to agree with lies that lead one to sin, or taking part in any practice or ritual that promotes agreement with truths that fall outside of Scripture. For example, I might agree with the lie that being involved in a fraternal order is the only way to participate in community service. We commonly see agreement with lies having to do with the issue of identity. When people agree with the lie that they were born in the wrong body or with the wrong gender, they invite evil into their life. This is a lie I've seen destroy people and families. Many lies relate to ideas of suicide, abortion, mass shootings, and other death-related activities. A recently developed lie people are believing in increasing numbers is that they need AI to survive.

- **Allowing bitterness and pride to settle into the mind (heart, soul, will, and emotions):** Hebrews 12:15 (NIV) states: "See to it that no one falls short of the grace of God and that no bitter root grows up to cause trouble and defile many." This can involve holding on to things, holding grudges, or feeling as if someone owes us out of our own pride. Bitterness that takes root within leads to many evil outcomes. Revenge is one example. A husband shooting his wife after she leaves him for beating her is an example of this type of bitterness and pride. Bitterness and pride often lead to social isolation.
- **Behaviors** and thoughts of unforgiveness: Matthew 5:40 (NIV) states: "And if anyone wants to sue you and take your shirt, hand over your coat as well." Deciding to not forgive oneself or others can to unimaginable self-destruction obscurity. Some even suggest unforgiveness is the root of most depressive symptoms. People are often hesitant to forgive because they mistake forgiveness with reconciliation. The two are not the same. Additionally, forgiveness doesn't mean we have to agree that the wrong carried out against us is acceptable. Neither does it mean that reconciliation is possible. Forgiveness is about deciding not to drink the poison that causes death. The poison of unforgiveness always kills the person who chooses not to forgive.

- **Making unlawful vows:** Matthew 5:33–37 says: "Again you have heard that it was said to those of old, 'You shall not swear falsely, but shall perform to the Lord what you have sworn.' But I say to you, Do not take an oath at all, either by heaven, for it is the throne of God, or by the earth, for it is his footstool, or by Jerusalem, for it is the city of the great King. And do not take an oath by your head, for you cannot make one hair white or black. Let what you say be simply 'Yes' or 'No'; anything more than this comes from evil." Our words mean something in the view of the Most High God. If we swear by something, He expects us to be truthful. If we promise something, we'd better fulfill the promise. Vows should be made with sincerity. We should use our words cautiously. Our decisions, in turn, should be made with eternity in mind. Evil can be invited in by making unlawful vows. Consider the courtroom practice of placing a hand on the Bible and swearing an oath to "tell the truth." If we then lie, we invite not only legal consequences, but more importantly, personal consequences: allowing evil into our life. In Judges 11, Jephthah made a vow that resulted in the death of his daughter. Today, we see narcissistic pastors take vows to shepherd their people and then they simply seek to rule over them. Unlawful vows are also made in the occult, within cults, and in paganism. Social media is full of harmful words and unlawful vows.
- **Making unfair judgments:** Matthew 5:38 says: "You have heard that it was said, 'An eye for an eye and a tooth for a tooth.' But I say to you, Do not resist the one who is evil. But if anyone slaps you on the right cheek, turn to him the other also." The idea of "an eye for an eye and a tooth for a tooth" represents equal or fair judgments. We don't take out the eye of someone who has slapped us on the wrist. That wouldn't be a fair response. The Most High takes judgments seriously

and expects us to treat others fairly. As an example, an unfair judgment might come in the form of kicking someone out of a church group for wearing the wrong attire. The social unrest in our society is heavily rooted in unfair judgments. If we judge folks unfairly, give out harsh punishments that don't fit the crime, et cetera, we are inviting evil into our life.

- **Involvement in the occult:** Deuteronomy 18:9–14 says: "When you come into the land that the Lord your God is giving you, you shall not learn to follow the abominable practices of those nations. There shall not be found among you anyone who burns his son or his daughter as an offering, anyone who practices divination or tells fortunes or interprets omens, or a sorcerer or a charmer or a medium or a necromancer or one who inquires of the dead, for whoever does these things is an abomination to the Lord. And because of these abominations the Lord your God is driving them out before you. You shall be blameless before the Lord your God, for these nations, which you are about to dispossess, listen to fortune-tellers and to diviners. But as for you, the Lord your God has not allowed you to do this." Scripture clearly forbids any engagement in astrology, witchcraft, black arts, fortune telling, magic, Ouija or spirit boards, tarot card, spiritism, parapsychology and/or Satanism. These practices are prohibited because they involve direct engagement with evil or fallen spirits/beings. Many engage in these practices in the hopes of speaking to a deceased loved one when, in fact, they are speaking with a dark being. They may find comfort originally but eventually darkness will ensue.

Captives: Being Taken Captive

Captives comprise the second category of spiritual manifestations. This refers to suffering due to things we can't necessarily control. Envision being taken captive by enemy forces, as this is exactly what can happen. Captives may include family or generational sin or iniquity. Unresolved trauma is also a form of captivity. These two categories cover a variety of actions that may result in evil bringing someone into captivity by the enemy.

- **Generational iniquity or familial wickedness (Exodus 34:7):** "Iniquity" comes from the Hebrew word *avan*, which means "twisted" or "crooked." It refers to corruption, immorality, corrupt or immoral character or nature, and the distortion or twisting of what is right or good. When I think of winding mountain roads, my stomach turns and I feel nauseated. This is how iniquity should make us feel. In generational iniquity, the twisted actions of one influence not only that person's immediate family but generations to come. An example could refer to a grandfather who molests his grandchildren. This is twisted and disgusting; it should make our stomachs turn. More accurately, it is pure evil, and it affects not just the victim but often has an impact on generations that follow in various ways. It takes people captive to the blackness of evil. Unhealthy attachments are evident here.
- **Unresolved trauma (Proverbs 18:14) or deep, dark trauma:** When someone holds on to dark, horrific, wicked, and twisted circumstances or events that have affected them, evil is allowed to stay until it's dealt with effectively. Some people dissociate to survive the worst forms of abuse; often they don't remember what's happened to them at times. Yet as they age, they begin to experience symptoms and eventually must resolve the dark trauma. In counseling, we see this frequently in those who have dissociative identity disorder. This can also come up for those with an abduction story.

General Symptoms Caused by Evil Influence/Spiritual Manifestation

Several biblical passages outline symptoms of spiritual manifestations of evil and the identification of an evil spirit—or, as some would commonly know it, demon possession. Again, there may be some overlap in mental health symptoms, and the best way to discern is through prayer and good assessment.

- **Dramatic changes in personality (Mark 5:1–20):** Changes often are seen because of dissociation; in other words, personality struggles include dissociative symptoms. These changes may make someone seem to be acting "out of character" or feel as if they have had an out-of-body experience.
- **Changes in sleep patterns (Mark 5: 1–20):** This often appears as sleep paralysis. It could also include excessive sleep or excessive periods without sleep.
- **Increased hostility (Acts 19:16):** Showing anger that leads to harm of oneself or others is one way to identify someone with increased hostility. An example of this might be a family member who loses his mind at a family gathering and starts shooting at others.
- **Self-harm (Mark 5:1–20):** Any attempt of self-harm or suicidal ideation is a symptom of an evil influence.
- **Behavior that humiliates or sabotages (Luke 8:27):** This behavior is often seen in those identified as having narcissistic personality disorder or virtually any other personality disorder. Someone who displays this behavior is extremely frustrating to those closest to them.
- **Aversion to Jesus Christ (Acts 16:17):** This is seen in a person who has a visceral hatred of the name of Jesus Christ in any form, someone who deliberately misuses the Lord's name, or someone who displays hatred for the Most High God.

- **Lack of restraint (Mark 9:22):** If someone is showing signs of superhuman strength in destructive ways, an evil influence is likely behind the behavior. A lack of restraint in other areas, such posting horrible statements or reels on social media and saying later, "I had to do it; I had no choice," might be a signal as well.
- **Trouble with speech/thoughts (Matthew 9:32):** Slurred or disoriented speech isn't always a sign that substance use or abuse is involved; it can be a sign of a demonic or evil presence. I've noticed this in face-to-face interactions and in text messages or other written communications. A vast difference from the person's norm is evident.
- **Physical infirmities or torment (mental) (Matthew 4:24):** This comes in the form of either mental torment to the extent that the person wants to do or take anything to make the thoughts stop or physical torment, like the literal pain of having a thorn in one's side.

In conclusion, *discernment* is key because often mental health struggles mirror spiritual struggles, and vice versa. They also always affect one another. Pray for guidance in discernment from the Holy Spirit. In exploring the root causes of mental issues (anything dealing with thoughts, feelings, and behaviors), good discernment involves good questions. Therefore, I recommend starting with a mental health or psychological assessment with a trained professional. I don't recommend doing online assessments to self-diagnose. Once someone has been assessed and it's been determined that mental health issues alone are not at play, a deeper exploration into spiritual matters is necessary. In other words, if you've discerned that something besides only mental issues is present, begin discerning spiritual matters.

As I began assessing more spiritual matters in counseling, I found that it became essential for me to provide the best service to clients. When I started doing that, however, a standard assessment hadn't yet been designed for mental health professionals to use in diagnosing spiritual influences presenting as mental health problems. So, I created one. In the next chapter, I will provide an assessment I've created to help assess what I call "Other Influences."

QUESTIONS FOR REFLECTION

1. Have you ever seen a spiritual manifestation of evil?
2. Have you ever miscategorized an occurrence in the past as being physical only and never considered whether it had a spiritual aspect?
3. Are any of your loved ones currently struggling with mental health issues? If so, what do you think is the cause?

PRACTICAL APPLICATION

Encouragement for pastoral counselors and mental health professionals:

- Be aware of the ways those around you may be unknowingly engaging in practice of spiritual darkness.
- Speak out against harmful wicked practices. This could be as simple as a social media post or as intentional as a sermon.
- Encourage those you have influence over to pray and fast regarding the growing darkness among those they love.
- Seek training on how to deal biblically with demonic oppression and possession.

Prayer Prompt: *Lord, give me eyes to see and ears to hear when any seemingly simple act is related to darkness. Give me courage to expose the deeds of darkness.*

SCRIPTURE TO CONSIDER

1 Corinthians 10: 20–21:

No, but the sacrifices of pagans are offered to demons, not to God, and I do not want you to be participants with demons.

> You cannot drink the cup of the Lord and the cup of demons too; you cannot have a part in both the Lord's table and the table of demons.

Acts 19:13–16:

> Some Jews who went around driving out evil spirits tried to invoke the name of the Lord Jesus over those who were demon-possessed. They would say, "In the name of the Jesus whom Paul preaches, I command you to come out." Seven sons of Sceva, a Jewish chief priest, were doing this. One day the evil spirit answered them, "Jesus I know, and Paul I know about, but who are you?" Then the man who had the evil spirit jumped on them and overpowered them all. He gave them such a beating that they ran out of the house naked and bleeding.

2 Peter 2:4–10:

> For if God did not spare angels when they sinned, but sent them to hell, putting them in chains of darkness to be held for judgment; if he did not spare the ancient world when he brought the flood on its ungodly people, but protected Noah, a preacher of righteousness, and seven others; if he condemned the cities of Sodom and Gomorrah by burning them to ashes, and made them an example of what is going to happen to the ungodly; and if he rescued Lot, a righteous man, who was distressed by the depraved conduct of the lawless (for that righteous man, living among them day after day, was tormented in his righteous soul by the lawless deeds he saw and heard)—if this is so, then the Lord knows how to rescue the godly from trials and to hold the unrighteous for punishment on the day of judgment. This is especially true of those who follow the corrupt desire of the flesh and despise authority. Bold and arrogant, they are not afraid to heap abuse on celestial beings.

PART FIVE

Overcoming Unseen Dark Influences Clinically and Biblically

Chapter 14

TREATMENT CONSIDERATIONS

The good physician treats the disease; the great physician treats the patient who has the disease.

William Osler

Years ago, I began working with a woman named Sarah, who struggled with anxiety related to health concerns. Every doctor's visit triggered intense apprehension, and anytime she had the slightest ailment, her thoughts were in continual turmoil. Cognitive-behavioral therapy provided some relief, and medication helped ease the tension, but nothing offered complete freedom from her anxiety. That changed when we began to dig deeper, prompted by the research I was doing related to evil influences and spiritual warfare. The change began when I started asking questions I had never asked any client.

Many counselors—both professional and pastoral—often don't ask the right questions in battling the darkness or evil influences in the world. Therapeutic assessments are used to gather information needed for diagnosing and treatment planning.[1]

If we hold to a biblical worldview and accept that battles can be against evil influences, we must learn how to assess these battles. A comprehensive assessment that includes the "weird" questions—those

1 Hawton, Keith, et al. "Assessment of Suicide Risk in Mental Health Practice: Shifting from Prediction to Therapeutic Assessment, Formulation, and Risk Management. *The Lancet Psychiatry*, Volume 9, Issue 11, 922–928.

otherwise not asked about how evil may have gained a foothold and led to the client's problems—is beneficial in counseling or in general. Good assessment can lead to better comprehension and answers! Jesus asked lots of questions to those He served. In fact, it was one of His primary tools for teaching.

Again, as no standardized assessment was available when I started incorporating this new approach to my practice, I developed my own using Dr. Michael Heiser's work (as discussed in previous chapters), alongside the work of other professionals such as clinical psychologist Dr. Laura Sanger (nolongerenslaved.com), since they helped me understand the spiritual battles people are truly in. I needed a clinical way to help clients identify how certain unseen influences might be affecting them, so I designed questions and, in turn, developed a biblical treatment model. The assessment seeks to provide deeper understanding and allows for tailored treatments; it's a comprehensive list of any factors known to open doors to the influence of spiritual darkness. In designing the assessment, I discussed the subject with other therapists and pastors, read books, listened to podcasts, and consulted with Dr. Sanger, who has done extensive work in this area, to provide the most comprehensive list of questions possible.

Back to Sarah. She was one of the first clients I guided through my assessment questions. After years of mental health sessions and treatments in our time together, I felt encouraged that these questions I developed would lead to the answers we had been looking for all along. Initially, I initiated a basic conversation about potential evil influences in her past.

After that session, Sarah spent time in prayer. She then went to a car wash, where she caught a whiff of marijuana; the smell transported her back to a childhood memory, triggering a forgotten experience: "The smell took me back to that Wiccan house," she later told me. "God clarified that was it. I hadn't thought about that friend or her house or the smell since sixth grade. The smell connected it all. Insane. I have only smelled marijuana twice in my life: at her house and at that car wash."

Through prayer and discernment, Sarah remembered exactly *when* the anxiety about her health began: when she had gone to a neighbor's house in the sixth grade. The neighbor's mom was a practicing Wiccan. She knew smoking marijuana was wrong and she felt as if it could make her sick. This, coupled with the mom's dark involvement as a Wiccan, seemed to be the cause of her anxiety about feeling sick. Therefore, each time she felt sick or had to go to the doctor from that moment on it was as if dark forces were influencing her to feel anxious. Seemingly, shame was a feeling she associated with sickness or a doctor due to her being at a house she associated with evil. Sarah finally felt a sense of freedom, having identified the root of her anxiety about health problems. Once we knew the root, the application of biblical treatment began, leading her to a place of ultimate healing!

Many who have struggled for years eventually believe full healing is not possible. The good news is that full healing is always possible! Healing may come instantly or gradually but bringing the matter before the Lord and finding a godly counselor or minister to help find the root of the problem may be a vital aspect of and first step toward treating the issue.

"Treatment" is a term I use as a mental health clinician to describe how I encourage healing among individuals. It may involve a variety of different strategies and methods, depending on the individual. The Most High God has given counselors and others many approaches, skills, and other ways to help those who have mental health problems. Some considerations should be reviewed within each category discussed: Mental health, spiritual warfare, and spiritual manifestations.

Treatment for Those with Mental Health Problems

In addressing matters of mental health and spirituality, specific considerations should include preparation for counseling (such as addressing physical concerns first); having a basic understanding of counseling; finding a good counselor; and learning about different forms of treatment. Mental health involves the heart, will, emotions, and brain, which are all part of the physical body. However, the medical community makes major distinctions between physical and mental health.

Resolve physical matters first. As a counselor, one of the first things I encourage clients to do is to get checked out by a medical doctor, if possible, to rule out any ways there might be a physical source of pain leading or contributing to mental health problems. Physical problems are often the easiest to treat and thus should be the first area explored. For example, someone might have a hormone imbalance that is causing insomnia, which in turn results in relational problems, leading the person to seek help from a counselor. Once the hormone issue is diagnosed and corrected, the person sleeps better and, consequently, relationships improve.

Have a basic understanding of counseling. Professional counselors are trained to help people with social and emotional problems in many areas of life by building safe and trusting relationships and implementing a diverse set of strategies and techniques. Counseling options can include individual, couples, group, pastoral, retreats, or any combination of these options. Proverbs 11:14 states, "When there is no guidance, a nation falls, but there is success in the abundance of counselors."

Find a good counselor. Anyone seeking mental health support should look for someone who is a good fit personally. It may help to get a referral from a trusted source and check out counselor profiles online to try to pick up on any points of connection, shared values, or agreement on treatment approaches. It's also appropriate to contact counselors being considered and ask them about their style, approach, and/or religious views. A good counselor is willing to meet people where they are by allowing them the freedom to be genuine and honest as they share their stories and struggles without judgment—all while coming up with a treatment plan. Finding a counselor who is a good fit is vital for healing.

Understand basic forms of treatment. Treatments include talking with a professional (talk therapy) to address problematic thoughts, emotions, and behaviors. Specific types may include cognitive behavioral therapy, dialectical behavior therapy, and interpersonal therapy, among others. Cognitive behavioral therapy is one of the most effective evidenced-based treatments—and I believe it is a biblical one that involves "taking thoughts captive." At times and when appropriate, medication may be discussed in addition to therapy.

In fact, a common question I receive as a Christian counselor is, "Is it okay for a Christian to take medication for mental health struggles?" My answer to that would be invalid outside of a biblical view. So, looking at the Bible, we often see medication or medicinal forms of substances used for healing; see, for example, Isaiah 38:21; Jeremiah 30:13; Ezekiel 47:12; and Revelation 22:2). With this in mind, I answer within this context by saying, "Yes, at times, it is beneficial. However, it should never serve as a crutch or as a stand-alone treatment for serious issues." This is similar to saying a cardiologist wouldn't recommend heart medication without including in the treatment plan other changes or therapies, such as exercise or physical therapy. Healing may be a long, nonlinear journey. In other words, it doesn't necessarily feel like moving toward optimum mental health at a steady pace, one step after another. It most often feels like a roller coaster ride, but eventually healing will happen. That said, if mental health treatments have been ineffective for an extended period (my recommendation is at least three months or twelve weekly sessions), it may be time to consider exploring supernatural/unseen realm factors such as oppression and/or possession of evil that may be manifesting as a mental health struggle. One exception may be if someone clearly discloses aspects related to spiritual darkness.

We should also be aware of attempts to "over spiritualize" issues or to forcibly translate deep trauma into their own personal faith or spiritual issues. This has often been called "spiritual bypass." Issues may or may not be dealt with this way, especially at first. This isn't about looking for root causes, which could be spiritual from an influence standpoint, but rather when individuals blame themselves for not "doing enough" in the past or present, resulting in a misinterpretation of the Most High God's justice. It could also include blaming evil influences without considering a person's choices or free will.

Treatment for Those in Spiritual Warfare (For Believers)

When considering treatment for those living in the oppression of spiritual warfare, Scripture is the ultimate authority. Therefore, biblical instruction is essential in that it establishes the foundation of obeying commands of the Most High God daily; crucifying the flesh or human desires (dying to oneself); putting on the full armor of the Most High God; following Jesus' example; and destroying arguments and opinions against the Most High God.

Daily obeying the Most High God's commands: The Ten Commandments are a great place to start working on behaviors that honor the Most High God and are for our good. Above all, it's important to remember to love God and others in words and actions. This should involve sharing the gospel. For example, even when we're angry, we need to obey God and not let that anger rise to the level of hatred. Hatred will lead to the enemy's camp and defeat. Ephesians 2:1–2 states:

> As for you, you were dead in your transgressions and sins in which you used to live when you followed the ways of this world and of the ruler of the kingdom of the air, the spirit who is now at work in those who are disobedient.

Crucifying fleshly desires, thoughts, and behaviors; dying to self: This involves evaluating self-centered tendencies and unhealthy behaviors and changing them to be in line with what Christ would honor. For example, we should kill any desire we have for someone who is not our spouse. This starts with prayers for that person as a brother or sister. If we give into the desires of the flesh, the enemy wins. Galatians 2:20 says:

> I have been crucified with Christ and I no longer live, but Christ lives in me. The life I now live in the body, I live by faith in the Son of God, who loved me and gave himself for me. (NIV).

Putting on the armor of God: This involves daily and even multiple times a day, visualizing putting on salvation, righteousness, truth, and peace (of the gospel) and picking up the sword of the Spirit (the Bible) and the shield of faith. We should stay alert and pray without ceasing about everything. This armor is effective in combatting the enemies of the Most High God. One example of using the armor is to hold tight to the truth as a belt when the enemy whispers a lie! Ephesians 6:13–18 states:

> Finally, be strong in the Lord and in his mighty power. Put on the full armor of God, so that you can take your stand against the devil's schemes. For our struggle is not against flesh and blood, but against the rulers, against the authorities, against the powers of this dark world and against the spiritual forces of evil in the heavenly realms. Therefore, put on the full armor of God, so that when the day of evil comes, you may be able to stand your ground, and after you have done everything, to stand. Stand firm then, with the belt of truth buckled around your waist, with the breastplate of righteousness in place, and with your feet fitted with the readiness that comes from the gospel of peace. In addition to all this, take up the shield of faith, with which you can extinguish all the flaming arrows of the evil one. Take the helmet of salvation and the sword of the Spirit, which is the word of God. And pray in the Spirit on all occasions with all kinds of prayers and requests. With this in mind, be alert and always keep on praying for all the Lord's people. (NIV).

Following Jesus' example of combatting the enemy: When face to face with the enemy, we should fast and pray, respond with the truth of Scripture (which requires studying and memorization), remember who we are as imagers of the Most High God, and command Satan to flee. Then we should raise a "Hallelujah!" and praise Him with thanksgiving as we worship. When the enemy tempts us with worldly pleasures, we can simply remind ourselves that we serve the Most High who owns it all. Matthew 4:1–11 states:

> Then Jesus was led by the Spirit into the wilderness to be tempted by the devil. After fasting forty days and forty nights, he was hungry. The tempter came to him and said, "If you are the Son of God, tell these stones to become bread." Jesus answered, "It is written: Man shall not live on bread alone, but on every word that comes from the mouth of God." Then the devil took him to the holy city and had him stand on the highest point of the temple. "If you are the Son of God," he said, "throw yourself down. For it is written: 'He will command his angels concerning you, and they will lift you up in their hands, so that you will not strike your foot against a stone.'"
>
> Jesus answered him, "It is also written: 'Do not put the Lord your God to the test.' Again, the devil took him to a very high mountain and showed him all the kingdoms of the world and their splendor. "All this I will give you," he said, "if you will bow down and worship me." Jesus said to him, "Away from me, Satan! For it is written: 'Worship the Lord your God and serve him only.'" Then the devil left him, and angels came and attended him.

Destroying arguments and opinions against the knowledge of God: As we obey God by taking thoughts captive, we should destroy any argument the enemy is trying to use and throw out any opinion that goes against the Most High God. Hiding His Word in our hearts (through studying and memorization) will help us discern what arguments and opinions are against the knowledge of God. If the enemies of the Most High say, "You are worthless," we can destroy that argument by saying, "I am fearfully and wonderfully made by the Most High God."

> For though we walk in the flesh, we are not waging war according to the flesh. For the weapons of our warfare are not of the

> flesh but have divine power to destroy strongholds. We destroy arguments and every lofty opinion raised against the knowledge of God, and take every thought captive to obey Christ, being ready to punish every disobedience, when your obedience is complete. (2 Corinthians 10:3–6)

Spiritual warfare is ultimately about persevering. It is having an unwavering faith in the Most High God as we continue to share the gospel. We will each time we obey the Most High's holy commands and prayerfully follow Jesus.

Treatment of Those under Evil Influence (Oppression/Possession)

Those seeking healing for the effects of evil influences should take the following steps: 1) Above all, be willing to engage in the treatment process. In addition, 2) look for qualified help: a counselor, pastor, or minister who has the specific ability to deal with folks who've been affected by spiritual influences. Finally, 3) the professional should assess how evil was introduced into the person's life and then follow a biblical and clinical model of treatment.

Let's look more closely at these steps:

Willingness to engage in treatment: Treatment of those affected by evil influences is only effective if it's evident that someone who's suffering really wants help. This willingness to go through the treatment involves accepting Christ as Lord and Savior—a decision that may begin with something as simple as attending a church or asking a pastor for prayer.

Treatment should never be forced; it's important for the person to be actively seeking help. *This is because people under demonic or evil oppression or possession don't respond well to therapy.* They may change their mind during treatment (which is likely), but at some point, they need to have expressed the desire to get help. The Apostle Paul teaches in the book of Ephesians how to battle evil, yet he never encourages believers to confront or seek out evil spirits.

Seeking a qualified help: A counselor, pastor, or minister should have the specific ability to deal with those who have been influenced by evil spirits. One of the first and most important aspects is the willingness of the helper to combat evil influences. Often counselors feel unskilled at helping clients with spiritual issues or with very dark issues that could be related to spirituality. Pastors and ministers at times may feel the same.

A lack of skill should not stop those who want to help those who are engaged in this type of battle. The most important qualification, in fact, isn't skill, a degree, or training, but rather the ability to let the Holy Spirit work in and through them to display the fruit of the spirit (love, joy, peace, patience, kindness, gentleness, longsuffering, self-control, and faithfulness) as they sit with those battling darkness. I propose a specific treatment model in the next chapter, but the fruit of the spirit is foundational, as is walking in the authority of Jesus. Skill will come but will never supersede a posture of *love* for the human imager in need of help. Preparation should also include understanding what scripture teaches about when and how to address an evil spirit.

Assess for darkness accurately and treat clinically and biblically. First assess a person's willingness to get help. One way to do so is by giving them homework to be completed between the first and second sessions. The assignment could be as simple as getting a medical evaluation. Use trauma-informed care that includes making the person feel safe (physically and emotionally), building trust, giving the person choices, empowering him or her and allowing for collaboration. Medical and mental health evaluations should be completed prior to spiritual-specific treatments before it's possible to properly evaluate the presence of evil influences.

Assessment is vital in treating the effects of evil influences successfully and it allows counselors to identify where evil could have been introduced and thus where treatment should begin.

QUESTIONS FOR REFLECTION

1. Which mental health, spiritual warfare, and/or spiritual manifestation treatment considerations stand out the most?
2. Why is a person's willingness to be treated important?
3. What prevents most people from helping others who are battling darkness?

PRACTICAL APPLICATION

Encouragement for pastoral counselors and mental health professionals:

- Review current practices and adjust according to the suggestions.
- Adapt referral practices based on whether a counselor regards Scripture as the ultimate authority for truth.
- Always evaluate a person's willingness to engage in treatment before beginning treatment of the symptoms of any evil influence.
- Provide a sermon or teaching on how willingness to be healed is vital.

Prayer Prompt: *Lord, fill me with the Holy Spirit as I trust in you to heal others. Show me what I need to know each step to effectively help each person you allow me to assist.*

SCRIPTURE TO CONSIDER

Galatians 5:22–23:

> But the fruit of the Spirit is love, joy, peace, forbearance, kindness, goodness, faithfulness, gentleness and self-control. Against such things there is no law.

1 Corinthians 16:14:

> Let all that you do be done in love.

1 John 4:16:

So we have come to know and to believe the love that God has for us. God is love, and whoever abides in love abides in God, and God abides in him.

1 John 4:7–8:

Beloved, let us love one another, for love is from God, and whoever loves has been born of God and knows God. Anyone who does not love does not know God, because God is love.

1 Corinthians 13:4–8:

Love is patient and kind; love does not envy or boast; it is not arrogant or rude. It does not insist on its own way; it is not irritable or resentful; it does not rejoice at wrongdoing, but rejoices with the truth. Love bears all things, believes all things, hopes all things, endures all things. Love never ends. As for prophecies, they will pass away; as for tongues, they will cease; as for knowledge, it will pass away.

Philippians 4:13 (NKJV):

I can do all things through Christ who strengthens me.

Chapter 15

ASSESSING THE ISSUES: ASKING THE RIGHT QUESTIONS

To ask the right questions is already half a solution of a problem.
CARL JUNG, Swiss psychiatrist and psychotherapist

From law enforcement officers to attorneys and judges, questions are an essential part of the legal system. The enemies of the Most High God are legal in nature. They love to take our choices to the divine council to try to bring charges against us. Their charges involve the ways they've been able to access people and influence them to allow evil in. Of course, the charges also involve times when people have harmed others. So, in battling these evil entities, we must determine where the darkness entered so we know what they're holding over us. At the very least, assessing the entry point of the darkness is a form of exposing it. In his letter to the Ephesians, Paul instructs us to "take no part in the unfruitful works of darkness, but instead expose them" (Ephesians 5:11, ESV).

A good assessment should be comprehensive and should include open-ended questions to allow those being treated to give more comprehensive answers.[1] People are often more comfortable writing or giving verbal answers to open-ended questions versus other forms of assessment questions.

Assessments of evil influence should also address internal issues such as mental health problems that haven't been helped by traditional

1 Geer John G., "What Do Open-ended Questions Measure?" *Public Opinion Quarterly*, Volume 52, Issue 3, Fall 1988, Pages 365–367, https://doi.org/10.1086/269113

mental health treatments. Questions about involvement in the occult or witchcraft, engagement in dark-themed entertainment, owning cursed items, or an obsession with social media are considered internal. Personal addictions, strange or unbiblical sexual practices, or any use of hallucinogenic or dangerous substances should also be included when assessing internal issues.

External struggles include family challenges or influences. Ideally, those being treated should be asked to go as far back as four generations to identify external struggles. Some suggest going farther back, but the Bible teaches that our sins impact the third and fourth generations, and God's grace covers us beyond that point. However, going back as far as possible wouldn't hurt. Conversely, some may have no knowledge of their family history. In these cases, they should be encouraged to ask family members, do other research, and pray. The Most High is faithful; if people really want healing, He will reveal what needs to be healed. Just like assessing internal issues, evaluating external issues should include asking about foreign objects that might have attachments to the occult (for example, home décor that may have been cursed), addictions, unresolved illnesses (mental or physical illnesses that have been passed down), abuse, negative words, broken homes/divorce, and/or sexual sin. These external issues aren't caused or introduced *by* those who are suffering; rather, they've been done *to* the person or in the presence of the person. For example, although someone may not have bought a haunted house, the person's parents might have.

When assessing for the presence of evil influences, pray for discernment and protection as you try to help the person identify potential areas of healing. As mentioned in the previous chapter, when I became interested in the spiritual dimension of mental health, I realized there simply wasn't any kind of a standard assessment mental health professionals could use. Although some deliverance ministers and Catholic priests have evaluation protocols, health providers and everyday pastors likely have nothing. Therefore, I created the assessment that follows—doing so prayerfully and over time amongst other trained professionals, and with the approval of someone I respect in this space, Dr. Laura Sanger. The assessment includes internal and external issues and features open-ended questions.

Overview: Other Influences Assessment by Dr. Natalie Atwell

Note: I gave this assessment its title intentionally not mentioning "evil spirits or influences" to not scare some practitioners or clients. "Other" simply refers to matters not addressed in typical mental health assessments.

This assessment may serve as a guide in understanding possible, non-traditional influences that could be affecting health (physical, mental, relational, and spiritual) in various ways.

The overview provides a general idea of what the assessment is about and what questions it will likely include.

- **What is it?** This assessment may be used to shed light on the struggles someone may be experiencing that may be unexplained by other types of evaluation.
- **Who can use it?** Those who find this useful may include counselors, therapists, pastors, teachers, parents, law enforcement, investigators, faculty, researchers, and anyone else who's interested in learning more about non-traditional influences on mental health.
- **When is it used?** This may be considered for use when traditional mental health treatments (including counseling and/or medication) have been found unsuccessful over an extended period.
- **What types of questions are included?** The assessment features open-ended questions about a variety of topics, including strange sexual, spiritual, emotional, or physical behaviors, happenings, and/or involvement; familial involvement in organizations that may be involved in rituals; occult

involvement; and more. Some questions may seem vague or open-ended, which is intentional because this approach allows people to share their experiences without being "led" to what they might consider are the "expected answers." A few of the questions may seem confusing to some people, they will be clear to those who need to respond.

The information collected via the assessment is used for exploratory purposes. Each provider may use it differently to determine a treatment plan and/or to decide the next steps to take in collaboration with those they're treating. If the clients being assessed confirm involvement in or experience with any of the potential influences mentioned in the questions, they may be referred to a professional (counselor, therapist, or pastor) who's willing to discuss and treat any concerns with a biblically and clinically sound perspective.

Other Influences Assessment by Dr. Natalie Atwell

Please answer each question below honestly and provide any details or information you are comfortable sharing or believe it's important to note.

The example responses below are not included in the assessment given to clients. Assessment questions may be asked verbally by a counselor, or the clients may write their answers.

1. Does anyone in the household or family have what you would consider strange or different beliefs? If so, please explain.
   Examples: My father's cousin was a psychic. My grandmother has an altar in her home. My mother was raised in a legalistic, cult-like church.
2. Do you know your family history from the third or fourth generation back? If so, please explain. List any problematic issues you know of (i.e., addiction, adultery, abuse).

Examples: My grandfather was an alcoholic. My grandfather cheated on my grandmother.

3. Has anyone in your family ever gone missing or disclosed some type of abduction story?
   Examples: I have a cousin who went missing for a year. I was told it was drug related but I'm not sure. I have no memory of a few days during summer camp, and they found me in a field where I do not remember going.
4. Have you ever had a near-death experience (i.e., wherein you felt you died and came back to life)?
   Examples: Maybe. I had surgery when I was a child, and can remember what the operating room looks like. My mom went into cardiac arrest and was said to be dead for ten minutes when I was younger.
5. Have you ever been what some would consider obsessed with horror movies (very dark-themed) and/or dark music? If so, please explain.
   Examples: When I was a teenager, I loved watching scary movies. I play video games that have dark magic in them. I enjoy dark music or something called suicidal music.
6. Do you live near or normally visit any places associated with any strange happenings or dark history (i.e., Stonewall Jackson Training School is rumored to be haunted, and it has a dark history associated with child abuse)? If so, please explain.
   Examples: I live on a lake where there have been many horrific accidents and even some suicides in certain areas. It has been said to be filled with large, scary sea creatures seen by men who work at a nuclear plant near the lake. Bigfoot is said to be in the woods in a town near where I grew up.
7. Have you ever routinely engaged in fantasy/role-playing games, and/or would you or someone you are close to consider you addicted to technology (including social media, i.e., TikTok)? If so, please explain.

Examples: I likely have an obsession with social media. I often compare myself to others, and I want to become an influencer. My sister is an influencer, and it was crazy how, one day, her social media seemingly took off. I watch TikToks about astrology. I used to have relationships with people online through chat rooms and gaming applications. I'd rather talk to people online than in person.

8. Have you ever mentally attempted to travel outside of your physical body or had someone try to convince you to do so? If so, please explain.
   Examples: When I was in my twenties, I dabbled in New Age practices such as dream journaling, wherein I tried to engage in astral projection.
9. Do you believe in alternative approaches to spirituality? (i.e., not mainstream faith practices). If so, please explain.
   Examples: I used to meditate as a part of my New Age spirituality. I do yoga often and lean into its spiritual aspects.
10. Have you ever participated in any mystical practices? If so, please explain.
    Examples: I often chant to a higher power. I believe the divine is in nature.
11. Do you engage in daily or occasional astrological readings? Add any details you want to share.
    Examples: My mom taught me to read my horoscope daily. I rely on this and find comfort in the readings.
12. Have you seen a psychic, healer, or spiritual advisor? Add any details you want to share.
    Examples: My dad's girlfriend had a psychic come to our house for a reading. I haven't been able to sleep in that room since. My friends and I had readings done on a girls' trip.
13. Have you ever been hypnotized? Add any details you want to share.

Example: I attempted to be hypnotized to relieve anxiety once by a mental health person. It helped for a while, I think.

14. Do you or have you ever used crystals? Add any details you want to share.

    Example: One time I was going through a tough time emotionally, and while getting acupuncture, the lady asked if I wanted to put a crystal near my heart to help with my emotional pain. I got rid of the crystal later, but I used it at the time.

15. Do you believe in alternative medicines like reiki, kratom, hallucinogens, psychedelics, et cetera.? If so, please explain and discuss any usage or experiences.

    Examples: I take kratom occasionally. I've thought about going on a retreat to do ayahuasca.

16. Have you ever engaged in witchcraft? If so, please explain.

    Examples: When I was younger, I was friends with a girl who liked to put curses on kids who were mean. My grandmother uses Santeria practices that involve cursing items.

17. Have you ever used tarot cards, a Ouija board, or other divination materials? If so, please explain.

    Examples: I use tarot cards occasionally. When I was a teenager, my friends and I played with a Ouija board.

18. Have you ever tried to channel (entered a meditative or trancelike state to convey messages from) things? If so, please explain.

    Examples: I have tried to channel energy to speak to my dead grandmother. I like to meditate to get out of reality for a moment.

19. Do you believe in manifesting as inspired by Hermeticism, transcendentalism, or other spiritual practices outside of monotheism? If so, please explain.

    Example: I have read books about manifesting success. I have tried this and continue to manifest what I want.

20. Are you or is anyone in your family a member of a fraternal secret society or similar type organization outside of a church, mosque, or synagogue? Add any details you want to share.
    Examples: My paternal great-grandfather was in the Woodmen of the World fraternal organization. My father is a Freemason.
21. Would you or someone else consider a church or group experience you've had to be similar to something that might take place in a cult? If so, please explain.
    Example: When I was in my thirties, I was a part of a church that felt like a cult. There were expectations for members to do certain things, like pay certain amounts of money. If you didn't do those things, you were kicked out. You were required to dress and act certain ways.
22. Have you ever been sexually abused in a ritualistic way (abuse that occurs or occurred in a context where symbols or activities have superstitious, supernatural, or religious connotations)? Add any details you want to share.
    Example: My grandmother molested me and told me it was for my good and that there were big plans for me for not telling and being obedient.
23. Have you ever engaged in pornography to the extent that it became addictive? Add any details you want to share.
    Examples: I have struggled in the past with pornography. My spouse also struggles with pornography.
24. Have you ever engaged in sexual activities that involved symbols or activities that had superstitious, supernatural, or religious connotations; or that had an interest in bondage, dominance, discipline, submission, masochism, sadism (i.e., BDSM), or other alternative sexual practices? Add any details you want to share.
    Examples: When the book *Fifty Shades of Gray* came out, I read it and wanted to try some of the things it mentioned.

25. Have you ever engaged in or attempted to become involved with any nontraditional sexual practices or relationships with humans, animals, objects, et cetera? Add any details you want to share.
    Example: My grandmother who molested me made me do things to her dog.
26. Have you ever been trafficked (been compelled or coerced into providing) for sex or other services? Add any details you want to share.
    Example: When I was younger, my uncle used to have his friends come over and I was made to have sex with them for money.
27. Do you have a history of sexual abuse as a child?
    Examples: My parents abused me physically. My grandmother molested me. A pastor abused me sexually.

Please add anything else you would like to share:

____

____

____

____

____

____

Disclaimers/Results: The information collected on the assessment is used for exploratory purposes only. Each provider or individual may use it differently to determine treatment planning and/or necessary next steps in collaboration with the individual.

If someone confirms involvement in or experience with anything on the assessment, the person may be referred to a professional (counselor/therapist, pastor, et cetera) who is willing to discuss and treat any concerns in any way related to answers.

Please use our digital Assessments Form to be connected with a Mental Warrior Consulting counselor.

•••

While most people won't answer all these questions, examples are provided for context. Meanwhile, every person who has been assessed at my counseling practice has answered at least one or more of these questions. We're actively collecting data to enable us to do more research and continue improving treatments to help our clients find healing. A sample assessment is included in the appendix. If you would like to use it in your own practice, please feel free to do so. Please consider sharing results by entering the data for those you serve at the following: https://forms.gle/NQBVZkGYSYTNdHpZ7.

By understanding and addressing the root cause or potential way evil was introduced, whether mental, physical, or spiritual, true healing can be achieved by the power of the Holy Spirit. Once the assessment has been completed, each area of concern should be dealt with through a biblically sound and clinically effective plan. This should include following a biblical model of dealing with evil, such as we find in Mark 5:1–20. A clinically effective plan should include trauma-informed language and evidence-based techniques such as cognitive behavioral therapy.

Reflect on and Review Dr. Atwell's Assessment

Examine and explore areas of potential odd or nontraditional influences in your own life.

QUESTIONS FOR REFLECTION

1. How do you feel about the questions on the assessment?
2. Which questions were the hardest to answer personally?
3. Will you consider discussing issues assessed with a counselor or pastor?

PRACTICAL APPLICATION

Encouragement for pastoral counselors and mental health professionals:

- Use a good assessment when helping others understand what might have influenced their struggles.
- Be bold in asking the right questions.
- Encourage those you have influence over to use good assessments such as the Other Influences Assessment included here.
- Seek out training on assessment as needed
- Teach others the art of asking good questions.

Prayer Prompt: *Lord, make me bold as I ask hard questions and seek deeper answers to my own struggles and the struggles of others. Lead me to the right answers.*

SCRIPTURE TO CONSIDER

James 2:19:

> You believe that there is one God. Good! Even the demons believe that—and shudder.

Jeremiah 33:3:

> Call to me and I will answer you and will tell you great and hidden things that you have not known.

Matthew 16:13–15:

> Now when Jesus came into the district of Caesarea Philippi, he asked his disciples, "Who do people say that the Son of Man is?" And they said, "Some say John the Baptist, others say Elijah, and others Jeremiah or one of the prophets." He said to them, "But who do you say that I am?

Philippians 4:6:

> Do not be anxious about anything, but in everything by prayer and supplication with thanksgiving let your requests be made known to God.

Chapter 16

EQUIPPED FOR BATTLE: SUGGESTIONS FOR TREATMENT

The devil can cite scripture for his purpose.

WILLIAM SHAKESPEARE, The Merchant of Venice

The devil is a better theologian than any of us and is a devil still.

A. W. TOZER, American missionary, pastor, and author

The devil, the proud spirit, cannot endure to be mocked.

THOMAS MORE, English statesman, theologian, and author

Many do not recognize the fact as they ought, that Satan has got men fast asleep in sin and that it is his great device to keep them so. He does not care what we do if he can do that. We may sing songs about the sweet by and by, preach sermons and say prayers until doomsday, and he will never concern himself about us, if we don't wake anybody up. But if we awake the sleeping sinner he will gnash on us with his teeth. This is our work—to wake people up.

CATHERINE BOOTH, co-founder of the Salvation Army

If you've ever met someone who has been healed from a mental or physical ailment, you will know it—most likely because they talk about it often. I love the stories in Scripture of the times Jesus healed people. In the story of the man healed of leprosy, Jesus told him to tell no one:

> Then Jesus said to him, "Don't tell anyone about this. Instead, go to the priest and let him examine you. Take along the offering required in the law of Moses for those who have been healed of leprosy. This will be a public testimony that you have been cleansed." (Matthew 8:4, NLT)

In Mark 7, we learn that although Jesus told people not to tell others what He had done, they couldn't help themselves. I'm not sure about you, but I understand. Whether I find a supplement that helps me with an ache or a prayer has been answered, I can't help but tell others!

Have you ever had this experience? You found something that worked, so you want to tell others. Maybe it came from people noticing changes in you and asking about the difference. This is likely why TikTok influencers can sell products—because they've had a personal experience with something positive. When healing is personal, it's very hard not to share the good news with those we love.

It's the same in counseling. Since I've started doing this work, many people have asked to see clinicians at my practice for treatment of spiritual matters and darkness. While we are humbled by and grateful for the referrals, we want and need *many* therapists and pastors all over the world to begin assessing and treating evil influences because they're becoming more prevalent as time passes. Just like the leper who was healed didn't want to keep the good news to himself, neither do I. So, since God has given me the knowledge about new ways to assess potential evil influences in clients' lives, I can't keep the information to myself; I want to share a clinical and biblical way of treating evil we're using.

Treatment Foundation

Once the root of the evil has been discovered (exposed) through the assessment, biblical treatment can be administered if the person is willing and is walking in the authority of Christ and Scripture. Biblical treatment of evil influence that can mirror mental illness should be based in love and not fear, shame, or other negative emotions. Jesus gave us the perfect example of how to get rid of evil and find freedom in Him, so we should model what He did. This also requires us to sit with people in a posture of love, to remind them or teach them what it means to be a human imager of God, and to encourage them to speak the name of Jesus as they live.

1. **Following Jesus' model:** My proposed method of treatment includes modeling the way Jesus dealt with unclean spirits in Mark 5:1–20 and other passages of Scripture, such as 2 Chronicles 7:14, while also using evidence-based, cognitive behavioral therapeutic techniques. We'll discuss Mark 5:1–20 in detail below. Second Chronicles 7:14 states: "If my people who are called by my name will humble themselves, and pray and seek My face, and turn from their wicked ways, then I will hear from heaven, forgive their sin and heal their land" (NIV). Good theology matters!
2. **Sitting with others in a posture of love:** The foundation of treatment must be a trusting relationship. *Panim/paneh*, the Hebrew word for "face," is mentioned in Scripture more than 2,100 times. In addition to "face," it is also translated as "presence," "surface," "front," "before," and "countenance." It involves a relationship and closeness. When we seek God's face, we are seeking His presence. *When we sit with others in a healing setting, we're asking God to allow us time in the presence of another as we invite the Holy Spirit to do the work of healing through us.* We must sit as God would with others in a posture and mindset of love.

People may frustrate us along the way; they may even bring up trigger issues. But in all matters throughout this process, *love* must be our posture for treatment to be effective. Jesus came in love and remained in it through the end. When we combat darkness, lots of evil things may manifest, but we are to remain in love. Love is what the enemies of the Most High God hate; they cannot stand to be in its presence. This love also must be the love of Christ working in us; no other form of love will work. Memorizing 1 John 4:16–21 may be a great foundational step to solidify this in our minds so that love flows out of all we do:

> And so, we know and rely on the love God has for us. God is love. Whoever lives in love lives in God, and God in them. This is how love is made complete among us so that we will have confidence on the day of judgment: In this world we are like Jesus. There is no fear in love. But perfect love drives out fear, because fear has to do with punishment. The one who fears is not made perfect in love. We love because he first loved us. Whoever claims to love God yet hates a brother or sister is a liar. For whoever does not love their brother and sister, whom they have seen, cannot love God, whom they have not seen. And he has given us this command: Anyone who loves God must also love their brother and sister. (NIV)

3. **Reminding or teaching the definition of "human":** We must remember the importance of teaching or reminding those we're counseling what it means to be human, and we need to make sure they understand this as the foundation of their identity. This involves good theology. As humans, we are imagers of the Most High God on earth; this is a very high calling. The "human" status is our identity and what our lives should be about: representing the Most High God on earth. It's the very thing the enemies of the Most High God hate and envy.
4. **Speaking the name of Jesus as we walk with Christ:** Many people believe we can simply "speak the name of Jesus" and the enemies of the Most High God will retreat. This can be effective if we're speaking the name of Jesus in all that

we do. It isn't just about what we say. It's about the character we're operating in, whose ways we're imitating, and who we're representing. Christ overcame our enemies, and we can overcome temporary daily battles as we look to what He did on the cross, but our actions must back up our words for us to walk in victory. Our lives should be examples of effective Christ-followers who image the Most High God.

Biblical Example

So they came to the other side of the lake, to the region of the Gerasenes. Just as Jesus was getting out of the boat, a man with an unclean spirit came from the tombs and met him. He lived among the tombs, and no one could bind him anymore, not even with a chain. For his hands and feet had often been bound with chains and shackles, but he had torn the chains apart and broken the shackles into pieces. No one was strong enough to subdue him. Each night and every day among the tombs and in the mountains, he would cry out and cut himself with stones. When he saw Jesus from a distance, he ran and bowed down before him. Then he cried out with a loud voice, "Leave me alone, Jesus, Son of the Most High God! I implore you by God—do not torment me!" (For Jesus had said to him, "Come out of that man, you unclean spirit!") Jesus asked him, "What is your name?" And he said, "My name is Legion, for we are many." He begged Jesus repeatedly not to send them out of the region. There on the hillside, a great herd of pigs was feeding. And the demonic spirits begged him, "Send us into the pigs. Let us enter them." Jesus gave them permission. So, the unclean spirits came out and went into the pigs. Then the herd rushed down the steep slope into the lake, and about 2,000 were drowned in the lake.

Now the herdsmen ran off and spread the news in the town and countryside, and the people went out to see what had happened. They came to Jesus and saw the demon-possessed man sitting there, clothed and in his right mind—the one who had the "Legion"—and they were afraid. Those who had seen what had happened to the demon-possessed man reported it, and they also told about the pigs. Then they began to beg Jesus to leave their region. As he was getting into the boat, the man who had been demon-possessed asked if he could go with him. But Jesus did not permit him to do so. Instead, he said to him, "Go to your home and to your people and tell them what the Lord has done for you, that he had mercy on you." So he went away and began to proclaim in the Decapolis what Jesus had done for him, and all were amazed." (Mark 5:1–20, ESV)

Biblical patterns of dealing with evil influence from the Old Testament to the New Testament involve the following:

- **Confessing and repenting:** This involves clients' willingness to engage in treatment and to deal with the evil in their lives.
- **Identifying evil influences:** Assessment is the best way to identify influences that may not be obvious. Even if evil influences are noticeable, consider a thorough assessment to make sure all areas are dealt with.
- **Casting out and renouncing the demonic:** Clients must refuse association with evil and sever any bonds or claims associated with any sin surrounding the evil.
- **Praying for healing in all areas:** Take a comprehensive approach to healing. Leave no stone left unturned.
- **Replacing lies with truth:** This is vital as a final step so the enemy cannot continue to lie and seek to defeat.

Elaborating on Mark 5:1–20 based on the pattern above, in verse 6, the man ran and bowed down before Jesus. Note that Jesus did not approach the man; the man ran to Jesus. This shows a willingness to be healed. It was an act of humility that involved confessing who Jesus is and acknowledging that the evil resident in him needed to bow down to Him; or in other words, he needed to repent. Verse 9 identifies the unclean or evil influence, evident when he told Jesus he had a "legion." Casting out and renouncing the demonic/unclean spirits occurs in verses 12–13 as the demons realized they would have to leave the man. Next, Jesus dealt with the unclean spirits. Verse 19 indicates the man was healed of all the unclean spirits. Finally, in verse 20, the display of how he replaced lies (from the enemy) with the truth of his healing was evident when he went home and shared the news of his healing with all!

The ultimate victory came when he shared the good news! I believe the man may have said something like what Paul said in the passages below:

> I pray that the eyes of your heart may be enlightened in order that you may know the hope to which he has called you, the riches of his glorious inheritance in his holy people, and his incomparably great power for us who believe. That power is the same as the mighty strength he exerted when he raised Christ from the dead and seated him at his right hand in the heavenly realms, far above all rule and authority, power and dominion, and every name that is invoked, not only in the present age but also in the one to come. (Ephesians 1:18–22)

> He is the one we proclaim, admonishing and teaching everyone with all wisdom, so that we may present everyone fully mature in Christ. To this end I strenuously contend with all the energy Christ so powerfully works in me. (Colossians 1:28–29)

> Dr. Michael Heiser stated:

> Only the Great Commission accomplishes the ends to which God has been working as well as the defeat and punishment of rebellious evil spirits. The Great Commission is thus a comprehensive plan for spiritual warfare.

> I believe the healed man understood this and shared accordingly.[2]

2 Heiser, *Unseen Realm.*

Dr. Natalie Atwell's Specific Method

This is an overview. Treatment worksheets and other details are provided in the appendixes. Also, if you are a licensed professional, adding a statement about this and/or similar types of treatments to your disclosure statements or informed consent is vital.

Remember to treat by using trauma-informed care that includes making those you're seeing feel safe (physically and emotionally), building trust, giving them choices, empowering them, and allowing for collaboration.

Step 1—Confession/identification (may take multiple sessions): Once a trusting relationship has been established, in a posture of love, encourage those you're counseling to share about their struggle(s) and listen to their story (their confession, in a sense). Do not advise at this point; just listen and assess. Also, *never* force clients to share; invite them to do so on their own terms and in their own timing.

- Do a thorough **assessment** (The Other Influences Assessment is recommended) that includes an exploration of how evil might have been introduced.
- After the assessment has been completed, construct a **genogram** or some other means to organize familial influences to the third and fourth generation mentioned.
- Next, list the specific issues assessed in relation to when they began (i.e., paternal mother: alcoholism)

Between sessions, pray and listen to what the Holy Spirit may be leading you to say or do.

- Homework:
  - Encourage those you're counseling to research past family history (three to four generations back).
  - Have them write out any ways what they've disclosed or discovered may have influenced them for good, bad,

or neutral (neither). Not everyone will believe certain things have influenced them negatively, but this is a great place for them to begin seeing potential connections.
  - Ask them to start identifying any feelings, thoughts, and potential lies they've believed as a result of any discoveries.

Step 2—Repentance (may take multiple sessions): In a posture of love, invite (this allows for choice) those you're helping to repent of any sin the Holy Spirit has revealed. It will likely start with their personal sins and then move on to things that have been done to them.

- Also encourage them to go back to their third or fourth generation and repent of any sin committed by past generations that are still negatively influencing the family. Make sure they don't blame themselves for the sins (that would be toxic shame); rather, ensure they're repenting as a way of cleansing the evil influence from their family bloodline.

> Keeping mercy for thousands, forgiving iniquity and transgression and sin, and that will by no means clear the guilty, visiting the iniquity of the fathers upon the children, and upon the children's children, unto the third and to the fourth generation. (Exodus 34:7)

Repentance is always the cure; also see Judges 3:9 and 1 Samuel 12:10–11. It is also important to note these past struggles so they're not repeated.

- Homework:
  - Have clients write a reflection on the repentance session(s).
  - Encourage them to identify any lies they have believed in addition to the ones already noted.

Step 3—Casting off/renouncing (may take multiple sessions): After confession/repentance, the promise for those who follow God's commands is a blessing for a thousand generations. Blessings come as people cast off and renounce associations with evil. Encourage healing in all areas (i.e., habits, nutrition, physical activity) and allow for collaboration.

- See Exodus 20:6. Once repentance has taken place, the next step is to cast off and renounce. "Casting off" means refusing to have any further association with the sin. This is not about casting out personal characteristics such as the personality; rather, it's about ending associations with sin. "Renouncing" means severing any bond or claim associated with the sin. So, in a posture of love, help the people you're serving explore any areas they need to deal with by casting off/out and renouncing relationships, beliefs, items, et cetera.
- Encourage clients to pray for healing in all areas. James 4:7 states that we must submit to God (this is done through repentance, renouncing/casting off) and then resist the enemy. This is a great time to do what Jesus did in Matthew 4:10: "Then Jesus said to him, 'Be gone, Satan!'" Empower individuals to resist the enemy! In a posture of love, make sure there are no hidden toxic shame messages they may be holding on to. Explore all areas that need to be healed, including the physical, mental, and spiritual realms.
- Finally, remind them that people overcome struggles by the blood of the lamb (saying "Jesus' blood is speaking a better word over this area of my life" [Hebrews 12:4] as the new testimony to overcome the issue [Revelation 12:11]). This is when those who have been healed in the name of Christ know where their victory comes from.

- Homework:
  - Have clients list all items, beliefs, feelings, et cetera, they cast out and/or renounced. The repetition will solidify the work done in session(s).

Step 4—Empowering clients to replace lies with truth (ongoing): Once doors of evil have been discovered/confessed, repented of, cast out, and renounced, it is essential to replace lies with truth to fully heal and overcome.

- The next step is to identify any lies clients have come to believe about themselves, others, and the Most High God because of the evil identified. Remind them of their high status and calling as human imagers. Often lies attack this in essence. Lies are always the "welcome mat" leading to the doorway to evil. They entice us in. In other words, lies are like saying "welcome" to evil influences.
- Next, remind or teach the clients spiritual truths about identity and other matters to combat the lies believed.
  - (Matthew 4) Emphasize the importance of combating lies with Scripture (encourage meditation/memorization of Scripture).
  - Replace lies with truth (take thoughts captive) daily, as we're urged to do in 2 Corinthians 10:5: "[First] we destroy arguments and every lofty [or proud] opinion raised against the knowledge of God, and [second] we take every thought captive." It's like strategy for a battle: First destroy the fortress, then take the captives. We "take every thought captive" to bring it to be obedient to Christ by hiding God's Word in our heart, putting on the armor of God, praying like warriors, and *sharing* the gospel.

When clients focus on the truth of the Most High God, they will be set free and that freedom cannot be manipulated by the enemy.

- This is a great time to use **cognitive-behavioral therapy** (CBT, which is clinically sound/effective), a structured form of therapy that helps people identify and change unhelpful thoughts, feelings, and behaviors. Techniques may include journaling cognitive distortions, identifying negative beliefs, or identifying and writing out lies believed and replacing them through writing with truths. Cognitive restructuring is a form of replacing lies with truth.

Writing things out and using repetition is a way to commit important truths to memory and to establish new thought patterns. We learn. We practice. We grow.

Treatment for Nonbelievers

For clients who aren't Christians/believers, we can still follow this pattern as therapists; we just need to change the language a bit. Ultimately, my prayer is that the Most High God will ultimately open the door leading nonbelieving clients who are struggling with the challenges wrought by evil influences to the saving knowledge of Christ.

Step 1—Encourage them to share their story/struggle(s) (may take multiple sessions): Once a trusting relationship has been established, in a posture of love, encourage clients to share about their struggle(s) and listen to their story (confession, in a sense). Do not advise at this stage; just listen and assess.

- Do a thorough **assessment** (the Other Influences Assessment is recommended) that includes an exploration of how evil could have been introduced.
- Construct a **genogram** or some other means to organize familial influences to the third and fourth generations mentioned after the assessment has been completed.

- Next, **list the specific issues** assessed in relation to when the issue began (i.e., paternal mother: alcoholism)

Between sessions, pray and listen to what the Holy Spirit may be leading you to do or say/do. The unbelievers don't need to know that you are praying for them.

- Homework:
  - Encourage those you're helping to research past family history (three–four generations back).
  - Have them write out any ways something they have disclosed or discovered may have influenced them for good, bad, or neutral (neither). Not everyone will believe certain things have influenced them negatively, but this is a great place to begin seeing potential connections.
  - Ask them to start identifying any feelings, thoughts, and potential lies they've believed because of things discovered

Step 2—Exploration and discovery: In a posture of love, invite the nonbelievers to "explore") any ways they have been involved in harmful practices or experiences leading to symptoms of what might be perceived as mental health struggles. (Use the term "explore" instead of "repent"; we must encourage repentance, but the Holy Spirit is the only One who can draw people to the place of repentance and salvation.) It is also important to note the past struggles so they are not repeated. This, we hope, leads to the discovery of issues that need to be dealt with.

- Encourage the clients to also go back to their third and fourth generation and explore any harm done in past generations that is still negatively influencing the family today. Make sure they don't blame themselves for these sins (that would be toxic shame) but rather are exploring as a way of cleansing the evil influence from their family line. It is also important to note these past struggles so they are not repeated.

- Homework:
  - Have clients write a reflection on the exploration session(s).
  - Identify any lies believed in addition to the ones already noted.

Step 3—Dealing with the issue: After exploring harmful behaviors and/or ways evil has been introduced, in a posture of love, encourage clients to deal with any areas that need attention by refusing any further association with the causes of the struggle ("casting off") and severing any bonds or claims associated with it such as relationships, beliefs, or items, et cetera ("renouncing"). Encourage healing in all areas (i.e., habits, nutrition, physical activity).

- Homework:
  - Have clients list all items, beliefs, feelings, et cetera, that were dealt with. The repetition will solidify the work done in session(s).

Step 4–Replacing lies with truth: Once some of the doors of evil have been discovered, confessed, repented of, cast out, and renounced, the next step is to identify any lies the clients have come to believe about themselves, others, and spiritual beings.

Next, in a posture of love, help them uncover truth to combat the lies believed. Teach the truths about identity. Treatments that may be effective are cognitive-behavioral and trauma-based.

Stories of Healing

Teaching truth—good theology: Since my time in the Philippines doing mission work sharing about the divine council worldview/

Deuteronomy 32 and mental health, life-changing truths have helped many people who are dealing with inner turmoil. Since the time we've staged suicide-prevention rallies, reports are that many people with suicidal ideation have been helped by understanding the truth that these thoughts are not coming from them but from "other influences" that are not from themselves or from the Most High God. *Good theology matters.*

Treating issues biblically: Counselors in my practice who are using the Other Influences Assessment and treating mental health concerns biblically are helping people find freedom. They're helping clients rid their homes of ungodly influences such as crystals and other items that would be viewed as objects of idolatry or as the source of a negative influence. Clients are learning to renounce and cast off items and ideas keeping them from reflecting God's image the way they're created to do. Long-term problems are being resolved in clients as they understand the root causes of their issues related to evil influences. To God be the glory!

Treating unbelievers: Often counselors who are Christian are fearful of treating nonbelievers with any biblical guidance. As I began this work, nonbelievers have been very interested in exposing and ridding themselves of darkness. I don't push my beliefs on anyone. Cognitive-behavioral therapy is a great treatment I consider a form of the biblical principle of "taking every thought" captive. One client dealing with dissociations was being triggered by water. I asked her if I could share a story with her from the Bible, knowing that passages from ancient texts can be helpful in therapy. I told her that Jesus had walked on the water as a way of showing the evil spirits in the abyss (the sea) that He was above them and would defeat them. She said, "I like this story, and I will think of it when I have bad thoughts about water from now on." I didn't force her to believe. I didn't tell her to recite the "Sinner's Prayer." I simply related a story. Dear friend, don't be afraid of telling the truth in love. The truth of Jesus will set people free.

Trust the Holy Spirit to help you discern, assess all areas of potential struggle, and be bold enough to help people heal in a posture of love.

Proverbs 3:1–6:

> My son, do not forget my teaching, but keep my commands in your heart, for they will prolong your life many years and bring you peace and prosperity. Let love and faithfulness never leave you; and bind them around your neck, write them on the tablet of your heart. Then you will win favor and a good name in the sight of God and man. Trust in the LORD with all your heart and lean not on your own understanding; in all your ways submit to him, and he will make your paths straight.

Final Treatment Encouragement and Conclusions

This isn't easy work, but it is rewarding. If the Most High God allows you to help someone overcome a battle with darkness, be thankful for the opportunity and relinquish any selfishness or attempts to control the process. Be patient, as it will likely take time with each person. Continue to encourage treatment as needed for individuals struggling with evil influences in their lives. Continue learning. Don't engage in the darkness but expose it! Refer as needed to trusted pastors and other professionals who are willing to help.

Overall, my conclusions are that humans live in a world with the influence of evil from divine beings and the consequences of our own choices. When we choose our own ways or decide to follow any spirits or beings other than the Most High God—in any action, belief, or thought—the path is death and destruction not only for ourselves but possibly for our loved ones as well. The Most High provided a way for our enemies to be defeated through His Son, Jesus.

Finally, remember that spiritual war needs to be understood as a conflict between two kingdoms: the *kingdom of the Most High God* and the *kingdom of Satan*. Jesus said, "If I drive out demons by the Spirit of God, then the kingdom of God has come upon you" (Matthew 12:28). As the kingdom of God grows, the kingdom of darkness shrinks and loses ground. So, if all else fails, continue to share the gospel to combat the darkness in the world as we know it.

QUESTIONS FOR REFLECTION

1. Do you believe evil can be treated effectively?
2. What lies have you believed that have held you back in any aspect of your life?
3. In moments of overwhelming thoughts or emotional turmoil, how easy or difficult is it for you to "take thoughts captive" to Christ? What practices (meditation, journaling, worship) could help you cultivate greater discernment?
4. What will you do differently in treatment now or in the future because of learning this model?

PRACTICAL APPLICATION

Encouragement for pastoral counselors and mental health professionals:

- Learn about trauma-informed practices and language, and practice using what you've learned as you interact with the suffering people you serve.
- Support counselors who offer clinically sound and biblically based treatment models such as the one above by referring clients to them. Share this treatment model with counselors you know.
- Preach a sermon about trauma and how to interact with others using trauma-informed language.
- Develop and use a treatment based on the guidelines shared and treatment plan above for those you serve.

Prayer Prompt: *Lord, order my steps as I refer, treat, or love those who've experienced harm at any level. Prepare me in all ways to treat clients effectively so your healing work can be complete.*

SCRIPTURE TO CONSIDER

2 Corinthians 10:3–6:

> We destroy every lofty opinion raised against the knowledge of God, and take every thought captive to obey Christ.

Matthew 10:1:

> And Jesus called to him his twelve disciples and gave them authority over unclean spirits, to cast them out, and to heal every disease and every affliction.

Revelation 12:10–11:

> We can overcome the accuser.

Revelation 10:12:

> Rejoice, woe to the devil, his time is short.

Revelation 10:17:

> Keep God's commands.

Revelation 14:12:

> Persevere under persecution, which is evidence of sound obedience.

CONCLUSION

Over the past several years, my journey has led me to examine the spiritual darkness behind circumstances and events in my own life and in the experiences of clients and others. The growing darkness being seen in our population's mental health is evident not only in mental health practice, but in society and, sadly, within our churches as well. With my research and discovery, I now have no doubt spiritual forces of darkness are seeking to influence humans toward evil with their ultimate goal of killing, stealing, and destroying. There is an unseen realm behind humanity. There are unseen forces for good that help humans directed by the Most High God. Conversely, there are unseen forces of darkness (fallen unclean spirits) that influence humans for evil.

The "killing" is carried out in society through mass shootings, abortion, isolation, cult and occult involvement, social unrest, and the rise of artificial intelligence. The "stealing" is evidenced by narcissism, paganism, and a lack of healthy relationships within our churches. The "destruction" is visible in uncommon symptoms such as dissociation, sleep paralysis, suicide/self-harm, gender dysphoria, unexplained physical symptoms, dark sexual behaviors, and strange abductions.

Graciously, the Most High God led me to discover the truth of the unseen realm in Scripture, which has provided life-giving answers. My worldview now includes the divine council from Deuteronomy 32, which taught me who the influencers of evil are and why they're trying to destroy humans. Understanding what it means to be human is where it all began. Humans are given the status of being the Most High's imagers, or representatives, on earth.

As an imager of the Most High God, I see in Genesis 3 the force of darkness, the serpent, trying to kill humans because of his jealousy of our status as imagers of God. As a result, I see this dark force as being potentially behind aspects of death. The battle is from an outside source, a dark one; it's not always from within.

In Genesis 6, I see the beginning of sexual sin, addiction, wars, and depravity. The fallen ones in Genesis 6 are the influencers today, in some way, of the dark choices being made. The battle to defeat humanity is raging all around us. The lie is that the battle is solely within us or our fellow humans.

The final rebellion of fallen beings in Genesis 11 influenced humans to be self-serving narcissists fighting against good. These dark forces are still seeking to destroy humans through anti-God governments and by causing us to fight against one another.

Realizing that many mental health problems can be traced back to the beginning of the human story on earth in the battle between our good, Most High, Creator God and the forces against Him has been enlightening. It's been freeing. Being able to tell those struggling with thoughts of suicide that the ideas about self-harm are likely coming from a dark force and not always from somewhere deep inside themselves is life-changing. Sharing with someone suffering with sexual sin that the temptation may be coming from fallen beings who are trying to destroy the image of God in them has been transformative.

While the world says the mental health battle is only within us or caused by the actions of others, I say the battle began long ago when the rebellious divine beings tried to stop humans from fulfilling their purpose of representing the Most High God on earth. This by no means takes out the element of human choice; it simply suggests the potential influences behind many troubles. Not all mental health issues spring from the activity of fallen beings; I'm just taking us back to the origin of human difficulties in Genesis. This has changed how I view not only problems, but also how I see my clients and decide how to treat them.

Currently, when a problem arises with clients and the standard mental health treatments have proven ineffective, I assess them to try to find out whether dark or evil influences might be in play. Asking different questions is essential in getting to the root of an issue. My desire is for more mental health professionals, pastoral counselors, and others to begin assessing the dark influences that could be causing their clients to experience problems or make unwise choices.

Along with the assessment I created came the design of a treatment plan to address any darkness the assessment exposes. Treating people biblically using clinically effective techniques has resulted in mind-blowing changes for clients—the kind of changes I hope to see among many others.

My prayer is that you won't keep this information to yourself, but will share this book, assessment, and treatment guidelines with anyone who is called to help people who are experiencing mental illness. My staff and I cannot do this work alone. We need others to fight alongside us in war in the unseen realm. If you would like to join a network of caring professionals who use my assessment and treatment plan, please visit mentalwarriorconsulting.com to join our referral network.

> May the God of hope fill you with all joy and peace as you trust in him, so that you may overflow with hope by the power of the Holy Spirit. (Romans 15:13, NIV).

Appendix A

OTHER INFLUENCES TREATMENT PLAN WITH WORKSHEETS

Step 1: Story Sharing

Confession and Identification
(This may take more than one session.)

Once a trusting relationship has been established, in a posture of love, encourage clients to share their struggle(s) and listen to their story (confession, in a sense). Do not advise at this point; just listen and assess. Also, *never* force people to talk; invite them to share on their own terms and in their own timing.

- Conduct a thorough assessment (i.e., the *Other Influences Assessment*), which includes exploring how evil influences may have been introduced.
- Construct a genogram or some other means of organizing familial influences to the third and fourth generations after the assessment has been completed.
- List and categorize the issues assessed in relation to when the problem began (i.e., paternal mother: alcoholism)

Confession and Identification Activity

Directions: After completing the assessment, use a genogram (similar to the example below) to help identify and categorize the struggles mentioned. This can assist in the treatment process.

GENOGRAM EXAMPLE

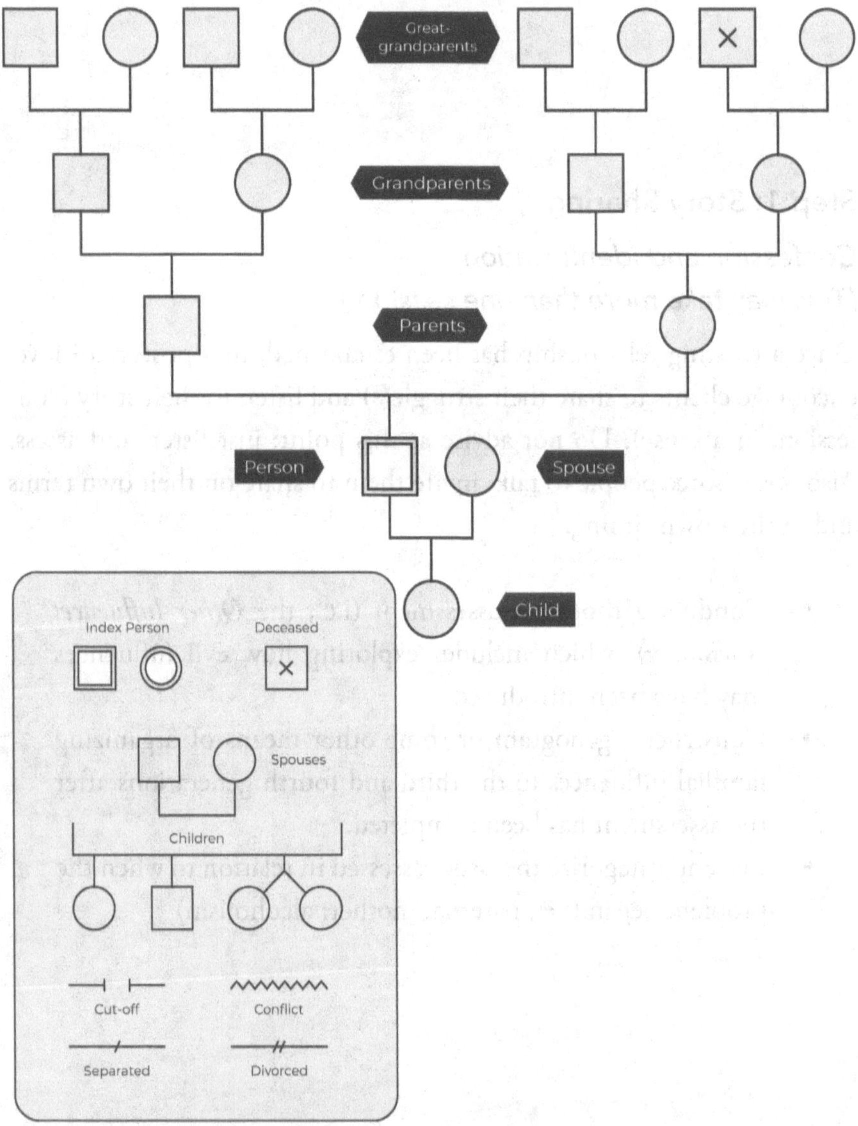

CATEGORIZATION CHART

Next, categorize the issues assessed using the sample chart below.

Issue Assessed	Potential Cause	Action Committed By	Treatment Implication

CATEGORIZATION CHART EXAMPLE

Issue Assessed	Potential Cause	Action Committed By	Treatment Implication
Dissociation	Family involvement in fraternal order	Paternal grand-father, father	Renounce association with fraternal order, cognitive behavioral therapy, prayers to break curses.
Alcohol Addiction	Agreement with lies: "I am just like my mother and I can never change."	Self, mother	Cognitive behavioral therapy, prayers to break generational patterns.

Homework

- Encourage clients to research past family history (three to four generations back).
- Have them list ways something they have disclosed or discovered may have influenced them for good, bad, or neutral (neither). Not everyone will believe certain things have influenced them negatively, but this is a great place to begin seeing potential connections.

- Ask them to start identifying any feelings, thoughts, and potential lies they've believed because of what they've discovered.

Step 2: Exploration/Discovery

Repentance

In a posture of love, invite clients to repent of or "explore/discover" any sin the Holy Spirit has revealed. Encourage them to go back and repent for generational sins (up to the third and fourth generations) that may still be negatively influencing the family today.

> Keeping mercy for thousands, forgiving iniquity and transgression and sin, and that will by no means clear the guilty, visiting the iniquity of the fathers upon the children, and upon the children's children, unto the third and to the fourth generation. (Exodus 34:7)
>
> Repentance is always the cure. (Judges 3:9)
>
> They cried out to the Lord and said, "We have sinned; we have forsaken the Lord and served the Baals and the Ashtoreths. But now deliver us from the hands of our enemies, and we will serve you." Then the Lord sent Jerub-Baal, Barak, Jephthah and Samuel, and he delivered you from the hands of your enemies all around you, so that you lived in safety. (1 Samuel 12:10–11)

It's important to acknowledge and note these struggles to prevent them from being repeated.

IDENTIFICATION AND REPENTANCE ACTIVITY CHART

Generation	Influence/Struggle Identified	Repentance Statement/Activity

IDENTIFICATION AND REPENTANCE ACTIVITY EXAMPLE

Generation	Influence/Struggle Identified	Repentance Statement/Activity
Self	Alcoholism	"I want no part in this influence and choose to walk the opposite way of these behaviors."
Parents	Divorce	"I choose to remain faithful to my spouse and not walk in adultery as my father did."
Grandparents	Sexual abuse	"I will seek out [x] person to see if forgiveness if possible."
Great-grandparents	Fraternal order involvement	

Homework

- Have clients write a reflection on the repentance session(s).
- Identify any lies believed in addition to the ones already noted.

Step 3: Dealing with the Issue

Cast Off/Renounce

After confession and repentance, the promise for those who follow God's commands is blessing for a thousand generations (Exodus 20:6). Encourage healing in all areas (i.e., habits, nutrition, physical activity).

Once repentance has occurred, the next step is to cast off and renounce.

- "Casting off" means refusing to have any further association with the sin.
- "Renouncing" means severing any bond or claim associated with the sin.

So, in a posture of love, help clients explore any relationships, beliefs, or items that need to be dealt with by casting off/out and renouncing. *Encourage them to pray for or seek healing in all areas.*

James 4:7 states that we must submit to God (this is done through repentance, renouncing/casting off) and then resist the enemy. This is a great time to do what Jesus did in Matthew 4:10: "Then Jesus said to him, 'Be gone, Satan!'" Empower individuals to resist the enemy! Finally, remind them that we overcome by the blood of the Lamb (by saying, "Jesus' blood is speaking a better word over this area of my life [Hebrews 12:4])" as the new testimony to overcome the issue (Revelation 12:11).

CASTING OFF/RENOUNCING ACTIVITY CHART

Category	Identified Issue	Casting-off Statement	Renouncing Statement

CASTING OFF/RENOUNCING ACTIVITY EXAMPLE

Category	Identified Issue	Casting-off Statement	Renouncing Statement
Issues	Anger due to the unforgiveness of parents	"Lord, I refuse to have any further association with anything that causes me anger due to unforgiveness (list specifics)."	"I sever any bond or connection to anything related to unforgiveness that leads to anger (memories that trigger will be worked through and processed)."
Relationships	Friends who encourage me to drink too much		
Beliefs to Change	I need to avenge my losses		
Items to Rid Self of	A family relic that has caused arguments		

Prayer Activity

Write a prayer renouncing and casting off issues. It can be as simple as: "Lord, I renounce ________. I cast off its influence from my life. I choose to walk in freedom and truth."

Sample Prayer 1:

In the name of the Lord Jesus Christ, I ask that the Holy Spirit bring to my mind all areas in which I have agreed with lies. Holy Spirit, help me discern good and evil. Show me the truth in Scripture. Align my heart, will, and emotions with your truth and not with the lies of the enemies of the Most High God.

Sample Prayer 2:

Father, I align with you, your will, and your ways. Bring my thoughts, feelings, and emotions into submission under you. I confess and repent of my sin and/or times I've agreed with or partnered with past-generational sin of ________. I repent fully as I turn to your ways and plans for me. I renounce any association or affiliation with ________. From this moment on, I replace the lie of ________ due to this struggle and believe the truth of scriptural evidence in ________.

Homework

Have clients list all items, beliefs, feelings, et cetera, that were cast out and/or renounced. This repetition will solidify the work done in session(s).

Step 4: Replace Lies with Truth

Once doors of evil influences have been discovered, confessed, repented of, cast out, and renounced, the next step is to identify any lies clients have come to believe about themselves, others, or God.

Remind them of their high status and calling as human imagers of God. Lies often attack this in essence. *When doors are actively opened to evil influence, there is always a lie waiting to entice us in.*

Next, teach clients spiritual truths about identity to combat the lies believed (Matthew 4). Emphasize the importance of combating lies with Scripture and encourage daily meditation and memorization of Scripture. Replace lies with truth daily and take thoughts captive. Second Corinthians 10:5 states: "[First] we destroy arguments and every lofty [or proud] opinion raised against the knowledge of God, and [second] we take every thought captive."

It's a battle strategy: First destroy the fortress, then take captives. We "take every thought captive to obey Christ" by hiding God's Word in our heart, putting on the armor of God, praying like warriors, and *sharing* the gospel (Ephesians 6).

This is a great time to use cognitive-behavioral therapy techniques such as journaling cognitive distortions, negative beliefs, or lies, and replacing them with truths. Often, I'll simply ask clients to list the lies and next to each one write the corresponding truth based on Scripture.

They may need to review this often to completely uproot the lies they've believed, but it can be done! Neuroplasticity indicates that the brain can change through the process of thinking differently and making different choices (epigenetics). It may take work and practice, but it is possible!

When working with clients who aren't Christian, therapists can still follow this pattern, changing the language a bit. My prayer is that God will ultimately open the door leading them to the saving knowledge of Christ.

REPLACING LIES WITH TRUTH CHART

Lie Believed	Truth	Scripture Evidence

REPLACING LIES WITH TRUTH EXAMPLE

Lie Believed	Truth	Scripture Evidence
"I was a mistake."	"God formed me in my mother's womb."	Psalm 139:13–16; Jeremiah 1:5

• • •

- Continue activities as needed until the person experiences freedom. Some parts of treatment should be a continual part of spiritual growth, such as identifying lies and replacing them with truth.
- All clients should keep their worksheets and writings so they can refer to them as needed.

These sample worksheets can be used as needed. Additionally, there may be other helpful resources that can and should be used at the counselor's discretion.

Appendix B

OTHER INFLUENCES ASSESSMENT

BY DR. NATALIE ATWELL

Introduction: This assessment may serve as a means to guide individuals in understanding possible, non-traditional types of influences in the lives of a person that could be impacting health (physical, mental, relational, spiritual, etc.) in various ways.

This assessment may be used for various purposes in seeking to understand struggles someone may be experiencing that may appear to be unexplained by other modes of assessment. It may also be considered for use when mental health treatments (counseling and/or medication) have been attempted yet found unsuccessful over an extended period.

Instructions: Please answer each question below honestly and provide any details or information you are comfortable sharing or believe is important to note. For children and minors, parents/guardians should be consulted prior to the assessment and in cases of younger children, parents/guardians may answer in place of or along with the child.

1. Is there anyone in your household or family with what you would consider to be strange/odd or different beliefs? If so, please explain.

2. Do you know your family history from the third or fourth generation back? If so, please explain. List any problematic issues you know of (i.e., addiction, adultery, abuse).

3. Has anyone in your family ever gone missing or disclosed some type of abduction story?

4. Have you ever had a near-death experience (i.e., wherein you felt you died and came back to life)?

5. Have you ever been what some would consider obsessed with horror movies (very dark themed) and/or dark music? If so, please explain.

6. Do you live near or normally visit any places associated with any strange happenings or dark history? (For example, Stonewall Jackson Training School has been rumored as being haunted, and it also has a dark history associated with child abuse.) If so, please explain.

7. Have you ever routinely engaged in fantasy/role-playing games and/or would you or someone you are close to consider you addicted to technology (including social media such as TikTok and other platforms)? If so, please explain.

8. Have you ever mentally attempted to travel outside of your physical body or had someone try to convince you to do so? If so, please explain.

9. Do you believe in alternative approaches to spirituality? (i.e. not mainstream faith practices). If so, please explain.

10. Have you ever participated in any mystical practices? If so, please explain.

11. Do you engage in daily or occasional astrological readings? Add any details you want to share.

12. Have you seen a psychic, healer or spiritual advisor? Add any details you want to share.

13. Have you ever been hypnotized? Add any details you want to share.

14. Do you or have you ever used crystals? Add any details you want to share.

15. Do you believe in alternative medicine like reiki, kratom, hallucinogens, psychedelics, etc.? If so, please explain and discuss any usage or experiences.

16. Have you ever engaged in witchcraft? If so, please explain.

17. Have you ever used tarot cards, Ouija board, or other divination materials? If so, please explain.

18. Have you ever tried to channel (entered a meditative or trancelike state in order to convey messages from) things? If so, please explain.

19. Do you believe in manifesting as inspired by Hermeticism, transcendentalism or other spiritual practices outside of monotheism? If so, please explain.

20. Are you or is anyone in your family a member of a fraternal order, secret society, or similar organization outside of a church, mosque, or synagogue? Add any details you want to share.

21. Would you or someone else consider a church or group experience you've had to be similar to a cult? If so, please explain.

22. Have you ever been sexually abused in a ritualistic way (abuse that occurs in a context wherein symbols or activities have superstitious, supernatural, or religious connotations)? Add any details you want to share.

23. Have you ever engaged in pornography such that it became addictive? Add any details you want to share.

24. Have you ever engaged in sexual activities that involved symbols or activities that had superstitious, supernatural, or religious connotations; had an interest in bondage, dominance, discipline, submission, masochist, sadist (BDSM), or other alternative sexual practices? Add any details you want to share.

25. Have you ever engaged or attempted to become involved with any non-traditional sexual practices or relationships with humans, animals, objects, et cetera? Add any details you want to share.

26. Have you ever been trafficked (being compelled or coerced into providing) for sex or other services? Add any details you want to share.

27. Do you have a history of sexual abuse as a child?

Please add anything else you would like to share.

Disclaimers/Results: The information collected on the assessment is simply used for exploratory purposes. Each provider/individual may use it differently to determine treatment planning and/or necessary next steps in collaboration with the individual.

If someone confirms involvement or experience with anything on the assessment, the person may be referred to a professional (counselor/therapist, pastor, et cetera) who is willing to discuss and treat any concerns in any way related to answers.

Please use our digital Assessments Form to be connected with a Mental Warrior Consulting counselor.

Appendix C

MENTAL WARRIOR COUNSELING TOOLKIT

The Mental Warrior Counseling Toolkit offers clinically informed and faith-based resources for lasting mental health impact. It features a thoughtfully curated collection of digital downloads for counselors, coaches, ministry leaders, and individuals pursuing healing and transformation. Each resource blends professional best practices with biblical wisdom to guide lasting change.

Whether you're helping clients process trauma, strengthen relationships, grow spiritually, or find clarity in the chaos, these tools are designed to support meaningful, restorative work in every season.

Appendix D

VITAL VOCABULARY

The following terms are defined in alignment with the following:

1. *The Unseen Realm: Recovering the Supernatural Worldview of the Bible* (Lexham Press, 2015). Dr. Michael S. Heiser's foundational academic work that lays out the divine council, cosmic geography, sons of God, Watchers, and rebellion motifs.
2. *Supernatural: What the Bible Teaches About the Unseen World—And Why It Matters* (Lexham Press, 2015). A popular-level version of *The Unseen Realm.* Easier to cite for non-academic audiences.
3. *Angels: What the Bible Really Says About God's Heavenly Host* (Lexham Press, 2018). Details the hierarchy, roles, and nature of heavenly beings.
4. *Demons: What the Bible Really Says about the Powers of Darkness* (Lexham Press, 2020). Covers Genesis 6, Watchers, Nephilim, territorial spirits, and spiritual rebellion.
5. Peer-reviewed academic work.
6. "The Divine Council in Late Canonical and Non-Canonical Second Temple Jewish Literature." (University of Wisconsin-Madison, 2004). Heiser's doctoral dissertation.
7. *1 Enoch,* for the Watchers, Nephilim, and celestial rebellion.
8. *The Ugaritic Texts,* especially the Baal Cycle—important for understanding *elohim*, divine councils, and ancient cosmology.

9. *The Dead Sea Scrolls*, especially the *Book of Giants*, which parallels the Genesis 6 narrative.
10. *Akkadian, Mesopotamian, and Canaanite Mythology*, for ancient cosmology and divine council patterns.
11. Biblical citations:

    - Psalm 82
    - Psalm 89:5–7
    - Job 1–2
    - 1 Kings 22:19–23
    - Genesis 6:1–4
    - Deuteronomy 32:8–9 (especially DSS and LXX)
    - Numbers 13:32–33
    - Jude 6, 2 Peter 2:4
    - Deuteronomy 4:19–20
    - Deuteronomy 32:8–9
    - Daniel 10
    - Acts 17:26–31
    - Genesis 3
    - Genesis 6
    - Genesis 11

12. *The Lost World of Genesis One: Ancient Near Eastern Thought and the Old Testament* supports ancient cosmology and ANE context.
13. The divine council in Canaanite and early Hebrew literature.
14. *God in Translation,* essential for ancient divine council literature.
15. Meredith G. Kline works on cosmic geography and theological patterns.
16. Jeffrey Tigay studies on ancient Israelite religion and ANE parallels.
17. Michael Hundley, *Gods in Dwellings*—ANE temples, divine presence, and governance.

Appendix E

VOCABULARY LIST

Ancient Mediterranean cosmology: The worldview of the ancient biblical world—heavens above, earth in the middle, underworld below—populated by spiritual beings. This is the "cosmic map" assumed by ancient Israelites and surrounding cultures.

Ancient Watchers: From 1 Enoch and hinted at in Genesis 6; spiritual beings ("sons of God") appointed to oversee humanity but who became corrupt. For Heiser, these beings sinned by descending to earth, mating with humans, and teaching forbidden knowledge.

Canonical patterns: Recurring theological and narrative patterns in Scripture (e.g., Edenic rebellion, Babel, exodus motifs) that reveal God's purposes and the spiritual conflict behind history.

Celestial corruption: The rebellion of spiritual beings who abandon their God-given roles, distort divine order, or harm humanity (e.g., Genesis 6 Watchers, Psalm 82 *elohim*).

Celestial hierarchy: The structured order of spiritual beings in God's divine council. Heiser emphasizes ranks rather than modern angel/demon categories.

Courts of heaven: A biblical metaphor for God's governing council in passages like Job 1–2; Yahweh presides as King and Judge while other *elohim* serve as participants.

Cosmic geography: Dr. Michael S. Heiser's term for the biblical concept that certain territories are under the rule of hostile spiritual powers after Babel (Deuteronomy 32:8–9). Israel belongs uniquely to Yahweh; other nations are overseen by lesser, often corrupt *elohim*.

Cosmic rebellion: The multilayered spiritual rebellion in Scripture:

1. **Edenic rebellion** (the *nachash* serpent).
2. **Watcher rebellion** (Genesis 6).
3. **Nations rebellion** at Babel (Deuteronomy 32).

Heiser sees these as the three pillars of the Bible's *supernatural backstory.*

Divine council: A key Heiser concept. A heavenly assembly of *elohim* who assist Yahweh in governing creation—analogous to a royal court. Not a threat to God's uniqueness, but expressions of His sovereign rule.

Divine insurgents: Spiritual beings (*elohim*) who rebel against God's order and attempt to exert illegitimate authority over humanity.

Divine rebellion: Any spiritual uprising against Yahweh's will—referring to Eden, Genesis 6, and Babel.

Divine transgression: A spiritual being crossing boundaries established by God—such as the Watchers descending or corrupt *elohim* ruling unjustly (Psalm 82).

Elohim: A Hebrew term meaning "disembodied spiritual being." It includes God, but also angels, demons, deceased humans, and territorial spirits. Yahweh is **the** *Elohim*—unique, uncreated, incomparable.

Fallen gods (*elohim*): Corrupt divine council members who rebelled, rule unjustly, or enslave nations. Heiser stresses these are not "fictional" but real spiritual powers judged in Psalm 82.

Heavenly governance: The administrative structure of God's rule, including loyal spiritual beings who execute God's will in creation.

Most High God: A title for Yahweh (*El Elyon*) emphasizing His supremacy above all *elohim* and His role as the sovereign ruler of all cosmic domains.

Nephilim: The offspring of the rebellious Watchers and human women (Genesis 6). Heiser interprets them as giant warrior clans whose spirits become part of the later demonic landscape.

Oppression: The unjust control or influence of corrupt spiritual powers over individuals, nations, or systems—often connected to the rebellious *elohim* of Psalm 82.

Principalities: New Testament category of high-ranking hostile spiritual powers (e.g., Ephesians 6:12). In Heiser's model, these are territorial or national *elohim*.

Ritualistic abuse: The exploitation of individuals through rituals that invoke or honor hostile spiritual powers. Scripture frames it as the demonic imitation of God's sacred rituals.

Sanctification: The process by which God transforms believers into Christlikeness, freeing them from the influence of rebellious spiritual powers.

Scriptural re-enchantment: Heiser's phrase for recovering the Bible's supernatural worldview—seeing Scripture as the ancient Israelites did, full of real spiritual agency.

Sons of God: Members of the divine council. Loyal or fallen *elohim*. In the Old Testament, this refers to spiritual beings; in the New Testament, it is applied to redeemed humans through adoption in Christ.

Spiritual authority: The God-given power believers possess in Christ to resist hostile powers and participate in God's kingdom rule.

Spiritual bureaucracy: The organized administrative system of spiritual beings outlined in Scripture—both loyal heavenly hosts and rebellious powers.

Spiritual entanglement: When hostile spiritual powers influence or bind a person through sin, lies, or oppression.

Spiritual formation: The lifelong process of developing into Christlike maturity, strengthened against spiritual deception.

Scriptural fragmentation: The disintegration of identity, purity, or wholeness caused by rebellion, sin, trauma, or demonic influence.

Spiritual inheritance: The believer's identity and future destiny in Christ—participation in the divine family and in the restored cosmic order.

Spiritual insurgency: Acts of rebellion by hostile spiritual beings against God's authority.

Spiritual rebellion: Any willful opposition to God by spiritual beings (Eden, Watchers, territorial spirits).

Stage-craft: The deceptive presentation or manipulation of appearances by fallen spiritual beings to mislead humanity.

Sub-created beings: Created spiritual beings (*elohim*) who are subordinate to the uncreated Creator, Yahweh.

Subversive forces: Spiritual entities or influences that undermine God's purposes and work clandestinely against His kingdom.

Supernatural hermeneutics: Interpreting Scripture through the lens of its original supernatural worldview—central to Heiser's approach.

Supernatural infiltration: Hostile spiritual beings inserting themselves into human affairs, institutions, or belief systems.

Supernatural interference: Actions by fallen beings that hinder God's purposes or obstruct human obedience.

Supernatural realm: The unseen dimension where *elohim* exist—interacting with the earthly realm in Scripture.

Territorial spirits: Hostile spiritual powers ruling over nations or regions (Deuteronomy 32; Daniel 10). These are the "princes" or corrupt elohim assigned at Babel.

Theological integration: Bringing together biblical theology, worldview, and spiritual reality into a coherent understanding that honors Scripture's supernatural framework.

Transdimensional intelligence: A modern phrase for spiritual beings (*elohim*) who exist in a nonphysical realm but interact with the human world.

www.ingramcontent.com/pod-product-compliance
Lightning Source LLC
Chambersburg PA
CBHW010503230726
48635CB00037B/549
* 9 7 8 1 7 3 2 5 4 7 8 2 7 *